TURNING TURK

EARLY MODERN CULTURAL STUDIES

Ivo Kamps, Series Editor

PUBLISHED BY PALGRAVE MACMILLAN

Idols of the Marketplace: Idolatry and Commodity Fetishism in English Literature, 1580–1680
by David Hawkes

Shakespeare among the Animals: Nature and Society in the Drama of Early Modern England
by Bruce Boehrer

Maps and Memory in Early Modern England: A Sense of Place
by Rhonda Lemke Sanford

Debating Gender in Early Modern England, 1500–1700
edited by Cristina Malcolmson and Mihoko Suzuki

Manhood and the Duel: Masculinity in Early Modern Drama and Culture
by Jennifer A. Low

Burning Women: Widows, Witches, and Early Modern European Travelers in India
by Pompa Banerjee

England's Internal Colonies: Class, Capital, and the Literature of Early Modern English Colonialism
by Mark Netzloff

Turning Turk: English Theater and the Multicultural Mediterranean
by Daniel Vitkus

Turning Turk: English Theater and the Multicultural Mediterranean, 1570–1630

Daniel Vitkus

palgrave
macmillan

TURNING TURK
© Daniel Vitkus, 2003.

First published 2003 by
PALGRAVE MACMILLAN™
175 Fifth Avenue, New York, N.Y. 10010 and
Houndmills, Basingstoke, Hampshire, England RG21 6XS.
Companies and representatives throughout the world.

PALGRAVE MACMILLAN is the global academic imprint of the Palgrave Macmillan division of St. Martin's Press, LLC and of Palgrave Macmillan Ltd. Macmillan® is a registered trademark in the United States, United Kingdom and other countries. Palgrave is a registered trademark in the European Union and other countries.

ISBN 0–312–29452–2 hardback

Library of Congress Cataloging-in-Publication Data

Vitkus, Daniel J.
    Turning Turk: English theater and the multicultural Mediterranean, 1570–1630 / Daniel Vitkus.
        p. cm. — (Early modern cultural studies)
    Includes bibliographical references and index.
        ISBN 0–312–29452–2
        1. English literature–Mediterranean influences. 2. English drama–Early modern and Elizabethan, 1500–1600–History and criticism. 3. English drama–17th century–History and criticism. 4. Theater–England–History–16th century. 5. Theater–England–History–17th century. 6. Mediterranean Region–In literature. 7. Multiculturalism in literature. 8. Orientalism in literature. 9. Exoticism in literature. I. Title. II. Series.

PR129.M48V58 2003
822′. 309321822–dc21   2003051797

A catalogue record for this book is available from the British Library.

Design by Newgen Imaging Systems (P) Ltd., Chennai, India.

First edition: October, 2003
10 9 8 7 6 5 4 3 2 1

Printed in the United States of America.

For my parents,
Paula and Rich

CONTENTS

Acknowledgments   viii

A Note on the Texts   xi

Series Editor's Foreword   xiii

1   Before Empire: England, Alterity, and the Mediterranean Context   1

2   The English and the Early Modern Mediterranean: Theater, Commerce, and Identity   25

3   Marlowe's Mahomet: Islam, Turks, and Religious Controversy in *Tamburlaine, Parts I and II*   45

4   Othello Turns Turk   77

5   Scenes of Conversion: Piracy, Apostasy, and the Sultan's Seraglio   107

6   Machiavellian Merchants: Italians, Jews, and Turks   163

Notes   199

Bibliography   221

Index   239

ACKNOWLEDGMENTS

It gives me great pleasure to acknowledge the help and support that I have received during the long process of preparing this book for publication. The research and writing that produced this book have been an extended labor, interrupted by two job searches and two moves, and by the editing of two additional books. Without the aid of many other people it never would have reached fruition.

This project began with my experience in Egypt, where I taught at the American University in Cairo for a period of six years. In 1991 I arrived in Egypt as a newly minted Ph.D., hopping the Atlantic from New York City to an even larger megalopolis, Cairo. Living in the Islamic world and in the multicultural Mediterranean, I learned a great deal about how cultures mix, overlap, and influence each other. Being there helped me to recognize that scholars in my field, early modern English culture, were largely unaware of the many important cultural connections that linked England and the Mediterranean world during the late sixteenth and seventeenth centuries.

First I want to acknowledge the hospitality and kindness that I encountered everywhere during the years that I lived and traveled extensively in the Middle East. I also want to thank my students at the American University in Cairo for what they taught me, and to recognize my colleagues there who helped me to think about theoretical and historical issues pertaining to this book. Anthony Calderbank, Richard Hoath, David Blanks, and Thabit Abdullah in particular were inspiring fellow travelers in teaching and scholarship during my years in Egypt.

I am grateful to the American University in Cairo for the generous research grants that enabled me to travel to the Folger Shakespeare Library, and I wish to express my gratitude to the Folger Institute for supporting me with a short-term fellowship. The Folger has been a home away from home for me, and this project has benefited tremendously from the impressive array of resources (both print and human) that are available to scholars who are lucky enough to conduct their research there. I would like to express my appreciation for all of the efforts made by the staff at the Folger Shakespeare Library on my behalf. Jean Miller deserves special recognition for the kind assistance she lent me. I received a huge boost from Natalie Zemon Davis and the other scholars who participated in her "cultural mixture" seminar at the Folger in 2000, and the conference held there in 2002 on "The Impact of the Ottoman Empire on Early Modern Europe" was an important coming together of people and ideas that helped me think through some of the refinements that went into the final revisions of *Turning Turk*. Many congratulations are due to Carol Brobeck, Kathleen Lynch, Gail Paster, Barbara Mowat, and the other key people at the Folger for the fine work they have contributed to make that place such an extraordinary, congenial zone of support for scholarship.

This book owes much to those who have been kind enough to read and comment on parts of the manuscript, and I reserve my special thanks for these people, who gave their valuable time and advice freely. They include Mark Garrett Cooper, Jennie Malika Evenson, Barry Faulk, Lindsay Kaplan, Barbara Mowat, Marcy North, and Mary Tonkinson. In a more general way, this book owes something to the intellectual exchanges that have taken place over the years at the annual meetings of The Group for Early Modern Cultural Studies. Members of the Group who have been particularly stimulating are Jonathan Burton, Ania Loomba, Mark Netzloff, Pat Parker, and Jyotsna Singh. They have demonstrated that academic conferences can be inspiring.

My original editor at Palgrave, Kristi Long, was willing to take a chance on this project when I was seeking a publisher, and Ivo Kamps, the editor of this series in Early Modern Cultural Studies, has been extremely accommodating—and patient. Their support and advice have been essential in getting this book into print.

I am indebted to my students at Florida State University, including Danielle Robitaille, whose hard work as my assistant in the final stages of revision was an enormous help. The graduate students in my seminar on "Shakespeare and the Exotic Other" were an inspiration to me, and our discussions helped me to clarify my thinking about cross-cultural encounters in the Renaissance. The English department at Florida State has been a hospitable, accommodating academic home. During my years here, I have experienced the institutional support that a scholar needs in order to get things done (including the glorious gift of a research semester, brought about by our Dean, Donald Foss). I especially wish to recognize the efforts of my hardworking chair, Hunt Hawkins, who has always tried to foster my development as a scholar. Finally, I would like to make a special declaration of thanks for the pleasure of having Bruce Boehrer as a colleague. He has aided me in more ways than he knows, and I admire him very much for his wit, generosity, and exceptional intellect. May the pagan gods smile down on him.

As long as I write books like this one, those writings will always bear the mark of three brilliant teachers whose work has profoundly influenced my own—Jean Howard, David Kastan, and Jim Shapiro. I don't always succeed, but I have tried to live up to their fine examples.

Finally, Jane McPherson is perhaps the one person to whom I owe the most—her trust, generosity of spirit, and understanding have been invaluable to me throughout the many years that I labored to complete this task. Thank you, Jane.

Much of chapter four appeared as an article in *Shakespeare Quarterly* and this material is reprinted here with permission, for which I am grateful. Columbia University Press and Palgrave have also kindly granted permission for me to publish versions of passages appearing in my introduction to *Three Turk Plays* and in an article that was published in *Travel Knowledge*, respectively. This book also draws, in a few brief passages, on two other essays that I have written—one in *Colonial and Postcolonial Incarceration* (ed. Graeme Harper) and the other in *Western Views of Islam in Medieval and Early Modern Europe* (ed. D. Blanks and M. Frassetto).

A Note on the Texts

All citations from Shakespeare are taken from the *Norton Shakespeare*, and all quotations from *A Christian Turned Turk* and *The Renegado* are taken from my edition, *Three Turk Plays from Early Modern England*. The reader will note that when citing from original spelling texts and manuscripts, I have silently modernized u/v, i/j, and long s. Italics in the original have not been preserved. The first time that a play is mentioned in this book, its title is accompanied by a date. This date is that of composition, not printing.

SERIES EDITOR'S FOREWORD

The Early Modern Cultural Studies series starts from the premise that as we enter the twenty-first century, literary criticism, literary theory, historiography, and cultural studies have become so interwoven that we can now think of them as an eclectic and only loosely unified approach to formerly distinct fields of study such as literature, society, history, and culture. This series furthermore presumes that the early modern period was witness to an incipient process of transculturation through exploration, mercantilism, colonization, and migration that set into motion a process of globalization that is still with us today. The purpose of this series is to bring together this eclectic approach, which freely and unapologetically crosses disciplinary, theoretical, and political boundaries, with early modern texts and artifacts that bear the traces of transculturation and globalization.

This process can be studied locally and internationally, and such a dual perspective is apparent in previous titles in the series as well as in Daniel Vitkus's *Turning Turk*. Vitkus's study centers on the English theater's representation and appropriation of the multicultural Mediterranean during the period 1570–1630, a time when English mercantile exploration began to expand its tentative mercantile proddings into "dark," exotic, and mysterious lands. By the end of this period there was already an intense and increasingly orchestrated national endeavor that sought to penetrate, understand, do business with, admire, learn from, and exploit the lands and people of the Mediterranean littoral. This period comprises a historical moment that can now be understood as a defining period in the prehistory of British imperialism and venture capitalism.

After theorizing his approach to the "exotic other" in relation to the work of Edward Said, Irvin Schick, Homi Bhabha, Aijaz Ahmad, and others, Vitkus offers an in-depth analysis of the nexus between English culture and the Mediterranean market. He argues that the Mediterranean sphere was in many ways far more important to English culture and commerce than the so-called New World. Drawing on a wide range of late sixteenth- and early seventeenth-century texts dealing with travel, religious polemics, and commerce, Vitkus creates both a vivid portrait of how the English imagined the Other and lays a foundation for understanding the crucial role the English theater played in providing the people with necessary knowledge about their new trading partners.

The necessity of this knowledge is apparent in the perceived dangers of engaging with the racial and cultural Other. Drawing on a variety of plays, Vitkus delves into the anxiety aroused in the English by the seductive qualities of Turkish culture and the power of Islam to convert English Christians into Muslims. A chapter on Machiavellian merchants broadens the discussion of religion and links the complex relations between Turks, Christians, and Jews directly to commercial interactions, including the burgeoning slave trade and a relatively new phenomenon in the English cultural imagination, namely piracy. Vitkus then turns to another complicating factor in the process of exchange between the English and Ottoman culture and demonstrates how ideas and language "gender" and sexualize commercial intercourse in ways that suggest sexual prowess but also center on fears of miscegenation and feminization.

Ultimately, Vitkus impresses upon us that the theater's manifold representations of cross-cultural exchange constitute a pedagogical effort to inform the English about the Other and to ready them for often unpredictable and even perilous encounters of bodies, minds, faiths, and desires that are an inevitable part of the economic future of the English nation as it gradually transforms itself into the British Empire.

Ivo Kamps
Series editor

CHAPTER 1

BEFORE EMPIRE: ENGLAND, ALTERITY, AND THE MEDITERRANEAN CONTEXT

> *When one uses the categories like Oriental and Western as both the starting and end point of analysis,... the result is usually to polarize the distinction.*
>
> —*Edward Said*, Orientalism

When cultural historians describe the relationship between England and other communities that existed outside England, they habitually refer to that foreign presence as "the Other." When employed in this sense, the term "Other" implies a radical, cognitive difference between the domestic and the foreign. In early modern studies, English identity is compared and contrasted to the Irish Other, the Spanish Other, the Islamic Other, the Amerindian Other, and so on. This use of the singular noun "other" to signify the status of a foreign entity beyond the pale of the homeland relies upon an analogy between individual consciousness and collective identity. The foundational psychoanalytic distinction between self (or ego) and other (or alter) becomes a model for our account of English culture's understanding of what is beyond its borders, outside its language and habitus. But already a problem arises: for the individual, alterity is everyone and everything but the self, but when we talk about an entire culture's "identity," we must speak using plural terms like "us" or "them." Perhaps the psychological mechanisms and processes that operate when one person perceives the world outside the self may be productively compared to the way that one society represents or apprehends another, but a strictly dualistic psycho-cultural phenomenology will inevitably fail to fit the form of "culture." Culture scatters and gathers in ways that are unlike a single mind at work.

Nonetheless, as any good cultural materialist knows, binary oppositions have an important rudimentary function in the dialectical process. One of the first steps in any basic cultural analysis is to distinguish the ideological function of binary oppositions. In the preliminary phase of interpretation, these binaries must be identified: for example, Shakespeare's *Othello* does rely upon a binary, one that was violently apparent to Protestant culture—that of heaven and hell, described in terms of white and black. But this binary does not remain stable, and in the next phase of analysis, we must trace the multivalent and multipolar significations that come into play in a text or a culture.

The routine usage in literary and cultural studies of "the other"—in a sense that relies upon a self–other binary—is a usage that has emerged from what Timothy Powell identifies as "the central project of Cultural Studies": "to deconstruct the epistemological structures of Eurocentrism and to recover historical voices that were overlooked because of an entrenched ethnocentrism that privileged the elite, white, heterosexual, abled, male, European perspective" (1). Powell goes on, however, to declare that "this initial phase of binary analysis" (1) has come to an impasse. While acknowledging that "One of the most effective strategies in this initial phase of the cultural *deconstruction* of Eurocentrism was the identification of theoretical binaries such as Self/Other, Center/Margin, Colonizer/Colonized" (1), Powell calls for a new theoretical order that would go beyond the binary in order to better describe cultural identity in a multicultural context. He writes,

> It has become clear in recent years . . . that a binary form of analysis that collapses a myriad of distinct culture voices into the overly simplistic category of "Other" defined in relationship to a European "Self" is theoretically problematic. The time has come, therefore, to initiate a new critical epoch, a period of cultural *reconstruction* in which "identity" is reconfigured in the midst of a multiplicity of cultural influences that more closely resembles what Homi Bhabha has called the "lived perplexity" of people's lives. . . . (1)

Powell's call for a more complex, non-dualistic paradigm to describe identity can and should be applied, not only to the analysis of the American, multicultural identities that concern Powell most, but also to early modern cultural identities in England and the Mediterranean, and especially to the formation and production of English identity under the influence of multicultural contact and mixture.

Consistent with Powell's manifesto, but directed toward early modern texts, is Daniel Carey's critique of what he terms "cognitive or symbolic incommensurability" (49). In a 1997 essay, Carey maintains, "much of recent scholarship on the subject of colonial encounter has been sustained by the conviction that unique, unassimilable cultures stared past one another in the Renaissance" (49). "The underlying assumption of fundamental oppositions between self and other," he writes, "...reflect[s] the endurance of structuralist readings of cultural contact, employing hermetic categories of self and other that result in an absolute rather than a variable account of incommensurability" (49).

The binary opposition of colonizer and colonized, so familiar in recent scholarship informed by postcolonial identity politics, cannot be maintained in a properly historicized description of England's early modern culture. The Tudor period was an age of plunder, not an "Age of Empire." English writers of the Elizabethan and Early Stuart era were not engaged in a foreknowing preparation for future empire (though British historians of the past century have often described the "Age of Discovery" in just this sort of teleological manner).[1] English authors writing before 1600 express imperial envy, ambition, desire, and fantasy. There was much rhetorical bluster and much interest in the New World, but there was no way of knowing if, when, or where the English (or British) would build an enduring empire.

Before the latter half of the seventeenth century, England's "colonial" discourse was merely the premature articulation of a third-rank power. From our perspective, this proto-imperialist discourse may appear to have prepared the way by providing ideological conditioning, but English fantasies did not comprise a precise blueprint for future conquest and rule. Nabil Matar and Daniel Goffman have argued persuasively against the ahistorical tendency to describe early modern Englishmen as "imperialist" before English imperialism began.[2] As Goffman points out, "the Englishman's imperialism is not innate" (1998, 4). The British empire of later centuries has an ideological prehistory, of course, and the roots of empire can be traced back to the sixteenth and early seventeenth centuries, but these roots are intertwined with other ideological developments. Cultural historians seeking the discursive origins of English colonial conquest and settlement have uncovered much evidence, but sometimes they fail to situate that evidence within a pre-imperial context that is complex, overdetermined, and ambivalent.[3]

There were certainly beginnings in Ireland, where a complex, multilayered history of colonization existed long before the British overseas empire did.[4] Nonetheless, before 1630 the English conquest and occupation of Ireland was only partially successful and was "imperial" only in its propaganda. The description of English colonization in Ireland outlined by the influential scholar Nicholas Canny must be balanced by the arguments of historians such as Steven Ellis and Bruce Lenman. While Canny points out that in Elizabethan writings one observes a growing perception of Ireland as a new sort of colony, similar to the Virginia plantation; Ellis and Lenman see events in Ireland in the larger, long-standing context of English royal efforts to consolidate its hold over unruly border zones that had always presented administrative challenges and engendered rebellion. Lenman describes, during the Elizabethan and Early Stuart periods, not the rise and development of an imperial power in Ireland or elsewhere, but "the bankruptcy of Elizabethan imperialism," followed by "the aborting of a three-kingdom overseas empire."[5] By 1600, claims Lenman, "...Elizabeth could hardly be said effectively to rule much more of Ireland than Henry VII had" (128). According to Lenman, this failure was not limited to Ireland:

> King James did not inherit an England within striking distance of imperial greatness. He inherited a financially and politically stressed monarchy whose peoples were dangerously divided....There was no imperial achievement. (142)

A series of setbacks occurred in both Ireland and North America during the period 1570–1620, as English ambitions and hopes were repeatedly dashed. Perhaps it was this experience of tense aspiration, followed by a series of failed expeditions and campaigns that generated so much imperial rhetoric as compensation for these setbacks, and as a strategy to conceal embarrassing and costly losses.

While Elizabethan Ireland was a disaster for would-be imperialists, the first attempted plantations in North America were not much better. Many of the early reports coming from the Virginia colony were not promising. In a recent study, Stephen Adams demonstrates that "Alongside the upbeat, propagandistic view of Virginia as Eden, Promised Land, gold mine, commodity warehouse, pastoral paradise...there emerges from the surviving texts another, opposite view of Virginia...as a hellhole where people die quickly and miserably and in breathtaking numbers—Virginia as a death trap or slaughterhouse" (Adams 2001, 156). John Smith, in one of his reports, acknowledged that some colonists saw Virginia as "a miserie, a ruine, a death, a hell" (cited in Adams 2001, 156). As late as 1625, Charles I's "Proclamation for setling the Plantation of Virginia" admitted failure in its opening words:

> Whereas the Colonie of Virginia, Planted by the hands of Our most deare Father of blessed memory, for the propagation of Christian Religion, the increase of Trade, and the enlarging of his Royall Empire, hath not hitherto prospered so happily, as was hoped and desired. . . . (Larkin 1983, 2:27)

At first, English colonizers in Virginia had hoped to supply the "plantation" by conquest, forcing the local population to provide them with food and shelter, but this approach failed miserably.

In literary studies, the material reality (i.e. failure) of England's early attempts at empire has been largely repressed. After the flood of New World scholarship that marked the five-hundredth anniversary of Columbus's voyage to the Indies in 1992, historicist analyses of early modern texts have tended to read "representations of the Other" according to a teleological historiography of Western domination, conquest, and colonization. Stephen Greenblatt's location of Shakespearean drama in the context of a nascent colonialism established the critical practice of reading all English Renaissance texts as the products of an imperialist culture that looked across the Atlantic—and across the globe—toward its colonies-to-be.[6] Kim Hall, in her important and influential study, *Things of Darkness*, conforms to this trend when she anachronistically locates "imperialist expansion" in the Elizabethan and Jacobean periods.[7] Though Hall mentions England's "subterranean anxieties of cultural impotence" (136), she emphasizes the notion of England as a society exercising "cultural hegemony" and driven by "the economic imperatives of imperial trade" (56). Similarly, Emily Bartels, in her study of Marlowe's drama, posits the historical presence of an imperial England that sought to "promote and justify imperialism," not only in New World plantations, but also in "the 'civilized' East" (1993, 59).[8] Jack D'Amico, in *The Moor in English Renaissance Drama*, also exaggerates England's presence abroad, referring to "budding colonialism" and an "expanding colonial empire" (61–62). More recently, Barbara Fuchs, in her discussion of early modern Spain, England, and Islam as cultural competitors, acknowledges that in the late sixteenth century, "England was painfully conscious of its own imperial belatedness with respect to Spain" (7), but having said this, she then maintains that sixteenth-century England carried out "the military imitation of imperial strategies on both Mediterranean and transatlantic stages" (7).[9] In her analyses of English texts and cultural tendencies, Fuchs frequently confounds "imperial claims" (11) with empire itself. All of these critics fall prey to the same postcolonial fallacy, a fallacy that is exemplified and encapsulated by Arthur L. Little, Jr., when he asserts, "To talk like an empire is to be an empire" (16), a statement that confuses the merely discursive with the material conditions of empire as an institution.[10] Foucault taught us to recognize the discursive and ideological circulation of power and its "net-like" organization, but he would certainly have agreed that imperial rhetoric without territorial possession—and without control over colonized bodies—does not an empire make.[11] This is not to say that a proto-imperial discourse did not have a key function in the development of an English empire: imperial fantasies did help to prepare the way for a real empire on the ground. Nonetheless, calling England an "empire" does not mean that England was in fact a conquering, colonizing power.[12] There is a danger here of confusing the discursive with the material, theory with practice, rhetoric with reality.

It is important to acknowledge that the "idea" of empire arose in England long before there was a real, material empire on the ground.[13] Describing the imaginative foundations of empire does not allow us to describe England in 1600, or even 1630, as an empire like that ruled by Spain, or ancient Rome. Using the term "British empire" brings further problems into play. It might be said that there was no "Britain," and thus no "British empire" until the Union occurred in 1707. Even a "composite monarchy," if that is what Jacobean "Britain" was, does not comprise a fully imperial power that holds sway over a variety of conquered subject peoples.[14]

Critical controversy surrounding Shakespeare's play, *The Tempest*, provides a striking example of how the misapprehension of an imperial telos deflects attention from more immediate, contemporary concerns. Much recent debate about colonialism and/in *The Tempest* has been obsessed with the premise that Prospero's control of the Mediterranean island represents the colonizing process—and some postcolonial authors have suggested that *The Tempest* prophetically prefigures decolonization when Prospero and the other Europeans leave the island at the end of the play.[15] More recently, David Scott Kastan and Barbara Fuchs have argued that specifically European and Mediterranean issues must be examined, along with the New World context, in order to fully historicize *The Tempest*.[16] One way to contextualize the play's ending is to see the departure for Italy as the conclusion of a provisional, unsuccessful effort to occupy Caliban's island, just as the Spanish failed to retain many of its outposts in North Africa, or the English failed to preserve early plantations like Roanoke.

Whether we focus on the play's literal setting in the Mediterranean, or its references to the New World, we see aristocratic characters who fail to sustain any empire-building projects. Instead, they are eager to retreat to their metropolitan homes in Italy. The only voice that celebrates the potential of the island for colonization, Gonzalo, is effectively mocked to scorn by Antonio and Sebastian. And, as Barbara Fuchs points out, "The vanishing banquet that tantalizes the starving Europeans in *The Tempest* serves well as a metaphor for the expected abundance that evaporated when the English arrived in the New World" (2001, 138). *The Tempest* is a play about a desperate struggle to maintain control over an isolated, unsupported outpost in order to recover lost power back home; it is not about the enforcement of an established imperial order.

At the same time that imperialist aspirations were going unfulfilled in under-supplied Jamestown, the English were developing a much broader and more successful enterprise in the Mediterranean, where English ships and men went to trade with the powerful empires that already existed there. While the leaders of the Virginia colonies begged for more supplies and people to be shipped to North America from England, ample resources were pouring into the lucrative trade in the Mediterranean. The early modern Mediterranean, it must be said, was a violent economy and replete with risk, but in spite of the hazards of doing business there, it offered a much more reliable site for English "ventures" whereby risks might be rewarded with a cargo of valuable commodities and then large profits back in London. In the Mediterranean, these profits were to be taken not by means of colonization or conquest, but primarily through peaceful trade, and secondarily through intimidation, piracy, and improvised violence at sea.

The assumptions of postcolonial theory and criticism simply do not apply to an early modern Mediterranean context that is nothing like the "Manichean world" (41) described by Fanon in *The Wretched of the Earth*. English representations of North Africa, Turkey, Greece, Italy, or the Middle East do not yet employ the "Manichean delirium" that Fanon and others have noted as the primary framework for Western imperial texts that describe thoroughly colonized peoples.[17] The cultural mixture and exchange permitted by the Ottomans and conducted in other Mediterranean entrepôts was quite unlike the rigidly compartmentalized and divided societies that developed later. The Mediterranean littoral formed an extensive network of "contact zones," but not of the colonial variety described by Mary Louise Pratt.[18] Before the eighteenth century, the Mediterranean world (including its Islamic and Ottoman components) was comprehended through residual history and contemporary cross-cultural encounters, not in terms of East-versus-West or colonizer-versus-colonized, but as a complex and unstable meeting ground for divergent cultural and religious groups. The humanist appeal to the classical past and the Christian appeal to the Biblical past were attempts to construct and impose a stable, definitive identity for the Mediterranean, its culture and geography; but often the rich variety of Levantine culture emerges uppermost, as the most visible and indelible part of the cultural palimpsest.

As Jonathan Burton points out in an essay on Marlowe's *Tamburlaine*, "early modern treatments of the East lack the 'internal inconsistency' which Said finds in eighteenth-century Orientalism" (2000, 126). Burton's observation is complicated further by the fact that "the East" was not yet the clearly defined geographic or cultural category that it would become under high British imperialism.[19] On the discursive map of England's imaginary geography, there was no unified space of "the other" called "the Orient." In early modern parlance "the Orient" had a very generalized geographic meaning: it did not refer to a particular imaginary entity with all of the features that post-Renaissance Orientalists would later attribute to that entity. Such an imaginary construct was yet to be built. It would be chronicled and unified later by the European orientalists, but no such academic or intellectual cadre existed before the late seventeenth century. From the perspective of an England without Orientalism, Mediterranean and Islamic alterity comprised many divergent identities, and these were defined by an overlapping set of identity categories, including race, religion, somatic difference, sexuality, and political affiliation. But alterity was also manifested in the *behavior* of foreign peoples—in the many specific practices, sexual regimes, religious activities, laws, values, and customs that were observed or made known to English subjects who went to the Mediterranean to travel, labor, negotiate, or trade. And as English identity mutated, acquiring, for example, a self-image that increasingly took on a mercantile, capitalist form, English subjects learned to change by incorporating what were initially foreign behaviors and practices.

In an essay on alterity and exchange in early modern culture, Ania Loomba makes this important point: "ideologies of racial differences have hardened as a direct response to racial and cultural crossovers; conversely, colonial enterprises have facilitated contact and exchange between people of different ethnicities, religions and cultures. Notions of alterity or exchange thus derive their meaning from one another" (2000, 201). She goes on to claim that the late sixteenth and early seventeenth centuries comprised "the last period in history where ethnic identities could be understood as fluid, or as the first moment of the emergence of modern notions of 'race'" (201). As contact with radically different cultures increased during the course of the seventeenth century, notions of racial identity rigidified, but as Loomba points out, this was not because of a heightened sense of difference experienced by English subjects who encountered Amerindians, Asians, Moors, and other alien peoples. It was the fear of becoming like "the Other"—of "turning Turk," or being Judaized, or taking on an Italianate identity, and the like—that generated the need for a rigidly defined discourse of racial alterity. As Daniel Carey demonstrates in his essay on early modern cultural exchange, English writings on colonization and travel stress "the potential interchangeability of self and other rather than the radical opposition between the two" (34). According to Carey, English authors "worried about the impact of travel precisely because they accepted the commensurability of human beings, and therefore the capacity of the English to become like those they observed and with whom they lived" (40). In their relations with cultural contestants like France, Spain, Portugal, Venice, and Turkey, the English were, in many ways, a society of mimic-men who were learning (or hoping) to imitate alien models of power, wealth, and luxury.

Not only in terms of identity politics, but also in the cultural history of England's foreign relations, the late sixteenth and early seventeenth centuries constitute a fascinating moment of ideological emergence. Where England's imperial ambition was concerned, rhetoric and cultural desire were far ahead of material achievement. English courtiers and adventurers strove to emulate the imperial accomplishments of the Spanish, Portuguese, and Turks, but the only empire the English had was an impoverished and besieged foothold in Ireland, and even as late as 1630, their "empire" had only been enlarged by a handful of miserable outposts in Virginia and Massachusetts. Many of the early voyages of "discovery" came to a bad end, and the earliest attempts at permanent English settlement in America collapsed completely: the Roanoke colony was wiped out by 1591, and the Plymouth Company's early attempts to found a colony failed in 1606 and again in 1607–08.[20] In 1612, it was necessary for Robert Johnson to publish, in *The New Life of Virginea*, an "apology...to free the name [of Virginia] from the injurious scoffer," in which he laments, "there is no common speech nor public name of anything this day...which is more vildly depraved, traduced and derided by such unhallowed lips, then the name of

Virginea" ("Epistle Dedicatorie"). Johnson goes on to claim that the domestic critics of the Virginia project have conspired with the playwrights of London: "not only the ignorant and simple minded are much discouraged, but the malitious and looser sort (being accompanied with the licentious vaine of stage Poets) have whet their tongues with scornfull taunts against the action it selfe" (sig. A3v). Johnson's parenthetical remark may allude to a lost play that represented and ridiculed the Virginia plantation's failure to live up to the Utopian rhetoric used to promote the nascent colonial project and to recruit willing colonists. This official concern with theatrical attacks on the colonizing project is also seen in a 1610 sermon by William Crashaw, delivered before Lord De La Warre and a group of colonizers about to depart for Jamestown. On that occasion, Crashaw declared that the three principle foes of the Virginia enterprise were the Devil, Roman Catholics, and players. It seems that the public playhouses provided satirical ridicule of imperial pretensions in North America, while at the same time, as I will discuss later, the public theater staged various models of imperial power and commercial profitability in the Mediterranean.

The evidence of early colonial failure on the part of the English makes it clear that, given the gap between the fantasy of dominance in exotic encounters, and the reality of frustration and insolvency, we cannot analyze pre-imperial English culture using the theoretical paradigms typically employed by first-wave postcolonial studies. Bart Moore-Gilbert and others have specifically addressed the possibility, incited by Edward Said, of medieval and early modern texts exhibiting an "orientalist" discourse.[21] Moore-Gilbert suggests not only that pre-Enlightenment contexts do not conform to Said's model in *Orientalism*, but also that Said's paradigm is too simplistic to render an accurately historicized account of any period:

> Western representations of Islam may be more complex than Orientalism characteristically assumes....Orientalism cannot be considered uniformly either as a discourse of mastery or even as the consistent and unvarying expression of the Western will to power through knowledge and representation....
> ...it is ambivalence rather than a simply dichotomizing and essentializing attitude which more accurately characterizes the western vision of the East. (61)

The general problem that Moore-Gilbert outlines here is compounded when we look for signs of orientalism in an early modern England that had not yet established a system of colonial mastery. If we take Said's analysis and apply it to the discourses produced by Elizabethan or Jacobean society, we commit the critical fallacy of back formation. By means of hindsight, and relying upon a teleological overview of history, imperialist fantasies may be misapprehended as evidence of empire. For an English subject to "know" about Islamic culture in 1560 or 1630 was not to maintain power over it.

The chief limitations of Said's *Orientalism* include its theoretical rigidity, "its insistence that the orientalist stereotype invariably presupposes and confirms a totalising and unified imperial discourse" (Gandhi 1998, 77), and its attempt to extend the historical limits of orientalism to include two thousand years of Western culture, from Homer to the present, arguing that during those two millennia every textual or imaginary construction of the non-Western world to the East was an orientalist construction. In describing orientalism as Manichean and binary, Said's *Orientalism* reproduces, in a mirror image, the distorting binarism that he rightly abhors in Western accounts of Islamic culture. His paradigm tends to define the project of resistance according to the very same semiotic opposition set up by the imperial discourse itself. Said's own precepts return to haunt him, and in a classic case of reinscription, what Said abhors in the orientalists reenters and defines his own logic: "When one uses the categories like Oriental and Western as both the starting and end point of analysis, research, public policy,...the result is usually to polarize the distinction" (45–46). Furthermore, the bipolar model fails to account for the mobility, interactivity, and variety of identity positions that emerge in texts about cross-cultural encounters. Thus, when we seek a theoretical framework to help us analyze the early modern representation of Islamic or Mediterranean alterities, we find that Said's postcolonial theory, which is based upon the historical experience of Western imperialism and colonization, must be deployed with caution, if at all. We should keep in mind that *Orientalism* first appeared over twenty years ago, and much theoretical work has followed in its wide wake. If *Orientalism*'s central paradigm, with its questionable melding of Foucault's "knowledge" and Gramsci's "hegemony," does not provide a valid model for our analysis of early modern cross-cultural encounters, perhaps more recent postcolonial theory can provide more useful terms and conceptual frameworks.[22]

This study draws upon postmodern theories of alterity and cultural identity that have contested modern philosophy's attempt to secure the legitimacy of knowledge on the basis of a self-conscious, Cartesian subject. Postmodern theory places in question and delegitimizes the Hegelian effort to secure self-knowledge and recognition by demonstrating that knowledge and recognition are mediated by a whole. It is not a "wholly other" that mediates and produces the self's identity; rather, the self is dispersed, fragmented, and always incomplete because there is no clear, stable distinction between individual subjectivity and the shared collective consciousness that is interpellated and produced by language and ideology. Just as the Cartesian subject has been disclosed as a philosophical delusion, so the notion of a unified, self-knowing cultural identity has been exposed as a fallacy. A better model for describing the construction of cultural identity, in relation to exogenous difference, might draw upon the insights of poststructuralism. The collective identity formation of an English culture that was experiencing, in powerful new ways, the shock of the exotic exhibited both attraction and repulsion simultaneously, and by oscillation between those poles came gradually to absorb and adapt various elements of alterity. Beyond selfhood, at a communal level, a kind of imitative receptivity altered the shifting foundation of an always precarious cultural condition. Culture constitutes itself, not on the basis of a coherent identity–alterity binary, but through a process of engagement with multiple "others" that precede and possess any given culture. Or to put it in Derridean terms, "every other is wholly other" (Derrida 82). This takes us beyond the limits of both a subjective singularity (or wholeness) and the dualism of the self–other binary.

A poststructuralist theory of alterity gives us a better description of how cultural identity is constructed, but we also need a more historically specific understanding of cross-cultural, multicultural, or transcultural phenomena. This is necessary if we are to analyze the development of early modern English culture in its relations with two other processes: English contact and interaction with other cultures in the Mediterranean, and the representation of the multicultural Mediterranean in English texts and performances. In this further effort to theorize the cross-cultural, it may be helpful to turn once again to the insights of postcolonial theory, though we must take care to adjust these theories in light of the differences between the precolonial and postcolonial moments. Some of the concepts developed more recently by Homi Bhabha, for example, might be adopted or adapted by early modern cultural studies. Bhabha, following the poststructuralist model of alterity articulated by Derrida and others, describes the process of identity formation:

> ...the question of identification is never the affirmation of a pre-given identity, never a self-fulfilling prophecy—it is always the production of

an "image" of identity and the transformation of the subject in assuming that image. The demand of identification—that is, to be *for* an Other—entails the representation of the subject in the differentiating order of Otherness. Identification ... is always the return of an image of identity which bears the mark of splitting in that "Other" place from which it comes. ("Remembering Fanon" 117)

He goes on to argue that the representation of the Other "is always ambivalent, disclosing a lack" (119). This description of alterity opens up a space of negation, negotiation, and confusion of identity that can be applied to the experience of early modern England, and much of Bhabha's work is concerned with the way that cultures meet and mix, adapting to each other, in that space. According to Bhabha there is a "liminal space, in-between the [binary] designations of identity" and "This interstitial passage between fixed identifications opens up the possibility of a cultural hybridity that entertains difference without an assumed or imposed hierarchy" (Bhabha, *Location of Culture* 4). This approach can be helpful because it eschews the rigid binarism of Said's polemic and offers a conceptual system that can accommodate the dynamic interaction that took place in the Mediterranean-Islamic region. English venturing and voyaging in liminal spaces and market-places, from Algiers to Venice to Constantinople, moved beyond the "primordial polarities" (Bhabha, *Location of Culture* 4) that were fixed in English ideology and rhetoric, into a multicultural zone that had transcultural effects on English culture. The representations of the Mediterranean world that were staged in early modern London are constructed in a cultural space that sometimes resembles Bhabha's "Third Space of Enunciation," where English cultural identity emerges under conditions that are contradictory and ambivalent. According to Bhabha, "...a willingness to descend into that alien territory...may open the way to conceptualizing an *inter*national culture, based not on the exoticism of multiculturalism or the *diversity* of cultures, but on the inscription and articulation of culture's *hybridity*" (Bhabha, *Location of Culture* 38). Here Bhabha suggests that cultural mixture (as opposed to a bicultural division or a multi-cultural patchwork) produces "intercultural, hybrid demands" (119) that, in the colonial context, can be effective in "challenging the boundaries of discourse and subtly changing its terms" (119). In the early modern context, however, the forms of hybridity that Bhabha describes were only beginning. And the kind of hybridity this study examines is produced, not by a blending of "native" and "colonial," but by a mixture of a "native," pre-colonial English culture with various "imported" foreign practices or "translated" discourses. Nonetheless, there are particular times and places where cultural hybridity is imagined or glimpsed by English subjects before 1630, and these moments are registered symbolically on the early modern stage; for example, when Othello and Desdemona elope and then succeed in defending and preserving their marriage against Brabantio's accusations. But just as often, English representations of cultural diversity serve to construct a border around some notion of Englishness or of White Christianity, and such representations oppose that bordered identity formation to various instabilities that surround it. This is the process that Michael Taussig describes in *Mimesis and Alterity*:

> Rather than thinking of the border as the farthermost extension of an essential identity spreading out from a core, this makes us think instead of the border itself as that core. Identity acquires its satisfying solidity because of the effervescence of the continually sexualized border, because of the turbulent forces, sexual and spiritual, that the border not so much contains as emits. (150–51)

This sexualized and eroticized border is redrawn at the end of *Othello*, when a paranoid vision of contamination destroys Othello and Desdemona's marriage. Centripetal forces, generated at the Cyprus borderland, are directed toward the core of Venice. Similarly, English contact with the Mediterranean continually challenged the borders of English culture, and English representations of its diversity and instability continually confront and express that challenge.

Fernand Braudel's work provides a useful historical mapping of this international, transactional structure.[23] Braudel's study of Mediterranean civilization emphasizes its hybridity:

> the extent and immensity of the intermingling of Mediterranean cultures, all the more rich in consequences since in the this zone of exchanges cultural groups were so numerous from the start. In one region they might remain distinctive, exchanging and borrowing from other groups from time to time. Elsewhere they merged to produce the extraordinary charivari suggestive of eastern ports as described by romantic poets: a rendezvous for every race, every religion, every kind of man, for everything in the way of hairstyles, fashions, foods and manners to be found in the Mediterranean. (Braudel 1973, 763)

Though Braudel's description retains touches of orientalism ("eastern ports as described by romantic poets"), he succeeds in demonstrating that the Mediterranean was a culturally fluid environment, to a degree that was shocking to English observers. In this "Mediterranean world" described by Braudel, English travelers found themselves within an environment that was defined by mixture, exchange, and hybridity; and they often reacted with amazement or bewilderment to the cosmopolitanism they observed in renowned Mediterranean centers like Venice, Constantinople, Cairo, or Jerusalem. This was the case for one traveler, William Lithgow, a Scot who recorded his extensive wanderings in *The Totall Discourse of the Rare Adventures* (1632).[24] Lithgow arrived in Jerusalem on Palm Sunday, 1612, only to find it occupied by a mob of Christians, Muslims, and Jews of various cultural identities. From the upper gallery of the Church of the Holy Sepulcher, during the three-day Easter festival, Lithgow looks down on "all the Orientall people" (266) and comments on their behavior. On this occasion, the "seven sorts of Nations, different in Religion, and language" who divide and occupy the church are for Lithgow a disorderly Babel, a manifestation of heresy and its capacity to divide and conquer the one truth. But on other occasions, when his irascible Protestantism was not set on edge, Lithgow could offer praise for the rich diversity he encountered. For example, while narrating his journey through Egypt, Lithgow reserves great admiration for the size and variety of Cairo, reporting, "This incorporate World of Grand Cairo is the most admirable and greatest City, seene upon the earth" (269). His description of the city's "infinite populositie" (271) spills over with verbal excitement:

> In this Towne a Traveller may ever happily finde all these sorts of Christianes[:] Italians, French, Greekes, Chelfaines [i.e. Chaldeans?], Georgians, Aethiopians, Jacobines, Syrians, Armenians, Nicolaitans, Abassines, and high Hungarians, Ragusans, and their owne Aegyptian Copties; the number of which is thought to be beyond two hundred thousand people: besides the infinite number of Infidels, whose sorts are these, Turkes, tawny Moores, white Moores, blacke Moores, or Nigroes, Musilmans, Tartars, Persians, Indians, Sabunks, Berdoanes, Jewes, Arabians, Barbares, and Tingitanian Sarazens. (271–72)

In this case, the very same variety of foreign peoples is celebrated, not reviled. Lithgow is able to characterize Cairo's multiculturalism differently from that of Jerusalem because he associates it, not with heresy or with the multiplicity of error, but with trade: he sees in Cairo "a great commerce . . . with exceeding many nations . . . wonderfully peopled with infinite numbers" (271) and offering a wide range of rich commodities for sale. Because it stood in contrast to the relative insularity, stability, and homogeneity of England itself, this multicultural mixture and movement of peoples, driven by market forces, made Mediterranean culture radically different (and therefore so fascinating) for visiting English observers. In one sense, this cultural difference, based on blending and variety of peoples, stood apart in contrast to Englishness, but in another sense it insistently offered to accommodate and absorb English subjects, by making them participants in the Mediterranean marketplace.

Lithgow was untypical of English visitors to the Mediterranean in that he was an intelligencer, whose primary aim was to bring back information to England. English merchants were perhaps more inclined to praise and embrace Mediterranean multiculturalism. Take, for example, John Eldred's remarks on Aleppo, made in 1583:

> This is the greatest place of traffike for a dry towne that is in all these parts: for hither resort Jewes, Tartarians, Persians, Armenians, Egyptians, Indians, and many sorts of Christians, and injoy freedome of their consciences, and bring hither many kindes of rich merchandizes.[25]

In places like Aleppo, the Ottoman empire functioned as a tributary economy within which Turkish elites cooperated with non-Turkish local elites in order to share power and wealth.[26] By 1588 there were English consuls and factors resident in Aleppo, Damascus, Alexandria, Cairo, Algiers, Tunis, Tripoli in North Africa, and Tripoli in Syria; and English mercantile activity in Italy and Greece also increased. At first, English visitors to the Mediterranean found it challenging to sort out the identities of the people they encountered, but by the end of the sixteenth century the continuous, expanding trade in the region made the Mediterranean world more familiar to English culture.

Seen through English eyes, what it meant to be a "Turk" was itself a disturbingly illusive and unstable identity. This could produce anxiety as well as admiration. The Turks and their "nation" were often depicted by European writers as a people without a deep-rooted, essential identity of their own. Instead of possessing a long-standing ethnic position, they were characterized as upstarts and thieves, or as an expanding, dangerously absorptive nation of renegades that had come into existence by feeding off other nations. The anonymous author of *The Estate of Christians, living under the subjection of the Turke* (1595) describes the systematic way that "the Turk" was said to draw his manpower from the very people he had conquered:

> Divers Countries and Nations are in subjection of the Turke ... insomuch that there be many thousandes of Christians subject to Turkishe

tyrannie. ... All the male children of Christians are written up at the day of their birth, and comming to ten or twelve yeres of their age, are presented to the Turkes officers, who take all such as they finde well made, and like to prove fit men for service in warre, from their parents...to become Turkes, and enemies to God, and their owne fathers and mothers, and kinsfolke, standing the Turke in more sted than his own naturall people. (1–2)

This text ascribes Islamic power to "unnatural" practices that were alien to English culture, but English and Continental authors also stood in awe of a social system that could produce mass conversion so effectively while European Christians engaged in violent conflict, Protestant against Roman Catholic, and saw many Christians become Muslims.

In early modern texts that were available to English readers, Islam itself is usually characterized as a hybrid religion, patched together out of other religions and as a false faith founded by and for deceivers, apostates, and renegades, rooted in the deluded or forced conversion of Christians to Islam. Islam was described as a religion founded on violent conquest, and Islamic conquests were said to be facilitated by religious fanaticism and proselytizing. Muhammed himself is described as a figure of hybridity and mimicry in *The Policy of the Turkish Empire* (1597): "His parents were of divers nations and different in religion: His father Abdallas was an Arabian: His mother Cadige a Jewe both by birth and profession" (lv). In the same text, following the typical narrative of anti-Islamic polemic, the Prophet is said to share the credit for the foundation of Islam with a renegade Nestorian priest named Sergius:

...these two hellhounds (one of them being an arch enemie to Christ and the truth of his religion, and the other seeming a meere Atheist or prophane person, neyther perfect Jew nor perfect Christian) patched up a particular doctrine unto themselves out of the olde and new Testament: depraving the sence of eyther of them: and framing their opinions according to their owne corrupt and wicked affections. They brought forth a monstrous and most divilish religion savouring partly of Judaisme, partly of Christianitie, and partly of Arrianisme. (sig. 2r–2v)

As for "the Turkish Alkoran," it, too, is denounced for its supposed patchwork nature: it is "for the most part full stuffed and replenished with vaine and fantastical conceits of feigned dreames, apparitions, visions, and revelations: And it aboundeth...with a number of fond tales and fables, which are every where entermingled with the deliverie of their superstitions" (sig. 14r). The Turkish language was also described as a hodge-podge: Lithgow reports of the Turks in Constantinople: "The better sort use the Slavonian tongue, the vulgar speake the Turkish language, which being originally the Tartarian speech, they borrow from the Persian their words of state, from the Arabicke, their words of Religion, from the Grecians, their termes of warre, and from the Italian their words and titles of navigation" (145). To communicate and trade in the Mediterranean, English subjects learned to use the *lingua franca* spoken in the region, or else they worked with "dragomen" or interpreters, many of whom were Jews, Armenians, or renegades.

In areas under Muslim rule, many tongues were spoken and many religious practices tolerated. Islam, unlike Christianity, was a belief system that allowed other religions, through the *dhimmi* system, to operate under its authority.[27] The Turkish sultan, like earlier Muslim rulers, permitted, and sometimes encouraged, other religious groups to live within his domains. Ottoman civilization was itself multi-layered and complex. This is one scholar's description of the art and culture of the Ottomans: a "Persano-Mongol-Turkic complex, enriched with a dash of Chinese art and technology, not to mention Indian mystical practices, all built upon an Islamic, Arabic base" (MacNeill 95).

Though they paid close attention to the religious differences that they encountered, English subjects who visited the early modern Mediterranean (including the Ottoman territories) experienced its openness and exotic variety primarily through the lens of international trade. When the circulation of English vessels between English ports and the Mediterranean began to increase dramatically in the 1570s, these merchants and their crews encountered a complex, fluid network of interlocking societies—not a monolithic "other." These seafarers dealt with alterity, all right, but it took many different forms: Spanish, French, Italian, Ragusan, Greek, Turkish, Arab, Berber, Muslim, Jewish, Orthodox, Roman Catholic, Morisco, "Marrano," "renegado," and more. The Islamic world overlapped with Christendom, and the Ottoman empire included a huge Jewish population. The Turkish empire was a porous body politic, allowing the entry and exit of various Christians, Jews, and Muslims who participated in its economic life.

The borders of the Ottoman empire were expanding and unstable. Throughout the sixteenth and seventeenth centuries, the Ottoman polity was extended through conquest: it incorporated border areas ruled by Christians who paid tribute, and it crossed over into

Christian territory with its fleets of galleys, its armies, and its *ghazi* border raiders. The North African regencies in Algiers, Tunis, and Tripoli were under nominal Ottoman rule but maintained substantial autonomy. The kingdom of Morocco was free of Ottoman sovereignty, and in the Balkans the Turks held tributary agreements with Christian rulers.

What Said seems to forget in *Orientalism* is that during the centuries that passed between the Crusades and Napoleon's invasion of Egypt in 1798, the Ottoman empire succeeded in colonizing large parts of "the West," and that throughout the early modern era, writers from Western Europe frequently wrote of their own cultural fragmentation and military inadequacy, which contrasted so radically, in their eyes, with the strength, power, unity, and discipline demonstrated by the Ottoman Turks and their Muslim subjects. As early as 1525, Piero Bragdin, the Venetian Bailo in Constantinople, wrote home to his son in Venice:

> I know of no State which is happier than this one [Turkey], it is furnished with all God's gifts. It controls war and peace with all, it is rich in gold, in people, in ships, in obedience; no State can be compared with it. May God long preserve the most just of Emperors.... (qtd. in Steensgard 74–75)

Writing in the mid-sixteenth century, Ogier Ghiselin De Busbecq, who served as the Archduke Ferdinand's ambassador at the Ottoman court of Soliman I, mixed his admiration for the Turks with considerable anxiety:

> I tremble when I think of what the future must bring when I compare the Turkish system with our own.... On their side are the resources of a mighty empire, strength unimpaired, experience and practice in fighting, a veteran soldiery, habituation to victory, endurance of toil, unity, order, discipline, frugality, watchfulness. On our side is public poverty, private luxury, impaired strength, broken spirit, lack of endurance and training. (112–13)

Throughout the sixteenth century, English translations of French and Italian accounts disseminated the kind of fear and admiration expressed by Bragdin and De Busbecq.

European anxiety was heightened by reports of the Turk's territorial advance into Austria and toward Germany and Poland. Hugh Goughe's *The Ofspring of the House of Ottomanno* (1569), a compilation translated and excerpted from Paulus Giovius, Bartolomeo

Georgievitz, and other Continental sources, praises the Ottomans'
military prowess:

> The Turkes do mainteine and kepe with such justice and severitie the
> discipline of war, the lawes and customes in battell, that in this behalfe
> they maye seme farre to passe the Gretians and Romains. Ther never
> chaunceth amonge them, eyther divisions, muttual slaughters, sedi-
> tions, or treason. For they ar fourthe with beheaded, being but for a
> trifeling offence convicted. The Turkish souldiers in many respectes do
> surmount the warriours of other nations. (sig. B7r)

While Turkish armies and navies were battling Roman Catholic powers
in Central Europe and in the Mediterranean, English Protestants were
forging commercial ties with the Ottomans. By the early decades of the
seventeenth century, it had become more common for Englishmen to
travel or trade in Turkey. Though still lacking an empire-building
capacity, English commercial, military, and colonial power began to
increase in relation to other European nations, but English subjects
were still vulnerable and insecure in the Mediterranean, where they
faced capture and enslavement at the hands of Muslim powers. In 1634
John Coke, the secretary of the Privy Council, wrote to Charles I to
complain about English humiliation in the Mediterranean: "It is...
notorious that all nations desire to bee served by their valor.... Yet
I know not how the world is posesed that our ancient reputation is not
only cried down, but wee submit our selves to wrongs & indignities in
al places w[hi]ch are not to be indurd."[28] Two years later, Sir Henry
Blount visited the Ottoman empire and described his firsthand experiences in *A Voyage into the Levant* (1636). He renders this account of
his "generall purpose" in going there:

> First, to observe the Religion, Manners, and Policy of the Turkes, not
> perfectly, which were a task for an inhabitant rather than a passenger,
> but so far forth, as might satisfy this scruple, (to wit) whether to an
> unpartiall conceit, the Turkish way appeare absolutely barbarous, as we
> are given to understand, or rather another kind of civility, different
> from ours, but no lesse pretending. (4–5)

In the end Blount comes to reject the idea that "the Turkish domination there were nothing but sottish sensualitie, as most Christians con-
ceive" (3). Instead, Blount is an unabashed admirer of the Turks, whom
he claims are "the only moderne people, great in action, and whose
Empire hath so suddenly invaded the World, and fixt it selfe such firme
foundations as no other ever did" (2). "I was of opinion," he goes on

to say, "that he who would behold these times in their greatest glory, could not find a better scene than Turky..." (2). Blount's praise for the Ottomans, as Gerald Maclean has shown, is symptomatic of English culture's tendency at that time to seek for an imperial model to emulate.[29] What Maclean terms "imperial envy" was born of England's inferiority complex, its collective desire for power and wealth, felt in relation to those nations that were truly imperial. This cultural attitude expressed itself through the rhetoric of empire, even before the English had an empire of their own. A strictly discursive "imperialism" was emerging, one that could be quite militant in its language, but there were also many texts and representations acknowledging English weakness and vulnerability. Insecurity and anxiety were sometimes projected into aggressive expression as English culture constructed a national identity. It was clear, however, that England's imperial desire, at least in the short run, was not to be fulfilled through bold European or Mediterranean conquests like those accomplished by the Turks. Nor were the English capable of mounting the sort of colonizing effort that the Spanish and the Portuguese had achieved since the late fifteenth century. Instead, the alternative path to power was through the acquisition of valuable commodities: gold, silver, and pearls taken from newly "discovered" lands, luxury goods obtained through trade in Asia or the Mediterranean, or booty taken by privateers from Spanish ships in the Caribbean, Mediterranean, or elsewhere. To pursue these goals, and to defend themselves against their maritime competitors, the English developed a fleet of armed merchant-privateers.[30] In order to deploy these ships profitably, the English required practical knowledge. Consequently, they worked to produce a new geography of profit and plunder. This was a period of intensive intelligence-gathering. In not only the Mediterranean, but wherever English maritime enterprise was carried out, those who traveled for the sake of trade helped to produce a body of knowledge that would serve the purpose of profit. The texts compiled by Richard Hakluyt and Samuel Purchas are the best-known examples of this data-gathering. These descriptions and accounts of exotic places were not produced or consumed for the sake of commerce alone: they also satisfied ethnographic curiosity and provided readers with the pleasures of the strange and the foreign. Thomas Palmer, in *How to Make Our Travailes Profitable* (1606), describes the need for traveling "intelligencers" to acquire and disseminate knowledge of foreign lands and peoples for the benefit of the state and the merchant class:

> ...the very point which every Travailer ought to lay his wittes about [is]
> To get knowledge for the bettering of himselfe and his Countrie: This,

being the object of their Countries defects and the subject of Travailers,
in a word containeth Six generall heads,...namely, the tongue, the
Nature of the People, the Countrey, the Customes; the Government of
the State; and the secrets of the same: the which are to be sought out
wheresoever these shall come. (52–53)

As more Englishmen traveled and traded in the New World, the East
Indies, and the Mediterranean, representations and descriptions of
alien peoples were produced in greater quantities. This intensified
flow of information (and misinformation) about foreign cultures produced a backlash, however, as xenophobic, ethnocentric energies
were directed against a variety of foreign, exotic alterities. The construction of English identity during this period involves a particularly
violent set of contradictions about alien cultures and peoples. They
are both demonized and exalted, admired and condemned.

When alien figures are presented on the early modern stage, they
partake of both the xenophobic and the xenophilic tendencies in
English culture. They are often heroic, and always dynamic, but they
are also potentially transgressive. They often figure a potential to trans-
form through exchange, and that exchange can be commercial, sexual,
or religious in nature—sometimes a combination of all three. The
space of "trade" in the early modern Mediterranean is an "in-between
space" of liminality and hybridity, where transformation takes place. In
an age when capitalism was emerging, Marlowe, Shakespeare, and
other English playwrights were obsessed with the transformative
power of commercial exchange. They recognized and responded to
the important function of Mediterranean trade in both economic and
cultural modes of production.

On the London stage, audiences encountered representations of the
Christianized "noble Moor," the Jewish merchant, the renegade, the
convert, or the shepherd turned emperor—all figures that embody
cultural flexibility, mobility, and adaptability. In the early modern
period, the cross-cultural exchanges that took place in the
Mediterranean were particularly paradoxical in their fusion of opposi-
tionality and mutuality, autonomy and dependency. The Mediterranean
was the site for transference, exchange, and mixture. These processes
were potentially contaminating, according to the ethnocentric pollution
anxiety of English culture, but the English were not in a position to
fight contamination by destroying or converting the supposed source
of that contamination. English anxieties about cultural pollution, miscegenation, or religious conversion were intense, but at the same time
the cultural, ethnic, and religious differences were often embraced

and internalized as English culture began to absorb and articulate those differences as a part of its own process of self-identification. The playwrights who wrote for the Elizabethan and Early Stuart stage were shrewd observers of this aspect of their culture's development, and their plays offered performances of just those allegedly alien behaviors that were being emulated by the English. Marlowe, in his *Tamburlaine* plays, to cite just one example, creates a figure who plays out England's proto-imperialist fantasy and achieves his imperial status through a process of aggressive transculturation that converts him from a Scythian shepherd (a nomad) to a king of kings. Originally a mere brigand, leading a small band of nomadic adventurers, he is able to speak and act the part of imperial conqueror. This stage Tamburlaine, played by the charismatic Edward Alleyn, was a hybrid figure—a Scythian played by an English actor. His rise to power enacts an English desire for imperial rule, but he also represents the fear of alien powers like the Turks—and a fear that the English themselves were learning to act like those aliens.

In English representations of the Mediterranean, various binarisms (English–foreign, friend–enemy, black–white, Christian–infidel) are broken down and deconstructed as often as they are upheld. This is what made texts and performances about the Mediterranean or Islamic world so startling and exciting for English audiences. The thrill of exotic transgression that these plays offered to their audiences was based on the violation of basic cultural constructions and taboos about religion, race, sexuality, and class. Many plays question and disrupt the violent hierarchies constructed by proto-colonialist binaries. Often, this is accomplished by the important role of a third term. In Marlowe's *Tamburlaine*, the Muslim Turks defeat a Christian army but are overpowered in turn by Tamburlaine, whose religious identity serves as a radically unstable third term. Shakespeare's *Othello* begins with the spectacle of a "noble Moor" who is neither "white" nor "black," in the sense that his spiritual "blackness" has been "whitened" by conversion to Christianity, but ultimately he reverts to "black" deeds. In *The Jew of Malta*, Christians, Muslims, and Jews become homologous rivals in moral corruption, who are willing to break vows and switch loyalties for the sake of a venal expediency. In both Daborne's *A Christian Turned Turk* and Massinger's *The Renegado*, we have a volatile triangulation that moves various characters between positions of Christian, Muslim, and renegade identity. These triangulations complicate and overturn the Manichean symmetries that were conventionally constructed by English culture. To resist the dominant discourse of ethnocentrism, it is necessary, not to reverse the terms of the binary (while preserving a hierarchical structure), but to create an imbalance or centripetal force that will topple the binaries, leaving a space for questioning, rethinking, reacting, and reconstructing. The ethnocentric certainties of the Elect Nation collapse under the pressure of these plays that both demonize and eroticize the ambivalent, hybrid heroes that cross the stage.

CHAPTER 2

THE ENGLISH AND THE EARLY MODERN
MEDITERRANEAN: THEATER,
COMMERCE, AND IDENTITY

Throughout the early modern period, firsthand contact with other cultures helped to define English identity and to alter English thought and practice. At the same time, the *representation* of cross-cultural encounters played an important role in the ideological development of English identity. The key process that generated this cross-cultural contact and influence was the movement of goods and people via international commerce. English merchants had always interacted with foreign economies, but after 1570 an unprecedented economic impetus sent an increasing number of English subjects to and fro, forming stronger and more extensive ties with what Fernand Braudel calls "world-economies."[1] At the midpoint of the sixteenth century, England was commercially unsophisticated and isolated, but by the end of the century, English merchants and mariners began to assert themselves as players in the world of international commerce and cross-cultural exchange.[2] One prominent economic historian has described this period, 1570–1630, as exhibiting "one of the most striking transformations in economic history," manifested in "...New forms of organization, a new breed of merchants and promoters, new sources of capital, a new sense of purpose, and a new vitality in economic enterprise..." (Rabb 1967, 2–3). London, where the public playhouses were located, was the center of this trade: "As new trades opened up in the later sixteenth and early seventeenth centuries, with Russia, the Baltic, the Mediterranean, the Americas and the Far East, they...were principally conducted from London, and in the cases of the Mediterranean and the Far East, completely monopolized by her" (Clay 1:200).[3] The English capital was a rapidly expanding super-port: "Shipping owned in London rose from a mere 12,300 tons in 1582, to 35,300 tons in 1629..." (Clay 1:202). London was the site of intense commercial and cultural absorption, defined by mixture and serviced by a literary and theatrical culture that received, engaged with, and reacted to all that London took in through its port. Other European polities were less centralized, and other European cities were more evenly distributed along multidirectional circuits and pathways of international exchange. London was, by comparison, simply a huge intake zone, the great One receiving the Many, and it was surrounded by rural and provincial areas that remained parochially static in relation to the destabilizing exotic influences that were impacting the capital so profoundly.

The Mediterranean was an increasingly common destination for English vessels because of the profitability of trading for luxury goods, mainly in North African, Greek, Italian, and Ottoman ports such as Tunis, Zante, Venice, and Smyrna. What Robert Brenner (1972) has called the "expansionary thrust" (363) of the English into the Mediterranean led to the establishment of an extensive commercial intercourse with foreign trade partners there, including Muslims. Soon after 1570, formal diplomatic relations with Muslim rulers in the Ottoman empire and in the autonomous principalities of North Africa were established. In 1575, two London merchants, Edward Osborne and Richard Staper, initiated a dialogue with the Ottoman sultan that led, first, to the queen's appointment of William Harborne as English envoy to the sultan; and, second, to the promulgation of commercial capitulations agreed between the English monarchy and the Ottoman sultanate. As a result of this agreement, the Levant Company was founded in 1581. By 1590, an English government official was able to make the following assessment of the Mediterranean trade: "It is well known that the parts of Italy and Turkey will bear a greater trade than all parts of Christendom now in amity with her majesty."[4] In Hakluyt's 1598 *Principall Navigations*, in an "Epistle Dedicatorie" to Walsingham, Hakluyt celebrates England's newly established role in the Eastern Mediterranean, asking, "Who ever saw before this regiment, an English Ligier in the stately porch of the Grand Signior at Constantinople?" (1:sig. 2v).

During the late sixteenth and early seventeenth centuries, as commodities, sailing vessels, and people moved back and forth between

English ports and Mediterranean destinations, the English sense of place and purpose was strongly affected by the flow of information and commodities that ensued. The English encounter with exotic alterity, and the theatrical representations inspired by that encounter, helped to form the emergent identity of an English nation that was eagerly fantasizing about having an empire, but was still in the preliminary phase of its colonizing drive. English subjects understood themselves by comprehending their difference from outsiders, but their identities were also changing as their outlook and behavior were affected and altered by foreign practices that they were learning to emulate.

In order to know and recognize what it meant to be properly English, Protestant, lawful, virtuous, masculine, noble, and so on, English subjects referred to the spectacle of variety and alterity that was played out in the representation of alien culture. I am in agreement here with Jean E. Howard, who has argued, "that even in Tudor-Stuart England . . . a discourse of national identity was emerging which, despite many differences, shares with modern nationalism a supposed fraternity of subjects within an imagined community defined in part by cultural and racial *differences* from other such imagined communities"[5] (Howard 1994, 101). This construction of a national identity, in contrast to *and* in correspondence with various alien identities, was not the self-conscious, propagandistic "writing of England" described by Richard Helgerson and Claire McEachern in their studies of England's emerging nationhood. Instead, I am concerned primarily with the ideological construction of English identity through commercial stage performances produced for a popular audience. These performances took place in the theaters and at other sites of cultural production that were marginal to the discursive communities where "official" (ecclesiastical, courtly, or academic) nationhood was promulgated.

The staging of outlandish plays offered a spectacle of what England was and was not, and presented those performances as popular entertainment for the urban populace. This study attempts to trace the relationship between a site of cultural production, the English theater in London, and a sphere of economic and cultural exchange, the Mediterranean. One thing that complicates this relationship is the fact that the theater itself was an economic enterprise, and its location within the domestic marketplace drew attention to many forms of economic life—not only those that were inscribed as *foreign* practices. As Douglas Bruster has pointed out in his important study, *Drama and the Market in the Age of Shakespeare*, ". . . English drama responded to the market, even as it sprang from it" (xi). Theater represented the world of foreign trade on stage, and foreign trade (and later, colonization) became an endeavor through which new roles, new forms of self-fashioning, could be staged—as Stephen Greenblatt has shown. The playhouses were exoticized by representing and selling exotic difference in many different forms. Foreign settings and foreign characters abound, and even in citizen comedies that presented London to London audiences, there are often foreigners like Franchesina in *The Dutch Courtesan*, or Englishmen who pretend to be foreign, like Lacy, who becomes Hans the Dutch shoemaker in *The Shoemaker's Holiday*, or Surly, who is disguised as a Spanish nobleman in Jonson's play, *The Alchemist*.

A further connection between international commerce and the commercial theater is the fact that Elizabethan theatrical companies (like the Lord Chamberlain's Men at the Globe) and mercantile joint ventures (like the Levant Company) were two of the earliest forms of the joint-stock company that was so important for the development of capitalism. Much anti-theatrical hostility was generated by the theater's combination of outlandishness, innovation, and autonomous commerciality. As Steven Mullaney has shown, the London playhouses functioned in a way that made this new combination threatening to the purity and cohesion of England's traditional social order and identity. Mullaney has shown us how "the place of the stage" was located at a marginal site and how it dispersed its messages like a foreign plague that emanated from the border between the city walls and the rest of the world. According to Mullaney, the theater presented

> a threat posed not by a merely foreign presence but by one that is both utterly alien—from outside the confines of Western culture—and hauntingly homegrown. Intimate yet foreign, an external threat nurtured from within and growing without restraint: such terms are equally commensurate, in London's apprehension, with plague and theatricality. (Mullaney 1988, 50)

But of course the theater was not only or simply a plague-like "threat": it was also a place to experience the pleasure of staged exoticism, and to consume images and words that sometimes celebrated the importance and appeal of commercial and cultural exchange with foreigners.

While the theater's concern with domestic, especially urban, exchange is clearly a central issue, there was also a strong interest in foreign trade and exotic settings because economic relations with the world outside were affecting and changing English society so profoundly, especially in London. Walter Cohen has traced the connection between England's commercial expansion and Shakespearean drama, arguing that "[Shakespeare's] plays register the rise of England's international trade, not least geographically" (132). Within English culture, the theater played a special role in adapting, articulating, and disseminating foreignness. Drama was an important medium through which the different appearances, behaviors, and beliefs of other cultures were imported, distorted, mimicked, and displayed. And it was not only exoticism that fascinated the English, but above all the *exchange* with or between exotic cultures (through armed conflict, trade, religious conversion, erotic encounter, and so on). In a sense, the theater took on a pedagogical role, offering examples of "foreign" action and English (or Christian) reaction. This is not to say that playscripts were transcripts of social or economic reality in England or the Mediterranean; rather, they provided scripts for the practice and performance of cultural behavior, modeling both virtuous and vicious conduct.

English playwrights and players were not attempting to provide accurate ethnographic reports of foreign peoples and their customs (though there were contemporaneous texts that did attempt to do so). They were mapping out an imaginary geography that was culture-bound, partial, and selective—as all maps and representations are. Many of the plays set in the Mediterranean merely deploy the foreign setting as an exotic framework in which to depict English concerns and English behavior, but the texts that I will analyze here are plays that have a tighter referential relation to contemporary events and conditions in the Mediterranean world. These plays refer to the international economy while translating those experiences into performances that explore many of the core issues, desires, and anxieties that new foreign influences brought to England. New ideas and attitudes that emerged at the onset of capitalism and imperialism were presented at the theater, and Mediterranean models were prevalent. The nearest and greatest empires of the day, the Spanish and the Turkish, were based in the Mediterranean world (almost dividing it in half); and Italy, at the center of the Mediterranean, was the birthplace of capitalism. English culture was moving toward both imperialism and capitalism, and the English experience in the Mediterranean encouraged the English, in both economic and ideological ways, to emulate imperialist and capitalist ways. The stage, in particular, functioned as an important site for ideological adaptation and reaction to invasive new economic practices that were transforming English society.

On the early modern stage, Mediterranean culture is represented as difference, but that difference is open, multiple, and unstable. In the London theater, the spectacle of Mediterranean alterity produces a space of deferral and possibility, not a clear, binary opposition between English self and exotic other. Levantine culture, for example, is represented in the drama by a series of alien characters who inhabit a dynamic, catalytic space in which cultures overlap, meet, clash, or engage in exchange. This is the space of international commerce, and until the late seventeenth century, power within that space was distributed evenly enough to create an environment that was not dominated by any one imperial system, but allowed for interlocking systems that mediated both cooperation and conflict. This was an unruly context, lacking the "order" and "stability" that comes from the asymmetry of power that we typically associate with the colonizer–colonized relationship.

By the early seventeenth century, the expansionary thrust of the English maritime economy was directed primarily toward the Mediterranean but voyages to the New World were also in progress. In the Americas, English venturers (most famously, Raleigh or Drake) could pretend to an imperial identity, but there was a much greater volume of trade going to the Mediterranean, where English pretensions to imperial hegemony were laughable. It is true that superior technology sometimes gave small groups of English vessels a competitive edge when encountering other vessels in the Mediterranean, but until the late seventeenth century, the English fleet there operated in the shadow of larger powers like the Ottoman sultanate, Habsburg institutions, or Venetian forces. When the English encountered these Mediterranean powers, they could not assume the role of potential colonizer. Instead, their pursuit of profit depended on the accessibility of markets that were controlled and managed by others whom they could not intimidate or coerce. English subordination and dependency produced a frustration and anxiety that was expressed in the theatrical representation of European encounters with Islamic wealth and power.

The predominant strategic function of the representations of Italians, Spaniards, Moors, Turks, Saracens, Mahometans, Africans, and other foreigners is not what Bhabha has called "the creation of a space for a 'subject peoples' through the production of knowledges... of colonizer and colonized" (Bhabha 1996, 41). Power in the Mediterranean world during the time of Marlowe and Shakespeare was a tricky, constantly renegotiated issue, but one thing was clear— the Ottoman empire was an institution to be feared and appeased.

Only rarely would English merchants who wished to turn a profit by dealing in "Turkish" markets choose to use force against the Ottoman sultanate and its fleet, and when they did the outcome was usually defeat, ruin, enslavement, or death. At the same time, many Christians "turned Turk," converting to Islam in order to enjoy the privileges of belonging to the Islamic community.

Nonetheless, the fantasy of colonial and imperial identity sometimes compelled English writers to represent themselves as potential colonizers, or at least as culturally superior. During the Elizabethan and Early Stuart periods, the commercial theater of London helped to lay the ideological groundwork for empire by presenting the Mediterranean world as a place where fortunes could be made by bold "adventurers" who joined with Christians, Muslims, and Jews in a competition for the control of bodies, souls, and profits. The proto-colonial fantasies produced in the late sixteenth and seventeenth centuries in England do not, however, comprise a colonial discourse that functioned as an instrument of power over colonized subjects. English subjects were well aware that the metropolitan centers of wealth, culture, civilization, and the imperial legacy of Greek and Roman culture, were located in the Mediterranean. They knew that London was on the periphery of Europe and far from the Mediterranean Sea, the sea designated as the middle of the earth, which had been home to the empires that really counted—Rome, Byzantium, then the empire of the Turks. The Mediterranean was not only the site of imperial history (from Alexander the Great to Suleiman the Great), but it was also, for Christians, the religious center of the world. Jerusalem and Constantinople were now ruled, however, by the Turks. From a vantage point of awe and deference (and sometimes envy), English writers began to gather knowledge about the Mediterranean world from a position of inferiority, not power, and so a Saidian "orientalist discourse" based on power and the control of knowledge was not possible.

In the early modern period, English texts expressed a will to power, but without the means. English culture demonstrated both hostility and admiration: the fantasy of reconquering Jerusalem, and a retention of the residual, nostalgic idea of the crusade; and at the same time a call for appeasement so that profitable trade could be carried on. Pragmatic merchants and monarchs dealt with the reality of Ottoman power while at home religious polemicists aggressively denounced Islam and called for its destruction. Many English authors of the early modern era recognized the West's inferiority to Islamic power, when measured by the extent of Turkish geographic control and by the vast resources available to the Sultan. They saw the need for Western rulers and merchants to establish friendly relations with the Ottoman sultanate and other Muslim rulers, so that they could do business throughout the Mediterranean. Under the threat of Spanish aggression, Elizabeth I and her councilors had forged an alliance with Turkey and had fostered the Levant trade, but when in 1603 James I succeeded to the English throne, he immediately expressed his dislike of this affiliation with the Turks. According to Thomas Wilson, James "denied absolutely" at the commencement of his reign in England to sign commercial agreements with the Ottomans, "saying, that for merchant's causes he would not do things unfitting a Christian prince" (qtd. in Baumer 36n).[6] Despite his personal animosity toward Islam, James discovered that it was not in his financial or political interest to hinder the very profitable trade between England and Turkey, controlled by the influential merchants of the Levant Company, and in December of 1605 a new charter was issued guaranteeing the continued prosperity of the Company.[7] English feelings about Islamic power continued to be complicated by commercial interests. In a pageant written for the Clothworkers' Guild, on the occasion of the inauguration of the Lord Mayor in 1633, Thomas Heywood gave these lines to Mercury, the god of trade and travel: "the potent Turke (although in faith adverse) / Is proud that he with England can commerce" (sig. B3v).

English trade with the Turks was not a bipolar enterprise: English merchant vessels took in many other destinations and commodities along the way to the Ottoman empire. They stopped in a variety of ports, from Spain and Morocco to harbors in Syria or Greece. Sometimes they sailed first to the Newfoundland fisheries, then to Spain or the Canary Islands, then on to the Mediterranean and finally back home. That way, they could leave England without carrying much cargo, load up on salt fish, and "trade up" until they obtained valuable Levantine goods toward the end of the voyage, perhaps wine and currants. Other vessels brought English textiles or raw materials like Cornish lead and tin more directly to Ottoman harbors. There were times when war or hostile relations closed certain ports to the English (most notably, during the Spanish embargo of 1585–1604), but this did not prevent the volume of Anglo-Mediterranean trade from increasing steadily.

While factors, merchants, and their crews sailed to the Mediterranean and bore witness to its cultural diversity, English subjects at home experienced that part of the world in a more symbolic and textually mediated way. The Mediterranean was a wildly overdetermined site in the imaginary geography of early modern England. It contained many meanings, many contexts: biblical history, the cultural achievements of ancient Greece and Rome, Hellenistic romance, the medieval and early modern romance traditions, the rise of Islam, the Crusades, the Ottoman conquests, and more. Representations of the Mediterranean evoked a range of responses, but power and wealth were usually part of the picture. It was a place where English merchants made money, and where, according to Richard Hakluyt, trade would lead "to the inlarging of her Majesties customes, the furthering of navigation, the venting of diverse generall commodities of this Realme, and the inriching of the citie of London" (Hakluyt 1903–05, 5:168).

In early modern England, attitudes toward the Mediterranean world were intensely conflicted: religious difference evoked hostile, demonizing descriptions of Spanish, Italian, Jewish, and Muslim peoples inhabiting the region; but many English writers maintained a positive attitude toward a classical and early Christian legacy with which English Protestants claimed an affiliation. Whether they were railing against religious "misbelief" or reimagining the glories of the ancient "world," English authors were fixated on the Mediterranean, both past and present; and English citizens were constantly encountering Mediterranean phenomena—news of Turkish conquests, currants imported from Crete, allusions to the papal "whore of Babylon," figures from classical myth appearing in civic pageants, letters sent by English captives in Algiers, and, of course, plays set in the Mediterranean but staged in the London playhouses.

The word "Mediterranean," derived from the Latin words for "middle" and "earth," is itself an interesting etymological case, and comes close to qualifying as a Freudian primal word. The term "Mare Mediterraneum" was first employed in late Latin during the seventh century to describe the body of water bounded by Europe, Africa, and Asia. In English, however, the adjectival usage of "mediterranean" meant both "inland; interior; remote from the coast" and (when referring to water), "nearly or entirely surrounded or enclosed by dry land" (*Oxford English Dictionary*). The *OED* cites Holland's translation of Pliny from 1601 in which Holland contrasts "The Mediterranean or midland parts of any country" with "the maritime or sea-coasts."

So the Mediterranean Sea was a body of water encircled by land at the center of the earth. This notion of centrality in relation to the rest of the world is basic to the medieval and early modern understanding of what we now call the Mediterranean region. The positioning of the Mediterranean in the middle of the earth was reinforced in medieval texts by the cartographic representation called the "T-O map." These cartographic images place the Mediterranean at the center of God's earthly creation, hemmed in by the three known continents, and surrounded by the great "Ocean Sea." T-O maps usually located the Holy Land and Jerusalem at the very center, at the meeting point of Europe, Asia, and Africa. After 1492, new geographic information began to alter this conception, but not as radically or rapidly as has often been claimed or assumed. From the perspective of early modern England, the Mediterranean "world" still represented the originary core of the civilized world, the place from which Brute came to found Britain. And of course a strong identification of the eastern Mediterranean with the Holy Land and with the events of the Old and New Testaments was still in effect during the early modern period. English subjects continued to think and act in terms of a Christian ideology that identified the Mediterranean world as the setting for the exploits of Moses, Jesus, Paul, and other figures from the Bible.

A map of the Mediterranean was printed in the Geneva Bible, arguably the most important and well-known book for Protestants in Shakespeare's England. This map, which was placed between Luke's Acts of the Apostles and the Epistles of Saint Paul, is probably the cartographic image of the Mediterranean that was most widely disseminated in late sixteenth and early seventeenth-century England. For readers of the Geneva Bible, the "Holy Land" was not just Palestine but included the entire eastern Mediterranean region. It is interesting to note that the list of "countries and places" that was printed on the same leaf as the map includes many of the settings of Shakespearean drama. For example, this map describes the imaginative space through which the characters of Shakespeare's late romance play *Pericles* travel by sea—Antioch, Tyre, Tharsus, Ephesus, Myteline—the same coastal cities and islands to which Saint Paul had journeyed. I will return to *Pericles* later in this chapter.

* * *

For the citizens of early modern England, the Mediterranean world was important both as the location for formative historical events in the past and as a sphere of contemporaneous economic activity. The Mediterranean was increasingly, for the English merchants of Shakespeare's London, a place where huge profits could be made. The technological edge that English sailing vessels acquired in the late sixteenth century and sustained in the seventeenth allowed them to move aggressively into the region in increasing numbers. In *The*

Mediterranean and the Mediterranean World in the Age of Philip II,
Fernand Braudel points out, "By the end of the [sixteenth] century
the English were everywhere in the Mediterranean, in Moslem or
Christian countries..." (628). Their guns and maneuverable, high-
decked ships were technologically and militarily superior to the older
style of open galley vessels that were still being built by the Venetians
and other Mediterranean states. But venture capitalism for the English
in the Mediterranean was fraught with risk. Merchants who journeyed
to Tunis, Alexandria, Venice, Crete, and other ports had to face the
considerable dangers of storm, shipwreck, and piracy. And they came
into contact with the Ottoman imperial power that ruled over
the Holy Land and continued throughout the early modern period to
expand at the expense of Christian rulers.

The Mediterranean was thought of as the original setting for
classical and scriptural histories, but it also represented the site of past
conflict between Christianity and other religions. The Islamic conquests, the Crusades, the strong presence of Jewish communities, and
the expansion of the Ottoman empire in the eastern Mediterranean
were all important events that contributed to a diachronic, geographic
conception of the Mediterranean in the minds of English subjects. So
it is not surprising that Mediterranean plays often represent the cultural and religious diversity of the region as a source of conflict. For
example, the Turkish threat is an invisible but terrifying force in the
first act of *Othello*, where the island of Cyprus, ruled by Venice, faces
an attack by a Turkish fleet that is subsequently destroyed by a providential tempest.

As John Gillies and others have shown, English culture constructed an imaginary Venice that is a site of tremendous uneasiness
about "trade, intermixture and miscegenation" (Gillies 1994, 136). It
is a place where a violent contradiction between "intrusion" and
"exorbitance" exists, "as if the dynamic outward thrust of the world-
city had imploded, drawing the transgressive and polluting energies
of the outside in upon itself" (Gillies 1994, 67). Like the Venetians,
English merchants were quite willing to work with Armenian and
Jewish dealers and middlemen who were employed by the Turkish
authorities. Nonetheless, most Londoners would have thought of
the Ottoman sultan or "Grand Seigneur," not as a friendly commercial partner, but as the absolute ruler of an evil empire that menaced all Christendom. To the people of Shakespeare's London, the
Mediterranean maritime sphere, including Cyprus and the Venetian
territories, must have seemed like a violently unstable sea of troubles—
and yet one where vast fortunes could be made by trade and plunder.[8]

It was the ultimate "free market" in which privateers under many different flags took what they could by force. The historian Molly Greene has argued that the seventeenth-century Mediterranean was no longer divided by clear, strict religious differences, nor was it yet a place where a "northern invasion" had installed an "economic competition between nation states [to replace] the old religious rivalry" (42).[9] According to Greene,

> The northern Europeans . . . were just one group among many in the complex of commercial activity in the seventeenth century. They were not in a position to impose their will on the marketplace; nor was anyone else. The result was a fairly egalitarian but anarchic commercial world where conventional distinctions such as European/local and Christian/Muslim are less than useful. (52)

Perhaps, for the English, the most fascinating and disturbing element in this mix was the presence of hybrid communities of "Barbary pirates" and "renegadoes" in places like Tunis or Algiers. The English translation of Nicholas de Nicolay's *Navigations, peregrinations and voyages made into Turkie* (1585) provides a typical Christian account of these Muslims' piratical activities:

> The most part of the Turkes of Alger, whether they be of the kings houshold or the Gallies, are Christians renied, or Mahumetised, of al Nations, but most of them, Spaniards, Italians and of Provence, of the Ilands and Coastes of the Sea Mediterane, given all to whoredome, sodometrie, theft, and all other most detestable vices, lyving only of rovings, spoyles, & pilling . . . and with their practick art bryng dayly too Alger a number of pore Christians, which they sell onto the Moores, and other merchauntes of Barbarie. . . . (8)

We see that "Turks" are not necessarily from Turkey proper—anyone who "turns Turk" and joins the Muslim pirates becomes a member of a group that is imagined as radically heterogeneous and, at the same time, united in depravity.

The Mediterranean littoral in the sixteenth and seventeenth centuries was a place where identity—in terms of political and religious affiliation—was frighteningly unstable. International alliances shifted rapidly and territorial changes were constantly taking place, including trade agreements and mutual-defense pacts between Christian and Muslim leaders.[10] The Turks and the Moors of the Barbary ports (principally Sallee, Tunis, Algiers, and Tripoli) sailed throughout the Mediterranean and preyed upon the Christians, who were themselves almost never united against the infidel foe (despite the ceaseless talk about mounting a general crusade). Furthermore, the widespread practice of piracy was not simply a practice undertaken by "wicked" pirates against "honest" merchants or by treacherous Muslim renegades against law-abiding Christian traders: rather, it was increasingly a free-for-all in which multiethnic crews fought each other for spoils, the strong preying on the weak. Many Christian sailors and ship captains had "taken the turban," formally converting to Islam, in order to enjoy the freedom and protection of the Barbary ports in North Africa, while corsairs manned by Christian crews roamed the Mediterranean attacking both Christian and Muslim targets.[11] Conversion to Islam and the practice of piracy were closely associated by the English, who feared and condemned both. In many cases, it was the temptation of lucrative employment that motivated Christian sailors and soldiers to turn Turk and become renegade pirates or join the Ottoman army.[12] All of this was a source of fascination and bewilderment to the English, citizens of a relatively homogenous and isolated kingdom.

Of course, we do not find the complex historical reality of the Mediterranean neatly "reflected" on the London stage. For the most part, Mediterranean plays written for the early modern stage tell us as much about English identity and culture as they do about actual cross-cultural interaction in the Mediterranean. Furthermore, it would be dangerous to make any sweeping conclusions about "Mediterranean plays" as if they formed some kind of coherent group within the body of extant plays written between 1570 and 1630. What we can discern in the drama of this period is a pattern of attraction and repulsion that emerges from the portrayal of various cross-cultural encounters. An anxious, conflicted attitude toward the Mediterranean, its inhabitants, and its economy is found in the early modern theater. According to the discourses that worked to construct English identity, interaction with Mediterranean peoples posed a threat to the integrity and coherence of English Protestant culture. This anxiety about contact with Mediterranean multiculturalism was part of a larger sense of cultural confusion that resulted from the intensifying influx of foreign commodities, texts, and ideas that were arriving in England, and especially in London. In the "Prologue" to his play, *Midas* (1587), John Lyly expostulates on the perplexing sense of change and variety produced by these exotic importations:

> Gentlemen, so nice is the world that for apparel there is no fashion, for music no instrument, for diet no delicate, for plays no invention but breedeth satiety before noon and contempt before night.

> ...There must be salads for the Italian, picktooths for the Spaniard, pots for the Germans, porridge for the Englishman.
>
> ...Traffic and travel hath woven the nature of all nations into ours, and made this land like arras, full of device, which was broadcloth, full of workmanship.
>
> Time hath confounded our minds, our minds the matter, but all cometh to this pass: that what heretofore hath been served in several dishes for a feast is now minced in a charger for a gallimaufrey. If we present a mingle-mangle, our fault is to be excused, because the whole world is become an hodgepodge.

Lyly jokingly excuses the generic mixing that characterizes his play by pointing out that cultures, like plays, are no longer pure or separate: English identity is being transformed by imported foreign commodities and practices into a "gallimaufrey," and the theater, reflecting this cultural mixing, "is become an hodgepodge," too. The prologue to *Midas* refers to a cluster of debates that were arising in English culture about how foreign exchange was affecting England. The implication that plays were being mingle-mangled was analogous to what English writers were saying about the English language, or about English travelers who came and went: in each of these cases, there was a mixed reaction in England. Traffic and travel were both adulterating *and* enriching, potentially contaminating *and* potentially empowering. Foreign words, people, and commodities were both welcomed and shunned. The English, like Lyly's Midas, imagined that an influx of gold would be the key to their happiness and success. But fears remained that the Midas touch could produce a deadly metamorphosis.

Lyly's play, which takes place at Midas's court in Phrygia, in the eastern Mediterranean, was written just at the time when England was opening up to increased exotic influences: by expanding its trade with the Mediterranean, by voyaging in the New World, Africa, and Asia, and by engaging in new forms of maritime aggression (against Spain, primarily). Lyly's prologue comments generally and proverbially on the "nice" way of the world that is always seeking something new and different, but the play's topical allegory identifies Midas and his fateful lust for gold with the overreaching Philip of Spain and his hunger for conquest and empire. Lyly's satire expresses a sophisticated humanist internationalism, but it is also conscious of Spanish power and other foreign threats to an English nation that was beginning to compete for the wealth that could be obtained through foreign adventurism. At such a time, both the fear of foreign powers and the allure of foreign commodities helped to construct English identity as heroic, masculine, and "venturesome."

After 1570, the extraordinary growth of English maritime traffic to North Africa, Italy, and the Levant, and the huge profits that accrued from this activity, brought the Mediterranean increasingly to mind for the inhabitants of early modern London. This renewed interest in the Mediterranean—its people, its culture, its commodities—may help to account for the fact that so many plays from this period take place there. If we look at the settings employed in Shakespearean drama alone, the list of Mediterranean locations includes Padua in *The Taming of the Shrew*, Ephesus and Syracuse in *The Comedy of Errors*, Verona in *Romeo and Juliet*, Venice in the *Merchant of Venice*, Messina in *Much Ado About Nothing*, Cyprus—and Venice again—in *Othello*, and many others. Taken altogether, there are twenty "Mediterranean" plays in Shakespeare's canon.

In the Mediterranean plays that appeared on the early modern stage, commercial discourse is pervasive; and yet economic discourse is only one element in the rich matrix of signification. There were other historical and cultural associations that defined the Mediterranean world, not only as a market, but also as the originary center of civilization. Roman plays like *Antony and Cleopatra*, *Sejanus*, or *The Roman Actor* express a nostalgia for an ancient imperial order, and Italy was still recognized as a place of rich cultural and economic production based in cities like Padua, Verona, Milan, and Venice. English writers looked to Italy as the place where classical civilization reached the peak of its imperial glory, and where the humanist revival originated. Humanist knowledge was gradually disseminated in the rest of Europe, and it took a long time to take root in distant England, where the Renaissance was both belated and marginal. In Shakespeare's *Richard II*, York reminds the audience of "proud Italy,/Whose manners still our tardy-apish nation/Limps after in base imitation" (2.1.21–23). England was geographically peripheral to the cluster of three continents that the English themselves believed to comprise the "civilized" world. For Londoners, acknowledging the centrality of the Mediterranean in geography, in history, and in the international economy, required an acknowledgment of English isolation, belatedness, and dependency. English cultural production had to work to compensate for this anxious marginality felt in relation to the Mediterranean cultural center— a center with an irresistible centripetal power into which the English imagination—and economy—was drawn. Part of the appeal of English Renaissance drama derives from the energy and effort put forth in order to appropriate, adapt, and nativize the narratives and histories that were engendered by the Mediterranean world.

Some Mediterranean plays are also placed distantly in time—in ancient Troy, in imperial Rome, in a mythical Athens ruled by Duke Theseus—but they all feature characters who speak and behave much like the English men and women of early modern London. These exotic settings were never naturalistically "real" or historically accurate: Shakespeare's audiences consumed representations of foreignness or ancientness that spoke in English verse—and sometimes in the local, London vernacular.

Inevitably, the speech of foreign characters from distant lands where other languages were spoken had to be "translated" into English for the London stage. In Shakespeare's *Pericles*, for example, Gower appears several times in order to transport the English audience from one Mediterranean locale to another; and in one of his speeches Gower asks the spectators to accept the theatrical illusion of an English-speaking world:

> Thus time we waste, and long leagues make we short,
> Sail seas in cockles, have and wish but for't,
> Making to take imagination
> From bourn to bourn, region to region.
> By you being pardoned we commit no crime
> To use one language in each several clime
> Where our scene seems to live. (18.1–7)

In this speech, Gower invokes the power of theater to represent actions from distant times and places, and he urges the imaginative participation of the spectators. In the lines that follow, the spectator's mind is compared to a ship, directed to "think his pilot thought" (18.18) and "fetch...home" (18.20) something valuable at the end of the journey. Gower asserts the ritual capacity of theater to enrich and transform the mind, and this marks a new sense of confidence in the power of the English language to contain and represent the world, including the ancient "world" that was located in the Mediterranean.

The analogy that Gower draws between the experience of theatrical "transportation" and that of sailing "from bourn to bourn, region to region" (18.4) is especially appropriate for a play like *Pericles*, one that is soaked in Mediterranean saltwater. The fortune of the seas that conducts the episodic plot of *Pericles* would have reminded Shakespeare's audience of the dangers faced by English sailors trading in the contemporary Mediterranean, and the providential capture of Marina by pirates refers directly to the economy of piracy and slavery that existed throughout the region during the early modern period. Marina's plight—captured in one coastal city and then sold as a sex slave in another—was similar to that of English subjects who were seized by corsairs and auctioned off to slave-dealing merchants in Mediterranean ports. The world of *Pericles* suggests the ancient, Hellenized East, but the play's location is also the site of an oriental despotism that was carried on by the Turkish "tyranny" and Ottoman power that came later and existed in Shakespeare's day. The Mediterranean was a place where slavery and the business of ransoming captives had been practiced continuously since ancient times.

In Shakespeare's *Pericles*, Marina is the object of international masculine desire, a piece of commodified flesh that attracts all comers, including men from Spain, France, and Greece. When Marina resists her new status in the Mediterranean market, the Bawd tells her: "Yes indeed shall you, and taste gentlemen of all fashions. You shall fare well. You shall have the difference of all complexions" (16.69–71). Marina's resistance to rape, her refusal to be prostituted in a cross-cultural marketplace where human bodies are bought and sold as chattel, is partly a projection of English anxiety about the economic conditions of the Mediterranean economy, an economy into which they were being increasingly integrated as profiteers, pirates, and slaves. The Bawd's advice to Marina speaks to the new merchant-adventurers of England: "...you must seem to do that fearfully which you commit willingly, to despise profit where you have most gain" (16.102–04). These phrases hint at the conflicted feelings of attraction and repulsion inspired by contact with the foreign economy of the Mediterranean. The English were hot for profit, but they feared that possession of alien commodities would give them a disease.

Referring to Marina's beauty, the Bawd declares, "if we had of every nation a traveller, we should lodge them with this sign" (16.99–100). In an international culture of bawds, prostitutes and customers, all are "creature[s] of sale" (19.73), and at Miteline the governor himself is reduced to the level of a stereotypical horny sailor, just off the boat and looking for "some private place" (19.90) to "do the deeds of darkness" (19.34). "Faith," swears Lysimachus, feasting his eyes on Marina, "she would serve after a long voyage at sea" (19.45–46). After her maidenhead is sold by the Bawd to Lysimachus, Marina succeeds in blunting the governor's "ill intent" (19.109). In spite of his failure to take possession of her, Lysimachus continues to identify Marina as a commodity, a "piece of virtue" (19.130), and pays her in gold for her service. At first, it appears that her virginity has been bought and sold, but it transpires that her service to Lysimachus is not sex; rather it consists of chastening him, curbing his unruly lust, and sending him away "as cold as a snowball, saying his prayers, too" (19.156–57). Ultimately, she turns the bawdy house into a place of respectable domestic labor, where profit is generated by practicing the typically English trades of sewing and weaving. At the time that *Pericles* was written and first performed, woven wool commodities comprised the mainstay of the English export trade to Turkey and the Eastern Mediterranean.

Once the governor is turned away from the brothel, Shakespeare's play gradually shifts from images of commodity, food, filth, and disease toward the motifs of healing and rebirth, preparing the way for the play's miraculous conclusion. At Miteline, one last cross-cultural encounter on the sea proves profitable for Marina's father, Pericles, who recovers his daughter and then sells her immediately to the ex-whoremaster Lysimachus. Lysimachus's initial gold payment to Marina is repaid in kind by her father, who concludes the play by exchanging her in marriage, which is thus a legitimized form of the prostitution she had avoided earlier. The bargain transacted between these two men, Lysimachus and Pericles, strikes a discordant note against the swelling music of the drama's final scenes, and it remains as an important sign of the new economic values and methods that were being adopted by the English, who were practicing and perfecting new modes of acquisitive aggression in the Mediterranean maritime context.

Conversion, exchange, trade—whether in gold, in souls, or in bodies—these transactions persist to the end of the play, and can be detected even in the moral pronounced by Gower in the epilogue. Virtue converts evil to good, Antiochus' "monstrous lust" (22.109) receives its "due and just reward" (22.109), and the citizens of Tarsus "turn" (22.120). Converted "to rage" (22.120) they burn Cleon and his wife in their palace. These homiletic symmetries are matched, however, by the pattern of economic exchange that the audience witnesses in Miteline and elsewhere. The value set on the chastity of Thaisa (who becomes a priestess of Diana) and the virginity of Marina makes these women commodified objects, prized for their purity. Their domestic, feminine virtue is expressed in their ability to preserve themselves patiently until they can be repossessed by their rightful male owners. This virtue endures in opposition to the exotic sexual aggression they encounter; but ultimately they, too, are consumed.

This sort of contradiction is typical of English representations of the multicultural Mediterranean. In *Pericles* and in the other plays set in the Mediterranean, the text does not simply validate or confirm a stable English identity constructed in direct opposition to a monolithic "other." Instead, these plays problematize the simplistic binary mechanisms that would locate the Protestant English "self" in polar opposition to Mediterranean "otherness." In Shakespeare's Mediterranean plays, English culture is repeatedly implicated in the practices of the Mediterranean characters who, after all, speak the English tongue when represented on the London stage. Figures like Barabas, Shylock, Cleopatra, and Lysimachus do indeed "use one language in each several clime/Where our scenes seem to live." Shylock as a Machiavellian merchant, Othello as a military absolutist committed to a deadly code of masculine honor, and Lysimachus buying himself a wife or a prostitute—all of these characters embody problematic elements of English culture, English thinking.

The heterogeneity and instability of identity that characterize the Mediterranean region made the English presence there a source of anxiety and contradiction: on the one hand, the English felt their difference as Protestant outsiders acutely, almost as alienation; on the other hand, they felt drawn into exchanges and relations that threatened to "convert" them to a foreign condition or, at least, contaminate them. This contradiction is what Stephen Greenblatt calls, in his analysis of *The Jew of Malta*, "[English] culture's bad faith, its insistence upon the otherness of what is in fact its own essence" (Greenblatt 1980, 209)

As a concluding example of Shakespeare's insistence that "the other is us," I would refer to the final scene in *The Merchant of Venice*, in which Shylock reveals the hypocrisy of his Christian adversaries. When asked to show mercy and relinquish his bond, he points to the practice of slaveholding among Christians:

> You have among you many a purchased slave,
> Which like your asses and your dogs and mules
> You use in abject and in slavish parts,
> Because you bought them. (4.1.89–92)

Shakespeare's audience is predisposed to identify and sympathize with the Christians, but in doing so the audience is implicated in the Mediterranean economy's most un-Christian form of property rights. Who is the spectator to identify with? The slave-holding merchants or the merciless Jew? They appear at the end of the play as homologous rivals, not distinctly different moral or cultural entities.

In *The Merchant of Venice* and in other plays from the period under study, oppositions between English "self" and foreign "other" are introduced only to be complicated or conflated. The Mediterranean context, which was so familiar and yet so strange, provided a useful framework for a drama of anxious difference. By asking the audience to identify with characters who were situated within an unstable nexus of exchange, trade and conversion, Mediterranean plays helped both to define and to problematize the development of English identity in the early modern era.

CHAPTER 3

MARLOWE'S MAHOMET: ISLAM, TURKS,
AND RELIGIOUS CONTROVERSY IN
TAMBURLAINE, PARTS I AND II

Question: What is the opposite of faith? Not disbelief.
Too final, certain, closed. Itself a kind of belief.
Doubt.

—*Salman Rushdie*, The Satanic Verses

Marlowe's drama, including the *Tamburlaine* plays, draws much of
its energy—derives its titillating, blasphemous edge—from the contradictions and paradoxes of theological discourse in a time of religious schism. Marlowe's *Tamburlaine* plays raise the same vexed
questions that both Protestant and Roman Catholic apologists sought
to answer: how does human power, both at the level of the individual and of the nation, manifest divine power? How can one authorize
the claim to know whose side God is on? How can we identify God's
will in these matters? These were (literally) burning questions for
Protestants and Catholics on the front lines of the sectarian conflict
in Europe. In the *Tamburlaine* plays, however, the Reformation's
intensification of the problem of knowing and recognizing the
one true faith is displaced from within the context of Western
Christendom to the Mediterranean world where many faiths coex-
isted, including Christianity, Islam, and Judaism. Though he stages

the dramatic action of the *Tamburlaine* plays in places like Constantinople or Jerusalem, Marlowe foregrounds—and lays open to questioning—the same providentialist approach to history that was invoked by Reformation and Counter-Reformation polemicists in Western Europe.

In two of Marlowe's plays, *The Jew of Malta* and *Tamburlaine, Part II*, Muslim–Christian antagonism is an important element in the unfolding of the plot, but in both texts Protestant Christianity is noticeably absent. The Christian cause is embodied in Roman Catholic characters who are figures of hypocrisy, not Christian virtue. At the outset, *The Jew of Malta* sets up a triangulation of religious identities—Jew, Christian (Roman Catholic), and Muslim (or "Turk"); and in *Tamburlaine, Part II*, there are also three religious positions established—Christian (again, Roman Catholic), Muslim (again, the "Turk"), and Tamburlaine's own religious identity, one that sometimes signifies as pagan but ultimately is uncertain and unstable. In both plays, Marlowe probes the ideological complications, anxieties, and uncertainties that arose from Christianity's confrontation and engagement with Islam in a specifically post-Reformation context.

In the *Tamburlaine* plays, the destabilization of deity operates in many forms, but with the recurrence of a basic subversive pattern: repeatedly, divine agency or metaphysical power is invoked and then shown to be unresponsive. This pattern is accompanied by a radical fragmentation of such powers—their exact name and nature is profoundly uncertain. Mahomet, for example, is identified as an idol, as a "friend of God," as a Christ-like divinity seated at the side of God, as a mere mortal prophet, as a devil, and as a damned soul in hell. This inconsistency in the references to "Mahomet" is part of a larger sense of uncertainty and multiplicity in the text's location of metaphysical presence. God's presence or clear evidence of his intervention is never directly felt in the world dominated by God's alleged "scourge," Tamburlaine. The apostrophic rhetoric deployed in so many different situations is not only shown to be impotent—it is also inconsistent and contradictory, referring to "God," Jove, the gods, "the stars," heaven, "Fate," "Fortune," Mahomet, "Christ," and so on. This confusion is not merely some sort of humanist syncretism of the variety commonly found in Renaissance art and literature; it is not a synthesis but rather a fragmentation, producing an unstable identity for divinity. Each new prayer to yet another version of "godhead," and each new failure of curse or prophecy, serves to further dissipate and undermine the notion of a unified, all-powerful God.

The plays begin by demystifying and ridiculing the idea of holy war (or its verbal equivalent, the invocation of divine wrath). Marlowe does this by means of a symbolic *reductio ad absurdum*: war is staged as a competition between gods or religions. The sixteenth century was a period of many victories and few defeats in the struggle between the Ottomans and their Christian foes. Luther himself stated in his 1529 tract *On War Against the Turk*, "we may perceive clearly that God is not with us in our war against the Turks" (5.85). A rationale was developed to deal with this situation: if the Christians were victorious, then God was on their side; if they were defeated by the Turks, then the Christian God was said to be scourging them for their sins. In the latter case, the triumphant Turks were not God's chosen people, but they were still instruments of God's will—His scourge. Clearly, the difference between being the leader of the Elect Nation and being the conquering scourge of God was not logically supportable. Tamburlaine, who is "enjoined...from above, / To scourge the pride of such as Heaven abhors" (2:4.1.147–48), claims to be elected and chosen by a variety of divine powers. If success in battle proves that God is on his side, then he is God's chosen warrior. Those that "Heaven abhors" just happen to be those that oppose his personal plan for self-exultation.

After the absurdity of the competing truth claims is established, the plays move on toward an indeterminacy or even an absence of divine agency. As the drama unfolds, there is a widening gap between a desperately reiterated sign and an elusive referent. Goldberg remarks, "The notion of Mahomet the intercessor as sleepy is amusing in itself, and the progression from sleepy to cursed to non-existent calls attention to the flimsiness of a faith based on anthropomorphism and expectation of personalized divine assistance" (575). While this absurdity is sometimes comic, it also had frightening implications for early modern Christians. Marlowe's "sleepy Mahomet," an Islamic deity who is impotent, presents the possibility that all belief in a metaphysical power that observes and responds to human words and deeds is a delusion. If God or Jove, or Mahomet—or at least some preordaining mechanical force of Fate or Fortune—do not respond to historical events involving the rise and fall of *empires*, then they certainly do not bother with the fall of a sparrow.

In the *Tamburlaine* plays, faith in the providential power and justice of God, which should provide solace for suffering and misfortune, results instead in compounding and exacerbating that very suffering. Pious fortitude becomes ignorant folly; prayer a joke. These impotent invocations of divine agency begin with Zenocrate's confident avowal that "The gods, defenders of the innocent, / Will never prosper your intended drifts / That thus oppress poor friendless passengers" (1:1.2.68–70) and Cosroe's assertion that Tamburlaine "opposeth him against the gods" (1:2.6.39). Later, when Bajazeth and the others call for divine intervention to put a stop to Tamburlaine's rise, or when they predict Tamburlaine's fall from pride, the futility of all their passionate prayers and prognostications merely adds frustration to their injury and despair to their helplessness. Their empty curses, intended to bring on Tamburlaine's downfall, instead provide humiliating confirmation of their own impotence. Throughout the two *Tamburlaine* plays, divine agency is defeated by Tamburlaine's human will. Only in the second play's final scene is there any suggestion of an efficacious divine power greater than Tamburlaine himself, but even that suggestion is compromised, and perhaps invalidated, by the uncertainty established earlier.

* * *

In late medieval Europe, under the unified Church of Rome, the demonization of Islam helped to produce solidarity among Christians who acknowledged papal authority and responded (in one way or another—emotionally, economically, or militarily) to the call for crusade against all heathens and heretics outside the circle of the true faith. The Reformation problematized this concentric, binary opposition: after 1517, Roman Catholics tried to define Protestantism as merely the latest heresy, one that would eventually be crushed, like those that came before; but the Reformation dealt a splintering blow to religious certitude from which Christianity has never recovered. The religious schism created an atmosphere of doubt that, paradoxically, produced an intensification of the rhetoric of certitude. The longer that Protestantism persisted, the louder grew the cries of "God is on our side"—from the followers of both Luther and the pope. Post-Reformation religious discourse includes a volatile polemic strain in which denunciations and affirmations of false or true faith escalated to new levels. The tendency of such religious rhetoric toward absurdity is something that Marlowe mocks in his drama, and as Dena Goldberg has noted, Marlowe specifically targets and parodies "the my-god-can-beat-yours motif" (570) in his *Tamburlaine* plays.

The intensification of intolerance that resulted from the Reformation is inseparable from the intensification of providentialism: certain faith required the evidence of events; God's will and his signs of favor were discerned in the unfolding text of history. The history of the Ottoman Turks' success was an important object of providentialist interpretation, and Turkish victories were generally received as evidence of divine wrath at Christian backsliding. Apart from the successful defense of Malta in 1565 and the defeat of the Turks by a Christian navy at Lepanto in 1570, the fifteenth and sixteenth centuries comprise a period of seemingly inexorable expansion and conquest for the Ottoman empire. In sixteenth-century England, it was the Ottomans who were customarily given the epithet Tamburlaine claims as his own: "the scourge of God and terror of the world" (2:4.1.154). In his 1542 translation of Antoine Geuffroy's history of Turkish conquests, Richard Grafton's letter "To the reader" laments the Turks' success, and Grafton compares his text to the lamentations of the prophet Jeremiah, who "so bewailed ye beatyng downe of the walles of Jerusalem and woofull captivitee of the people thereof." The letter goes on, asking the reader to

> consyder howe farre and howe wyde Antichrist hath dilated his kyng-
> dome by other his instrumentes, and namelye by Mahumet that pestif-
> erous false prophet: for not onely castelles, tounes and citees have been
> blasted with the deadly breath of this poysoned serpente, but also
> whole and soundrye provinces, realmes and nacions, have so dronken
> in his cankerde venome, that it hath been harde for the verye chosen
> to escape his terrible stynges. And where as other adders dooe onlye
> corrupte the bodies, this hell viper with his forked fierye tongue hathe
> perced even the verye soules of menne. (lxxviii)

In the text proper, Geuffroy gives all the credit for the Turks' success to the Christian deity, claiming that the sultan's "strengthe is permyt-ted of God, whyche for oure synnes sufferethe thys estate so farre swarvynge frome all good pollycie so to prevayle and not that it is maynteyned by their wisdom, strength, or vertue" (lxxviii).

At the time that Marlowe wrote, the expansion of Islam under the Ottoman sultanate seemed unstoppable. Fifteen years after Marlowe penned *Tamburlaine, I and II*, Richard Knolles, in his *Historie of the Turkes* (1603), would comment on the long-standing fear and uncertainty that Europeans felt about the Turkish threat:

> ...this barbarous Empire [is] (of almost nothing) growne to that height
> of majestie and power, as that it hath in contempt all the rest, being it
> selfe not inferiour in greatnesse and strength unto the greatest monar-
> chies that ever yet were upon the face of the earth...Which how farre it
> shall yet farther spread, none knoweth, but he that holdeth in his hand
> all the kingdomes of the earth.... ("Induction to the Christian reader")

When Knolles places his hopes in an appeal to a providential God, this is the conventional Christian reaction that Marlowe mocks in the drama of Tamburlaine, the scourge of God who succeeds in conquering the Turks. Clearly, the *Tamburlaine* plays were meant to provide pleasure in the spectacle of Tamburlaine defeating the imperial power that Knolles calls the "present terror of the earth," the Turk, and in subduing other Islamic potentates such as the Persian emperor and the sultan of Egypt. Anxieties about the Turks' growing dominion find relief in the fantasy of Turkish defeat and humiliation. This pleasing fantasy is initially what pulls the English audience in. Once they are implicated in Tamburlaine's actions, they are then made increasingly uncomfortable by his cruelty and pride, and by his blasphemous defiance or appropriation of divinity.

In the *Tamburlaine* plays, many of Marlowe's subversive insinuations work through the representation of Islam. The denunciation of Mahomet or the denial of the "gods" to whom Muslims or "pagans" pray was usually a way to validate, by contrast, the authority of the "true" Christian deity, but in *Tamburlaine, Parts I and II*, the demonization of Islam contaminates Christianity itself—indeed, all faith in metaphysical causality is shown to be futile. We can see how this works by looking first at the scene in which Tamburlaine orders the burning of the Koran.

Toward the end of Marlowe's *Tamburlaine, Part II*, having besieged and conquered Baghdad (referred to in the play as "Bagdeth" or "Babylon"), Tamburlaine orders a massacre of the city's inhabitants—men, women, and children. He then abruptly calls for a book-burning:

> Now, Casane, where's the Turkish Alcaron
> And all the heaps of superstitious books
> Found in the temples of that Mahomet
> Whom I have thought a god? They shall be burnt. (2:5.1.172–75)

Tamburlaine's words imply that until this point he had "thought" Mahomet to be a god—if not *the* God, at least one god among many. In this scene, however, he begins to speak of Mahomet as a mere mortal—and a damned one at that. Tamburlaine seems to have moved from one image of Mahomet to another. His attitude toward Mahomet shifts from one of the two images of Muhammed prevalent in early modern Europe to the other: the first is the notion of Mahomet as a pagan god or idol, the deity worshipped by the "Saracens" (in the *Chanson de Roland* and other romance narratives) and the second is the conception of Muhammed as a heretic and fraud, a renegade Christian who built a powerful new heresy in Arabia, an "imposture" allegedly cobbled together from plagiarized scraps of Judeo-Christian theology. During the course of the two plays, Tamburlaine converts from his initial position as a pagan polytheist to an acceptance of Mahomet as "a god"—and then later he becomes an anti-Islamic scourge and destroyer who seeks to annihilate Islam as an established religious culture. In this process of transformation, Tamburlaine's instability of religious devotion demonstrates that the rejection of one's native belief system (even if that entails a conversion from paganism to monotheism) indicates an infirmity of faith. When Tamburlaine turns Turk, it is a step on the path toward a more radical rejection of divinity. Ultimately, in the place of God or Mahomet, Tamburlaine asserts his personal power as a transcendent force, but in the end this claim is denied by his death.

It is important to note the distinction between an iconoclastic smashing of idols and what Tamburlaine does when he burns the Koran at the end of the second play. By calling for the destruction of sacred texts, Tamburlaine assaults the ideological foundation of expansionist Islam—its intense logocentrism. Logocentrism and iconoclasm were theological positions that Muslims and Protestants held in common, and in diplomatic relations between the rulers of England and Turkey, these shared beliefs were sometimes emphasized. Elizabeth I, in her letters to Amurath III (who in his letters to her titled himself as "he who is granted victory always"), downplayed the differences between her religion and that of the sultan: in one letter, she calls herself "the most invincible and most mightie defender of the Christian faith against all kinde of idolatries, of all that live among the Christians, and falselie professe the name of Christ" and promises that if the sultan will help to free her "subjects, who are deteined as slaves and captives in your gallies," she will ask "God (who onely is above all things, and all men, and is a most severe revenger of all idolatrie, and is jealous of his honor against against the false gods of the nations) to adorne your most invincible imperial highness with all the blessings of those gifts, which onely & deservedly are accounted most worthie of asking" (Skilliter 69–72).[1] As Jonathan Burton (2000) aptly puts it, these statements are part of an effort "to link Protestantism and Islam together in ersatz kinship" (136). The common cause of Protestants and Muslims against Roman Catholic "idolaters" (especially Spain and the Habsburg powers) helped in the negotiation of an Anglo-Ottoman alliance. And yet, in Marlowe's play, Tamburlaine seeks to destroy Islam, both its holy books and its holy warriors. He slaughters the Babylonians and abjures Mahomet, reducing the Ottoman powers from "millions" (2:5.2.25) to Callapine's "one host" (2:5.2.27). Then Tamburlaine and his followers wipe out that last remaining Islamic army. In the end, the Turkish threat simply evaporates "Like summer's vapours vanished by the sun" (2:5.3.116). When he accomplishes this feat, Tamburlaine fulfills a longstanding Christian-European fantasy—the complete elimination of Turkish military power.

Tamburlaine annihilates the fearsome Turkish armies, but he also attempts to defeat and delegitimize "Mahomet," the deity who was associated with the Islamic threat. Marlowe's Tamburlaine draws upon the anti-Islamic discourse that had developed over the centuries in Christian Europe, and specifically on the traditional misrepresentation of Islam as a religion that deified and worshipped Muhammed himself. (In fact, the notion that Muhammed is a god was and is utterly rejected by Islamic theology.) Tamburlaine tries to prove Mahomet powerless by locating the essence of Islam in its holy "writ" and then destroying those texts. Taking the idea of Muhammed's divinity as the keystone of Islam's validity, Tamburlaine then euhemerizes Muhammed when the Scythian leader declares that the Prophet is a mere man because no god would permit the destruction of the books that encapsulate and embody their religion: "Thou art not worthy to be worshipped / That suffers flames of fire to burn the writ / Wherein the sum of thy religion rests" (2:5.2.188–90).

For London playgoers in Protestant England, Tamburlaine's attack on the Book would glance at the logocentric principles of Protestantism. At the same time, it might remind them of the book-burning that took place as a result of the post-Reformation struggle between conflicting Catholic and Protestant interpretations of the Word. Nonetheless, many Protestants, as Christians opposed to Islam's spread, would approve of Tamburlaine's anti-Turkish violence. Marlowe's play thus evokes the uncomfortable contradictions inherent in England's cozy relations with infidel Turks.

Tamburlaine's bonfire of the vanities is lit onstage, and the Islamic holy books are tossed into the flames. While carrying out this spectacle of desecration, Tamburlaine declares that he will no longer invoke the Prophet's name in vain,

> In vain, I see, men worship Mahomet:
> My sword hath sent millions of Turks to hell,
> Slew all his priests, his kinsmen, and his friends,
> And yet I live untouched by Mahomet. (2:5.2.178–81)

In these lines, there is an implicit mockery of the notion of holy war (either crusade or jihad). According to Tamburlaine's logic, the god of those defeated in battle is no god at all. Victory in war proves that the god of the victorious is the true God. Might *is* right. The same reasoning leads to the conclusion that the Christians' God, the deity venerated by those whom the Turks had defeated in so many parts of Europe and the Mediterranean, had also been worshipped "in vain." This kind of thinking is seen, for example, in some of the occasional forms of prayer that were used in the Elizabethan Church—for example, the prayer for the delivery of Malta from Turkish siege that was read out in the city and diocese of Sarum:

> Suffer not thine enemies to prevail against those, that now call upon thy name, and put their trust in thee, lest the Heathen and Infidels say: "Where is now their God?"[2] (Clay 1847, 523)

The logic of this prayer, taken one step further, implies that because Islamic foes have indeed prevailed, there is authority to doubt the potency (and perhaps the very existence) of the Christian deity. After all, "the Heathen and Infidels" had occupied Jerusalem for centuries and the Turks continued to expand their empire at the expense of Christendom.

A reversal of this same logic is expressed in a narrative that celebrates a small Christian victory, "The worthy enterprise of John Fox, an Englishman, in delivering 266 Christians out of the captivity of the Turks at Alexandria, the third of January 1577," which was included in Hakluyt's 1589 edition of *The Principal Navigations*. Employing a conventional providential framework, the narrator describes the escape of Fox (not the same man as the martyrologist) and his companions, who had been held captive as galley slaves in Alexandria for many years. The fleeing slaves steal a galley and sail out of the harbor at Alexandria, but in order to gain their freedom, they must pass the cannons located on both sides of the harbor's mouth:

> There was not one of them that feared the shot which went thundering round about their ears nor yet were once scarred or touched with five and forty shot which came from the castles. Here did God hold forth His buckler. (Vitkus, *Piracy, Slavery, and Redemption* 2001, 65)

The Christian God is not the only deity invoked, though. A god much like Marlowe's "sleepy Mahomet" is also mentioned:

> And verily I think their god was amazed thereat. It could not be but he must blush for shame; he can speak never a word for dullness, much less can he help them in such an extremity. Well, howsoever it is, he is

very much to blame, to suffer them to receive such a gibe. But howso-
ever their god behaved himself, our God showed himself a God indeed
and that He was the only living God. (Vitkus, *Piracy, Slavery, and
Redemption* 2001, 66)

Sounding very much like the narrator of the Fox account,
Tamburlaine contrasts the impotence of Mahomet with the omnipo-
tence of the god he obeys, "a god full of revenging wrath, / From
whom the thunder and the lightning breaks, / Whose scourge I am"
(2:5.2.182–84). The reference to thunder and lightning suggests
either Jove the thunderer or the wrathful god of the Old Testament,
but in fact the exact identity of this god is never stated in Marlowe's
text. Tamburlaine's own religious faith is never quite clear: he appeals
to Jove's power but, at various points in the drama, Tamburlaine also
threatens or claims to rival Jove and other deities.

As Tamburlaine watches the Islamic texts being thrown into the
fire, he addresses Mahomet directly: "Now, Mahomet, if thou have
any power, / Come down thyself and work a miracle" (2:5.2.186–87).
It is perhaps these lines that Robert Greene had in mind when he
accused Marlowe of "daring God out of heaven with that Atheist
Tamburlan."[3] Tamburlaine's words echo those of the Gospel
(Matthew 27:40–42), where Christ on the Cross is taunted: "if thou
be the Sonne of God, come downe from the Crosse" and "let him
now come down from the Crosse, and we will beleve him." This echo
of the biblical text serves as a reminder that Christ himself was, in
some sense, "forsaken" by God—the moment of Christ's own doubt
and questioning ("My God, My God, why have you forsaken me?"
Matthew 27:46), and the notion that God did not prevent Jesus from
suffering a cruel, lingering death by crucifixion, are blasphemously
linked to Tamburlaine's challenge to Mahomet and his seemingly
successful demonstration that Mahomet lacks the "power" to work
miracles. Just as Marlowe's Mahomet fails to prevent Tamburlaine
from massacring the population of Baghdad and burning all of the
"superstitious books" in the city, so the Christian deity had failed to
save the Holy Land from subjection to bondage under the infidel.
William Lithgow, who passed through Jerusalem in 1612, wrote about
the Christian sense of dispossession in a despairing tone, lamenting,
"the holy Land together with Aegypt...being by Infidels detayned to
this day: and by likelihood shall keepe it to the consummation of the
world, unless God of his mercy deale otherwise [than] the hopes of
mans weaker judgement can expect" (214). In Marlowe's drama,
Tamburlaine accomplishes what the Christians hoped to achieve, but

the Scythian conqueror does so by asserting his own, indomitable will in the place of God's will.

As the sacred volumes burn, Tamburlaine ceases to address Mahomet and turns to his troops:

> Well, soldiers, Mahomet remains in hell;
> He cannot hear the voice of Tamburlaine.

The next three lines of this speech are oddly ambiguous:

> Seek out another godhead to adore,
> The God that sits in heaven, if any god.
> For he is God alone, and none but he. (2:5.2.197–201)

The question raised here—which God really "sits in heaven"?—calls for a response of absolute certainty, and Tamburlaine is not one who likes to admit doubts. And yet the precise name and nature of this "godhead" is not mentioned. These lines describe a God who sits "alone" in heaven, but at the same time Tamburlaine's words indicate a plurality of gods. Tamburlaine's suggestion that he and his followers should abandon one God and "seek out" another lacks the decisive conviction that normally accompanies conversion. Tamburlaine seems to mock and parody the call for conversion: for one thing, it is not clear which faith he wants his soldiers to convert *to*. And the phrase "if any god," seems to discourage the search for a true God altogether. If Tamburlaine is affirming the existence of God, one whose wrath he acknowledges and manifests, it is not at all certain which god that might be.

What would the sacking of Babylon/Baghdad and the burning of the Koran mean to Marlowe's Protestant audience in London? Certainly, the primary significance of "Babylon" for Londoners at the time would be biblical, and in particular would recall the references to Babylon in the Book of Revelation, a text that is so important for the Protestants' typological readings of history within an apocalyptic, providentialist framework. The destruction of the city, the mass slaughter of the inhabitants of Babylon, and the throwing of their bodies into the bituminous lake, are all suggestive of the description of the fall of Babylon in the New Testament. In the Geneva Bible, Babylon is repeatedly identified with Rome in the commentary to Revelation. But Babylon is also associated, in the Geneva Bible commentary, with the Turks. According to the propaganda of the Protestants, the Antichrist of Revelation, the scarlet whore, is the pope; and so the fall of Babylon is interpreted as the "fall of that great whore of Rome." The Geneva commentary also tells the reader that the collapse of the Roman Church shall be accompanied by the fall of "all strange religions, as of the Jews, Turks and others."[4]

Prophecies of Turkish doom were popular throughout Europe during the early modern period. Such texts always refer to the Book of Revelation, and sometimes they identify Muhammed with the Antichrist. They predicted the recovery of all lands lost to the Turks, and their conversion to Christianity; or they foretold the ultimate downfall of the Turks, but often after further victories (sometimes including the capture of Italy) before they would be turned back.[5] Perhaps these prophecies of Turkish doom express the collective desires and anxieties of the Europeans who were faced with the possibility of their own unthinkable defeat at the hands of the Muslims. These desires are acted out in Marlowe's *Jew of Malta* as well as his *Tamburlaine* plays, all of which look back at historical episodes of Turkish defeat and offer to English audiences the delightful spectacle of Turkish humiliation. In *Tamburlaine, Part I*, Tamburlaine reassures the audience, saying "Tush, Turks are full of brags / And menace more than they can well perform" (1:3.3.3–4), and when the bragging Turk, Bajazeth, appears in act 3, Tamburlaine proves the boasts of the "Great Turk" to be empty threats. The "Turkish arms / which lately made all Europe quake for fear" (1:3.3.134) are defeated by Tamburlaine who succeeds in out-scourging the Ottoman "scourge of God."

It has often been observed that the events that make up the episodic plot of the *Tamburlaine* plays are constantly subjected, by the characters in the play, to prediction and analysis in terms of a providentialist framework.[6] The characters in the play ceaselessly call upon divine or metaphysical powers in curse, oath, invocation, and prayer, in order to establish a causal link between higher forces and the events of the play. Defeated characters like Bajazeth and Zabina, try, again and again, to call down divine "justice" or retribution upon the alleged crimes of Tamburlaine. Conventional Tudor tragedy was a drama that fulfilled such expectations of divine retribution, but (as David Bevington has shown) Marlowe's tragedy is anti-homiletic.[7] In the *Tamburlaine* plays, the overweening pride of Tamburlaine is not punished by the hand of God; rather, the gods are silent, unlistening, asleep—passive and unheeding at best; at worst, nonexistent.

The followers of "sleepy Mahomet" are, in one sense, a version of the boasting Saracens of the romance tradition, whose invocations of Mahound and other idols prove ineffective in their confrontations with Christian knighthood. Bajazeth and Zabina sound much like the fictional Saracens who curse their own deities in the *chansons de geste* or in early modern romances by Tasso, Ariosto, and Spenser. But when Zabina asks, "Then is there left no Mahomet, no God, / No fiend, no Fortune...?" (1:5.1.239–40), her words go beyond the conventional anti-Islamic notion that Mahomet is a false prophet or idol, to suggest that there may be "no God" of any kind. Such insinuations of atheism would not have passed through the mechanisms of censorship had they not issued from the mouth of a non-Christian character.

Robert Greene's *Selimus, Emperor of the Turks* (1588) appeared soon after Marlowe's *Tamburlaine* plays were first staged during the winter of 1587–88. Greene's play was written to capitalize on the huge popularity of Marlowe's plays, and in Selimus we see a figure who closely resembles Tamburlaine. Like Tamburlaine, Selimus is never defeated or punished for his "unnatural" actions or bold blasphemies, but Selimus's moral identity is clearly that of a villain. Where Tamburlaine is an ambiguous figure, Selimus is plainly evil. It might be said that Greene's protagonist takes Tamburlaine's sacrilegious reasoning further, to its logical conclusion: Selimus is even more clearly and outrageously atheistic, rejecting the idea of an afterlife and declaring that the soul dies with the body. He declares that "religious observations" were "mere fictions" made by men to keep others "in quiet awe" (2.101–04): they are "Only bugbears to keep the world in fear / And make men quietly a yoke to bear. / So that religion (of itself a fable) / Was only found to make us peaceable" (105–08). These are not the words of an idol-worshipping "paynim knight" from the tradition of medieval romance. Rather, this is a scourge of God who claims to act alone, discounting the very notion of divine agency. In this sense, Greene's play picks up where Marlowe's plays left off.

Unlike the Christian knights of the romance tradition, the Christians who appear in *Tamburlaine, Part II*, are not victorious in their struggle against Islam. Frederick, the "lord of Buda," reminds Marlowe's audience of the "cruel slaughter of our Christian bloods / These heathenish Turks and pagans lately made" (2:2.1.5–6) in Hungary and Bulgaria. The opening scene of *Tamburlaine, Part II* features a powerful Turkish force whose leader, Orcanes, threatens a general massacre of Europe, promising to turn "the Terrene main" (the Mediterranean) into a "bloody sea" (2:1.1.37–38) by sending "The slaughtered bodies of these Christians" out on a grisly tide of blood and floating corpses that will be carried by the Danube River until "The wand'ring sailors of proud Italy / Shall meet those Christians fleeting with the tide / Beating in heaps against their argosies, / And make fair Europe...wear a woeful mourning weed" (1.1.39–44). It is only the arrival of Tamburlaine that prevents Orcanes from putting this plan into action. Menaced by Tamburlaine's invading forces, Orcanes forms a "league" (2.1.28) with the Christians, "Confirmed by oath and articles of peace, / And calling Christ for record of our truths" (2.1.29–30). When Orcanes subsequently moves most of his army to defend against Tamburlaine, the Christians see an opportunity to "work revenge upon these infidels" (2.1.13). Frederick and Baldwin persuade Sigismund to break the truce, and their sleazy arguments in favor of oath-breaking constitute a cynical perversion of providentialism: Frederick asks Sigismund, "should we lose the opportunity / That God hath given to venge our Christians' death / And scourge this foul blasphemous paganism?" (2.1.51–53). Just before Orcanes's Muslim army fights the Christian knights who have broken their oath, Orcanes invokes the Christian deity, saying "on Christ still let us cry— / If there be Christ, we shall have victory" (2.2.63–64). The Christians are vanquished, and for a moment, it appears that the battle is a clear case of divine intervention—Christ, it seems, has punished his own people for breaking their oath. In this scene Marlowe mocks the conventional Christian interpretation of victory and defeat on the battlefield: there is no Christian triumph to demonstrate the true God's backing of His chosen people. Instead Orcanes, a Muslim, acknowledges the doctrine of Christ's divinity because his outnumbered Turkish army has decisively defeated a Christian one. This might have been understood as a typical case of a non-Christian scourge (the Turks, in this case) scourging Christians for their oath-breaking sins, but such a reading of the Muslims' military success is immediately questioned: when Orcanes asks his viceroy, Gazellus, if the Christians' defeat constitutes a clear demonstration of Christ's power on earth, Gazellus replies, " 'Tis but the fortune of the wars, my lord / Whose power is often proved a miracle" (2.3.31–32). This statement undermines the providential interpretation of events and weakens Sigismund's previous claim (in the same scene) that God, the "just and dreadful punisher of sin" (2.3.4), "hath thundered vengeance from on high" (2.3.2).

The Sigismund–Orcanes episode suggests that all invocations of divine power and all claims to divine sponsorship are mere rhetoric. Orcanes tries to claim some divine authorization by declaring, "Christ *or* Mahomet hath been my friend" (my emphasis, 2.3.11), but this awkward equivocation only serves to intensify the already increasing sense of doubt about the exact location of godhead. Nonetheless, Marlowe's Protestant audience might well have been willing to believe that Christ would give victory to the Turks in order to scourge the Roman Catholic and Orthodox "idolatry" of Sigismund's Christian army.

* * *

I now want to situate the *Tamburlaine* plays' anti-providentialism and its representation of Islam and holy war within the context of sixteenth-century Protestant discourse—in particular, the Protestant response to the dual threat of Turkish power, on the one hand, and papal power on the other. While Protestants were confronted with a militant papal-Habsburg Counter-Reformation, the Habsburgs and their Roman Catholic allies faced the Turkish menace in Central Europe and in the Mediterranean. In the minds of some Protestants, there was a question as to who was the more threatening foe of the Reformed Church—the pope or the Turk? In fact, the Ottoman Turks have been called "allies of the Reformation," and they were much more tolerant of Protestants under their rule than were the Roman Catholic princes of southeastern Europe.[8] It was also the Ottoman threat that helped to place the early Lutherans in a position of strength in their negotiations for religious freedom.[9]

In England, Elizabeth I was pursuing a policy of commercial and military alliance with the Ottoman sultanate under Amurath III at the time that Marlowe wrote the *Tamburlaine* plays.[10] In 1585 Walsingham had instructed William Harborne, the English ambassador to the Ottoman Sultan, to urge a military alliance between England and the Turks. Walsingham hoped for a Turkish attack on Spain that would "divert the dangerous attempt and designs of [the Spanish] King from these parts of Christendom."[11] But more than that, Walsingham expressed the hope that Spain and Turkey, two "limbs of the devil" as he put it, might "be set one against another, by means thereof the true Church and doctrine of the gospel may, during their contention, have leisure to grow to such strength as shall be requisite for suppression of them both" (Read 1925, 3:226).

In the context of diplomatic and commercial relations, where the pressures of trade, war, and religious difference came together, it is apparent that the binary opposition of Christian to non-Christian or Protestant to Roman Catholic, quickly gave way to more complex configurations. At first, we observe a triangular structure emerge in sixteenth-century Europe: Roman Catholic/Protestant/Turkish.

The introduction of a third term into the conventional binaries of faithful–infidel, Christ–Antichrist, and Christian–heathen, disturbs and undermines the rhetorical operation of these oppositions. This triangulation of religious conflict is replicated in Marlowe's presentation of Sigismund's Christians and Orcanes's Turks, with Tamburlaine as the third term. This triangulation was a problem for Martin Luther, and it is seen in his conflicted attitude toward the Turks and Islam, which was a serious dilemma for him throughout his career—a weak point for which he was roundly attacked by his critics.[12]

Luther's attitude toward Islam must be seen in light of the Protestant critique of the papal theory of crusade, and in the context of the Protestant struggle for survival against the Habsburg effort to stamp out the new heresy. The Protestant attack on the idea of a crusade was part of the assault on papal prerogative and the Roman Catholic penitential system, particularly on indulgences that were granted to those who had donated to the cause of an anti-Islamic crusade. In 1518, Luther was accused (in the papal bull of excommunication) of a heretical opposition to holy war against the Turks. In his response to the pope, Luther defended the principle (one of his original ninety-five theses) that to fight the Turks is to resist the judgment of God upon men's sins ("Proeliari adversus Turcas est repugnare Deo visitanti iniquitates nostras per illos").[13] Interestingly, Luther's pronouncement about the Turkish scourge is identical to Tamburlaine's claim for himself: fight me and you are opposing God's just wrath. Although Luther's position may well have been an objection "less to fighting against the Turk than to fighting under papal leadership," it implies that to fight the Turk is to resist God's will (Vaughan 1954, 135).

Later, as the Turkish invaders drew closer to Germany, Luther was forced to explain, defend, and then modify his position. In a series of sermons and writings on the Turks and their religion, he advocated a united resistance against the Ottoman advance, but not in the form of a traditional religious crusade. At the same time, he began to equate the pope's "false faith" with that of the Turkish sultan. In his 1529 tract, *On War Against the Turk*, Luther states repeatedly that the pope and his religion are to be abhorred and resisted as much as the sultan and Islam, and in *Table Talk*, Luther is quoted as saying, "Antichrist is at the same time the Pope and the Turk. A living creature consists of body and soul. The spirit of Antichrist is the Pope, his flesh the Turk. One attacks the Church physically, the other spiritually" (qtd. in Setton 1962, 151). Luther continued to claim in his writings that Turkish power was brought by God to punish those who failed to join the Protestant Reformation. Like the Ottoman sultan, Marlowe's Tamburlaine takes advantage of his enemies' fighting amongst themselves (in the case of the Christians of Hungary versus Muslims of Turkey), and like the Turks he accomplishes a string of victories that rapidly expand the territory under his control. As a serial conqueror, Tamburlaine gains imperial momentum and followers: his success resembles and replaces the Turkish model, but in Marlowe's play he is not a conqueror whose accomplishments are founded on Christian schism and disarray.

In post-Reformation polemics, Catholics compared Protestants to the Turks, and Protestants returned the insult. The pope and the Ottoman sultan were frequently equated, conflated, or compared in antipapal literature. An important example of this occurs in John Foxe's *Acts and Monuments*, which includes a lengthy "history of the Turkes" that recounts "their cruell tyranny and bloudy victories, the ruin & subversion of so many Christen Churches, with the horrible murders and captivitie of infinite Christians" (1:675). Foxe goes on to declare that "…the whole power of Sathan the prince of this world, goeth with the Turkes," and he calls for a fortification of the spirit to strengthen the faithful against Turkish expansion: "though the Turke seemeth to be farre off, yet do we nourish within our breasts at home, that [which] may soon cause us to feele his cruell hand and worse, if worse may be, to overrunne us: to lay our land waste: to scatter us amongst the Infidels" (Foxe 1:675 and 677). Foxe's narration of the Christians' resistance to Ottoman expansion ends with a ten-page section on "Prophecies of the Turke and the Pope, which of them is the greater Antichrist" (1:701–10), and the concluding paragraph of this section gestures toward a distinction between papal and Turkish evil, but ultimately Foxe declines to discern the difference:

> …in comparing the Turk with the Pope, if a question be asked, whether of them is the truer or greater Antichrist, it were easy to see and judge, that the Turke is the more open and manifest enemy against Christ and His church. But if it be asked, whether of them two had bin the more bloudy and pernitious adversary to Christ and his members: or whether of them hath consumed and spilt more Christian bloud, he with sword, or this with fire and sword together, neither is it a light matter to discern, neither is it my part here to discusse, who doe onely write the history and the Actes of them both. (Foxe 1:710)

Foxe and other Protestant writers described the wars against Roman Catholic rule and religion as crusades against "the second Turk," the Antichrist, or the Eastern whore of Babylon. Roman Catholic polemicists returned the accusation in kind. In 1597, a Latin treatise called *Calvino-Turcismus, id est, Calvinisticae perfidiae cum Mahumetana Collatio* was printed in Antwerp, and within two years a ferocious response appeared in London, called *De Turco-Papismo, hoc est de Turcorum et Papistarum adversus Christi ecclesiam et fidem Conjuratione, eorumque in religione et moribus consensiene et similitudine.*[14]

While Protestants and Catholics accused each other of turning Turk, they both continued to cry out for a crusade against the real Turks. In the sixteenth century, incessant warfare between the Christian states of Europe actually served to intensify the exhortations for Christian unity and a crusade against the Turks. Despite their hostility to any crusade led by the pope, Protestants in England, at least, did not abandon the principle of a just holy war, waged by the "common corps of Christendom" against the predations of the infidel.[15] Such calls for a crusade were frequently trumpeted in the pulpit and in print, but such a pan-Christian unification in the cause of a holy war against the Turks never materialized.

The fantasy of Christian unity in a crusade was manifested in the continued popularity of legends and romances that described the heroic exploits of Christian knights defeating (and sometimes converting) various Islamic foes (including Moors, Saracens, Turks, Scythians, and Arabs). The imaginative geography of the *Tamburlaine* plays is much like that of early modern romance narratives by Tasso, Ariosto, and others. A similar sense of imperial scope and accomplishment is seen, for example, in both Tasso's Godfrey and Marlowe's Tamburlaine. They fight the same foes: in *Jerusalem Delivered*, the crusaders are opposed by three "pagan" empires that worship "Mahoun[d]"—Persia, Turkey, and Egypt. And Tasso's representation of Islamic might in *Jerusalem Delivered* is remarkably similar to the descriptions of the armies in Marlowe's Tamburlaine plays. The setting and the order of events are almost identical. The crusaders in Tasso's poem combat the same Muslim enemies in the same order: first, the Persians, then the Turks, then the Egyptians, and finally they attack Jerusalem. They move, as Tamburlaine does in Marlowe's play, from Gaza to Syria, to Damascus, and then to Jerusalem. Marlowe's *Tamburlaine* plays offer another version of the liberation of Jerusalem from Islamic rule. The similarities go further, including details: the battle against an Egyptian king at Gaza; the appearance of a governor of Damascus; and a scene in which Armida, like the virgins of Damascus, is sent out to appeal for pity to the Christian knights laying siege to Jerusalem. Tasso's characters share the obsessive concern with divine intervention expressed by the characters in the *Tamburlaine* plays, but for Tasso's Christians, prayer is an effective means to gain God's support. While Tasso asserts divine providence in order to support the idea of an omnipotent, responsive Christian deity, Marlowe dramatizes an impotent providentialism in order to undermine it. Stephen Greenblatt describes this tendency in Marlowe's work "to spurn and subvert his culture's metaphysical and ethical certainties," and Greenblatt (1980) reads *Tamburlaine, I and II* as a text that "repeatedly teases its audience with the form of the cautionary tale, only to violate the convention" (220). The effect of the play, he claims, "is not to celebrate the transcendent power of Muhammed but to challenge the habit of mind that looks to heaven for rewards and punishments, that imagines evil as 'the scourge of God'" (202).[16]

The conclusion of *Tamburlaine, Part II* shows that Tamburlaine's death is caused by a radically material disease of the body, an elemental imbalance that is not produced by anything above or beyond his own physical anatomy.[17] Nowhere does the play suggest that his death is the result of divine retribution. Tamburlaine is merely the last in a series of characters who arrogantly and then desperately invoke divinity only to find such invocation futile. Tamburlaine and his followers try to interpret the manner of his death as an apotheosis, but the doctor's diagnosis is clearly accurate, and this is confirmed by Tamburlaine's last words, "Tamburlaine, the scourge of God, must die" (2:5.3.248). In the death scene we have the final violation of audience expectations for a "theater of divine judgement." It is a double violation: neither do we see Tamburlaine punished for his pride and blasphemy, thereby confirming the existence of a divine agent that, in the end, scourges the un-Christian scourge; nor do we see Tamburlaine's claim to personal divinity validated. Tamburlaine is neither punished nor rewarded; he is merely the victim of materiality, of the body's elemental and temporal limitations.

The imperial, Islamic powers that occupied the Christians' Holy Land—and threatened Europe with conquest and conversion—are all destroyed or subdued by a virtual nobody who began as a landless nomad, and who ultimately dissolves in an elemental, material disintegration. The powers that initially competed to demonstrate that their God, like Fox's, was "a God indeed and that He was the only living God" join in denying the efficacy of all divine agency. The English fear of being conquered or colonized by Islamic powers is transformed, through the construction of an increasingly sympathetic audience position, into an identification with Tamburlaine's Islamic victims. Tamburlaine himself is also eliminated at the end. His son is crowned but his empire will not last: the map he brings out at the end will be used to divide his holdings, not to expand them further. From nothing came Tamburlaine, and to nothing he returns.

Under the guise of an anti-Islamic drama that superficially confirms and conforms to orthodox demonizations of the Turk, the play insinuates that the discourses of providentialism, prophecy, and holy war are merely empty rhetoric, and that if there is a God in heaven, he is no more than another "sleepy Mahomet" who does not hear the prayers of Christians. Christian faith in God's will to punish evildoers and preserve the righteous against infidels is denied in the case of Tamburlaine. In the end, the location and nature of divine power remain elusive, perhaps even unknowable.[18] What is tragic in these plays is the desperately misdirected attempts of human beings to make sense of events, and to seek for the source of their misfortunes in metaphysical causality, rather than material circumstances. Marlowe's play takes the Turks, who were traditionally understood as God's "scourge," and renders them impotent. Their desperate calls for divine intervention, and by implication the analogous prayers of Christians for protection, by means of divine intervention, against the Ottoman Turks, are futile. All such prayers are subjected to Marlowe's mockery. This demystifying message in the *Tamburlaine* plays is a product, perhaps, of the blasphemous attitude of which Kyd, under interrogation, accused Marlowe.[19] Indeed, the *Tamburlaine* plays ask their audience to consider "That things esteemed to be donn by devine power might have as well been don by observation of men...."[20]

* * *

Marlowe locates his anti-providentialist drama in exotic settings where outlandish characters question religious orthodoxies. The *Tamburlaine* plays subvert English Protestant beliefs about God's triple role as playwright, director, and spectator in the theater of the world, but scholars of Marlowe have also remarked on the way that these plays produce a fantasy of imperial ambition in the achievements of Tamburlaine.[21] Beginning in Persia, and ranging through the Mediterranean world, Tamburlaine and his followers trace their conquering paths across Ortelius's *Theatrum Orbis Terrarum* (published at Antwerp in 1570), the map that Ethel Seaton has convincingly shown to be Marlowe's main cartographic source.[22] According to Seaton, Tamburlaine's rise to power is charted by Marlowe "with the accuracy of a scholar and the common sense of a merchant-venturer" (54) and writing in 1924 she compares the playwright to one who plays "a great game of chess, with kings and conquerors for pieces, and for the chess board the *Theatrum Orbis Terrarum*: a *Kriegspiel*, such as many recently have played with the aid of flags on pins; but his game, being imaginary, without our bitter mercenary urgency, was excellent sport" (55). For Marlowe, it was not World War I, but the contemporary rivalries with imperial Spain and the Ottoman empire that provided an urgent sense of global ambition and international conflict for London audiences. It was also the contemporary "game" of planning for commercial and colonial expansion that informs Marlowe's portrait of the aspiring Scythian, who conquers and reaps rich booty at will.

Like contemporaneous English representations of Turks, *Tamburlaine* was a mirror, a "tragic glass" (Prologue, 1.7) in which the English saw a distorted, fantasmic version of themselves—a spectacle that was both admirable and frightening. For the English, Tamburlaine is a paradoxical model of what to be or do, and what not to be or do. He is both glorious and monstrous, an outrageous upstart; he is Alexander the Great and Satan combined, declaring in his first scene a transgressive ambition to rule the world. When Zenocrate questions his birth and breeding, he answers, "I am a lord, for so my deeds shall prove, / And yet a shepherd by my parentage" (1:1.2.34–35). He goes on to express an almost limitless hunger for territory that begins with the satisfaction of his sexual desire for Zenocrate, the Egyptian princess:

> But lady, this fair face and heavenly hue
> Must grace his bed that conquers Asia
> And means to be a terror to the world,
> Measuring the limits of his empery
> By east and west as Phoebus doth his course. (1.2.36–40)

The truth is that he is merely one of a band of "silly country swains" (1.2.47), a shepherd turned bandit. When Tamburlaine casts off his lowly shepherd's robes to reveal the "complete armor" and "curtle-axe" (1.2.43) that he wears beneath, this is a metamorphosis that signifies his status as a convert figure, a renegade or "runnagate," who has transgressed the social boundaries of class. He refuses to have a master and is therefore a masterless man who will go on to convert others, making them turn against their masters. The process that he sets in motion is much like that of the powerful Turk of Istanbul who also enlarged his empire by persuading potential enemies to join him, turning Turk. The Ottoman dynasty was usually given a genealogy much like Tamburlaine's, though more transgressive because it was recognized that through the institutions of harem and concubinage, and through the promotion of men who were taken as children and converted to become Turkish eunuchs or janissaries at court, the purity of the Ottoman court and royal line was continually being adulterated by the blood of foreign slaves and concubines. The similarity between Scythians and Turks is made clear in various European accounts of the rise of Ottoman power. For example, Stephen Wythers's 1563 translation of Johann Sleidanus's Latin history of empires says, "the Turckes...weare issued out of Scithia" and then offers a quick account that might have described Tamburlaine as well as the Ottomans: "the Turckes beyng of a small begynning beganne to enlarge their dominions by lytle and lytle, and to assault Asia: in such sort that encreasing daily their power, at length they have establyshed a Monarchye" (66). In Ralph Carr's dedicatory epistle to *The Mahumetane or Turkish Historie* (1600), a translation and synthesis of various Continental writings about the Turks, Carr marvels at the Turks' sudden appearance as an imperial power, and his account sounds exactly like a description of Marlowe's Tamburlaine:

> from how lowly and small beginnings the victorious and never degenerating race of these Ottamans, together with the invincible nations of their Turkes, are growen; that being but bare breach Tartars only, runne out of the caves of those horrid countryes of the Rifean and Caucasus mountaines, yet have with glorious successe in their attempts ledde captivitie captive, made themselves now conquerors over the whole East; and in fine are becoming even the terror of the West. Sacking infinit numbers of Citties and Countryes: dispoyling multitudes of Princes and high discended families of theyr lives, together with theyr crownes and kingdomes: and this done in so few yeares space above all opinion, or what else before was ever executed by the antique world. (sig.A3v)

In *The Policy of the Turkish Empire*, the Turks are said to be "naturally descended from the blood and brood of the auncient Scythians called Nomades: who, using to wander up and downe in Tents...not having any townes Cities or villages, and without any certaine habitation" (sig.7r). For the author of *The Policy*, Tamburlaine and the Turks share a common genealogy of rootlessness. The Scythian shepherd and the Ottomans themselves were considered upstarts and renegades when seen from the perspective of European Christians whose societies were subjected to an ideology that stressed and enforced a strict hierarchy and the authority of an exclusively hereditary ruling class. Marlowe's play registers the anxieties about social place and stability that accompanied the rise of "Turkish" or "Scythian" capitalists.

Tamburlaine is a fantastically successful stage version of real English renegadoes like John Ward or real converts to Roman Catholicism like the Sherley brothers or Thomas Stukeley, who also defied the political and social limits placed on them in order to give vent to their expansive ambition. The implication in Marlowe's play is that even the greatest and most renowned conquests are merely grand larceny. The basis of imperial power and conquest is twofold: it relies upon force and what Walsingham called "finesse," and these are driven, not by divine will, but by a human, all too human, will-to-power.[23] This idea is stated quite clearly in Lyly's 1587 play, *Midas*, when King Midas debates with his bellicose advisor, Martius, as to what comprises the true basis of monarchical legitimacy:

> Midas: Every little king is a king, and the title consisteth not in the compass of the ground but in the right of inheritance.
> Martius: Are not conquests good titles?
> Midas: Conquests are great thefts.
> Martius: If Your Highness would be advised by me, then would I rob for kingdoms, and if I obtained, fain would I see him that durst call the conqueror a thief.
> Midas: Martius, thy counsel hath shed as much blood as would make another sea. "Valour" I cannot call it, and "barbarousness" is a word too mild. (3.2.84–93)[24]

Tamburlaine's transformation from thief to emperor demonstrates the point made by Midas in Lyly's satire. For Marlowe, as for Lyly, this satirical barb is explicitly directed at external empires like those of Spain and Turkey, but it also carries a more self-critical valence. One man's barbarousness is another man's valor, and Tamburlaine is only a more transgressive, exaggerated, exoticized version of what the English themselves desired to be. In the voice and form of Edward Alleyn, who first acted the part and made the plays a huge commercial success, Tamburlaine was a common, English-speaking player trumped up as an exotic hero. In Alleyn's Tamburlaine, the English fantasy of upward social mobility is articulated by a masterless man.

Jonathan Burton argues that in *Tamburlaine, Part II*, in particular, Tamburlaine exemplifies "the aspiring mind of European selfhood even while he seems so threateningly Other. For the audience of the second play, it is impossible to fully distance Tamburlaine by attributing his actions to Islam, and impossible to see Christianity as an exemplary negation of Islam" (150). Tamburlaine is a classic example of that Renaissance "perspective" so popular with new historicists, the anamorphic device, appearing from one point of view as an admirable fantasy figure, the imperial conqueror that the English wanted to become, and from another point of view something quite different: a version of what they most feared, a ranting tyrant like Philip of Spain or the "Great Turk" who gains wealth, power, territory and converts, all at the expense of England and the Protestant church.[25] Like all of Marlowe's overreaching protagonists, Tamburlaine represents both powerful desires and deep anxieties.

Returning once more to the spectacle of Tamburlaine's unveiling and revelation, when the "shepherd's son" becomes the armor-clad conqueror, there is an additional set of associations, also paradoxical, that comes into play here. The story of the unknown shepherd, the man of humble origins who would be king, would certainly have both Davidic and Christological associations for an audience steeped in biblical allusion and Christian imagery. Tamburlaine figures both the shepherd who defeats the giant Philistine/Islamic Goliath and the wrathful, conquering Messiah who appears at the apocalypse to scourge the earth. The scene in which Tamburlaine cuts himself and bleeds offers a perverse and blasphemous typology of Christ's blood sacrifice. First, Tamburlaine calls on his followers not to "stand in fear of death" (2:3.2.102) and then he describes the "streaming blood" (3.2.105) of his wounded soldiers who return from battle as a parody of sacramental transubstantiation: "at night [Tamburlaine's men] carouse within my tent, / Filling their empty veins with airy wine / That, being concocted, turns to crimson blood" (3.2.105–08). The text's incessant use of the verbal imagery of bloodshed is then given a visual, ritualized form when Tamburlaine gashes open his vein and urges his sons to "Come, boys, and with your fingers search my wound / And in my blood wash all your hands at once" (3.2.126–27). Here, the audience would certainly think of the crucified Christ, washing away the sins of the world; and asking his disciple-like sons to search his wound recalls, of course, Christ's exhortation to "doubting Thomas." Tamburlaine's self-inflicted injury is that of a god-like figure who cannot be harmed by human beings and can only be wounded when he wills it to happen. Just as the Christian God sacrificed his son to redeem the sins of all, and just as the Eucharist is a ritual of remembering that sacrifice, so Tamburlaine, the quasi-divine father, bleeds so that his sons will remember, not to emulate Christ, but to copy the violent, merciless example of an almighty father who does not fear death and ignores the offer of eternal life.

The play's deployment of biblical language also encourages an ironic association of Tamburlaine with Christ the messiah. For example, in *Tamburlaine, Part I*, the Scythian warrior declares, "Then, when the sky shall wax as red as blood, / It shall be said I made it red myself, / To make me think of ought but blood and war" (1:4.2.53–55). This speech, and others like it, recall apocalyptic language from the Bible in passages like Matthew 24:30: "And then shal appeare the signe of the Sonne of man in heaven: and then shall all the kin[d]reds of the earth mourne, and they shal see the Sonne of man come in the cloudes of heaven with power and great glory."[26] Tamburlaine's sudden appearance on the stage of the world parodies the apocalyptic return of Christ as a figure of God's wrath who comes to defeat the (Turkish) Antichrist and establish his rule over the world. English Protestants were accustomed to hearing prophecies (from the pulpit or in polemical texts like Foxe's *Actes and Monuments*) that predicted in terrifying and "high astounding terms" the coming of a universal scourge that would destroy the corrupt old order and establish a new kingdom based on God's truth. English desire to imitate imperial models or to compete with other nations was commonly articulated through a religious discourse that included such apocalyptic prophecies. Mercantile expansionists also proposed and validated their projects within a religious ideology, and they often combined economic, patriotic, and religious justifications for their enterprises.

A good example of this kind of propaganda may be found in Sir George Peckham's *True Report of the Newfound Landes* (1583), in which a series of dedicatory poems preface a call for English subjects to leave their homeland in search of wealth and glory abroad. It is worth quoting at length from a couple of these poems because these texts give vent to a pent-up, aggressive desire for "liberty" from domestic limitations, combined with a lust for wealth, that typified the adventuring class of merchants and seamen who were already flexing their muscle in the Mediterranean and would soon target Spanish shipping. The explicitly neoclassical fantasy of creating colonies, which could not be established in the Mediterranean where the Greeks and Romans had done so, is projected onto North America. In his dedicatory poem, Sir John Hawkins, one of the first English sea captains to transport slaves from Africa to the Caribbean, sees a golden opportunity to serve God, queen, and country, and make "private gaines" at the same time:

> If zeale to God, or countries care, with private gaines accesse,
> Might serve for spurs unto th'attempt this pamflet doth expresse[,]
> One coast, one course, one toile might serve, at ful to make declard

> A zeale to God, with countries good, and private gaines regarde.
> And for the first this enterprise the name of God shall founde,
> Among a nation in whose eares the same did never sounde.
> Next as an endles running streame, her Channels doth discharge:
> That swell above theyr boundes, into an Occean wide and large.
> So England that is pestered nowe, & choakt through want of grou[n]d
> Shall find a soile where room inough and perfect doth abounde.

Hawkins endows the "intended voyage" with a Christian purpose, but most of his poem stresses the notion that a lack of colonial outlets for England has resulted in an overpopulated homeland. In subsequent lines, he cites the expansion of the ancient Greeks and Romans in the Mediterranean as a model and precedent for England's future colonies, but claims that the present need to release those who have been "pestered" and "choakt" in England is greater than it ever was for the ancients:

> But Rome nor Athens nor the rest, were never pestered so,
> As England where no roome remaines, her dwellers to bestow,
> But shuffled in such pinching bondes, that very breath dooth lacke:
> And for the want of place they craule one ore anothers backe.

Other contributors to the dedicatory apparatus include the explorers Sir Francis Drake and Martin Frobisher. One of the poems, by "a Marchant tailour of London," John Achelley, urges his readers not to delay but to lend their support to the Newfoundland project, either by joining the expedition or by investing their capital:

> Bee not for want of men and aide, through slackfulnes undoone.
> So shall you harbour in your hartes, the seedes of magnanimitie:
> A vertue where with all the Romaines did enlarge their Empery.
> Be you prepared for every foe, and be couragious then:
> For that you slippe through negligence will fall to other men.

Achelley and the others are aware of English belatedness in the competition to acquire colonies, and like Tamburlaine they must seize Occasion by the forelock in order to create an empire *ex nihilo*.

Tamburlaine is defined and motivated by the greatness of his fiery spirit. His bold rhetoric is the accidental but instrumental expression of that essential, elemental quality. The would-be colonizers assert the same providentialist self-assurance that gets Tamburlaine going. According to Achelley, if they keep "the seedes of magnanimitie" in their hearts and then take action when the right moment arrives, they will succeed. "No doubt that God will blesse th'attempt" says Achelley. As it turned out, the voyage planned and promoted in Peckham's *True Report of the Newfound Landes* (Frobisher's third trip to seek a northwest passage) was a dismal failure and a setback for English expansionists.[27] Frobisher brought back tons of a black ore that he believed contained gold but turned out to be worthless. Their hopes for the "plantation" of seeds that would grow profitably were dashed. It was only later, during the war against Spain and as plundering pirates targeting Spanish ships and territory, that Hawkins and Frobisher found ways to direct their aspiring "magnanimitie."

* * *

In *Spectacles of Strangeness*, Emily Bartels maintains that Marlowe's *Tamburlaine, I and II* comprise an exercise in "imperialist self-construction," and she rightly argues that "...Turkish imperialism provided a crucial impetus for England's own" (54). She goes a bit too far, however, when she claims that in Marlowe's day "the Orient's myths and realities had begun to capture, and be captured by, Europe's imaginative and imperialist interests" (54).[28] Empire was still beyond their grasp. And it is not "the East" per se that Marlowe dramatizes in the *Tamburlaine* plays: instead I would suggest, along with Stephen Greenblatt (1980), that "If we want to understand the historical matrix of Marlowe's achievement...we might look...at the acquisitive energies of English merchants, entrepreneurs, and adventurers, promoters alike of trading companies and theatrical companies" (194). In the remainder of my comments on *Tamburlaine*, I want to focus on the specifically Mediterranean location of that economic and cultural energy.

In *Tamburlaine, Part II*, Tamburlaine's success and ambition come to be measured globally, but from an increasingly Mediterranean-centered perspective. The play's staging of a competition for imperial control begins in the Mediterranean world and the neighboring region to the east that includes Persia. Persia was the primary gateway through which the luxury goods arrived from further east on their way to the Mediterranean and Europe, having been moved along the "silk road" and other important trade routes. Goods from China and the East Indies were transported through Tamburlaine's hometown of Samarkand and carried on to the southwestern termini of these routes. Along with Trebizond, Kaffa, and Tana, on the Black Sea, Constantinople was an important terminus for these land routes. In *Tamburlaine, Part I*, at the beginning of act 3, Marlowe introduces Bajazeth and his army as a force that is besieging "Grecian Constantinople" (3.1.6). By the fifteenth century, the Ottoman state had established a solidly founded political system, one that was sorely tested in 1402 when the Mongol invaders under Tamburlaine (or Timur) thoroughly defeated the Turks; but the staying power of the Ottoman polity was proven in the rapid recovery and reintegration of the Ottoman territories under Amurath II (1421–51). Constantinople was then captured in 1453 by Amurath's successor, Mehmed (or Muhammed) II. Marlowe's *Tamburlaine* plays represent an earlier historical moment, before Constantinople fell, in which the fearsome Turkish power (embodied in the bluster and pride of Marlowe's Bajazeth) was crushed. As it turned out, this was only a brief hiatus for Ottoman hegemony, but Marlowe's play never acknowledges that fact.

Marlowe's Turks are an Islamic threat to Christendom that relies upon converted Christians to maintain its imperial momentum. In consultation with the North African kings of Fesse, Morocco, and Argier, Bajazeth describes the Turkish army that invests Constantinople:

> As many circumcised Turks we have
> And warlike bands of Christians renied
> As hath the ocean or the Terrene sea
> Small drops of water when the moon begins
> To join in one her semicircled horns. (1:3.1.8–12)

This invocation of the crescent moon, image of Islam in general and of the Ottomans in particular, was employed by various Christian writers, for example, we find it used in Abraham Hartwell's 1595 translation of Minadoi's history of the wars between Turkey and Persia, where this passage appears in the dedicatory epistle:

> ...the power of the Turks growes so huge and infinite, and their enemies so divided and weakened, that unless God come downe as it were out of an Engine, to protect the Gospell of his Sonne Jesus Christe, and the Professors thereof, I feare greatly that the halfe Moone which now ruleth & raigneth almost over all the East, wil grow to the full, and breede such an Inundation as will utterly drowne al Christendoime in the West. (sig.A3v–A4r)

In Marlowe's play, it is the upstart Tamburlaine, not a *deus ex machina* that suddenly arrives to protect Christendom from inundation. This sense of a waxing Islamic force, carried by the natural

power of the tides, conveys a natural image that contrasts with
the unnatural or supernatural qualities used repeatedly to describe
Tamburlaine: for example, when Ortygius calls him a "god or fiend
or spirit of the earth, / Or monster turned to a manly shape"
(1:2.6.15–16). Bajazeth proclaims himself as the leader of a force that
"lately made all Europe quake for fear" (1:3.3.135), but the arrival of
Tamburlaine's army causes him to break off the siege.

Earlier, in *Tamburlaine, Part I*, the Scythian shepherd-turned-
warrior had promised to make the Mediterranean a safer place for
Christians to do business:

> I...
> Will first subdue the Turk, and then enlarge
> Those Christian captives which you keep as slaves,
> Burdening their bodies with your heavy chains
> And feeding them with thin and slender fare
> That naked row about the Terrene sea;
> And when they chance to breathe and rest a space
> Are punished with bastones so grievously
> That they lie panting at the galley's side
> And strive for life at every stroke they give:
> These are the cruel pirates of Argier,
> That damned train, the scum of Africa,
> Inhabited with straggling runagates,
> That make quick havoc of the Christian blood.
> But, as I live, that town shall curse the time
> That Tamburlaine set foot in Africa. (1:3.3.44–60)

After Tamburlaine makes good on his promise to defeat and humiliate
the Turks, Bajazeth acknowledges that this will give his Christian enemies cause to celebrate, as they did when the Turks were defeated at
Malta and Lepanto: "Now will the Christian miscreants be glad, /
Ringing with joy their superstitious bells / And making bonfires for my
overthrow" (1:3.3.236–38). Marlowe makes clear at the beginning of
Tamburlaine, Part II, that the Turkish armies, which have reformed
under Orcanes's leadership, will cease their attacks on Christian Europe
only because they "are glutted with the Christians' blood, / And have
a greater foe to fight against— / Proud Tamburlaine, that now in
Asia / ...doth set his conquering feet / And means to fire Turkey as he
goes" (1:1.1.14–17). But Tamburlaine's role as Christianity's friend
becomes less clear as the second *Tamburlaine* play proceeds.

As many critics have noted, Tamburlaine grows increasingly mono-
maniacal, changing from the underdog and liberator of Part I to the

tyrant and destroyer of Part II. In *Tamburlaine, Part I*, Tamburlaine disdains gold, rejecting Bajazeth's offer of ransom. At this point, what Tamburlaine appears to value and enjoy most is the dramatization and verification of his power through a public spectacle in which those who oppose his power are humiliated or killed. Later, in *Tamburlaine, Part II*, the Scythian conqueror calls on his sons and followers to pursue his goal of global empire, and the acquisition of gold becomes an important part of that mission. In act 1, scene 3, Theridamas, Techelles, and Usumcasane muster their troops and report to Tamburlaine that in the hiatus between plays they were busy exploring and conquering. Their separate journeys, to North Africa and the Canary Islands, throughout sub-Saharan Africa, and to central Europe and the Black Sea, sound much like colonizing voyages, but their wanderings also involve the acquisition of luxury commodities like those that the English obtained through the Levant trade. Tamburlaine's followers convey their booty back to the Mediterranean region where it is placed within the reach of European merchants.

Tamburlaine ends the first act with a call to consume the goods that his men have transported to his base at Larissa, a Mediterranean port located between Egypt and Syria:

> Then will we triumph, banquet, and carouse;
> Cooks shall have pensions to provide us cates
> And glut us with the dainties of the world:
> Lachryma Christi and Calabrian wines
> Shall common soldiers drink in quaffing bowls—
> Ay, liquid gold when we have conquered him,
> Mingled with coral and with orient pearl. (1:1.3.218–24)

Later, Tamburlaine describes his serial conquests as a process of material accumulation, calling himself a "scourge.../That whips down cities and will controlleth crowns, / Adding their wealth and treasure to my store" (2:4.3.99–101). He plans to conquer territory from Babylon to Persia to Samarkand, thereby controlling the silk routes and the flow of goods between the Mediterranean and the commercial centers further east. And in his death scene Tamburlaine calls for a map and tells his listeners that he "meant to cut a channel" (2:5.3.134) between the Mediterranean and the Red Sea, a Suez canal, "That men might quickly sail to India" (2:5.3.135). His dying plan for an additional set of conquests is motivated by a lust for valuable commodities:

> And shall I die and this unconquered?
> Lo here, my sons, are all the golden mines,

Inestimable drugs and precious stones,
More worth than Asia and the world beside. (5.3.150–53)

Perhaps these lines express something of the collective frustration felt by Marlowe's generation, who were full of imperial ambition and envy, but lacked the means to create a real empire, and who had to settle instead for an expansionist thrust that was commercial in nature and directed into the Mediterranean. English merchants sought to obtain access to commodities that flowed through the places that Tamburlaine names at the play's end. It is not so much the commodities themselves, but the power of mobility and access—the control or use of trade routes—that would make merchants and investors rich. Tamburlaine's mortality is therefore an emblem of England's ambition, a *memento mori* for Mediterranean merchants. The man who began as a model for a radically aggressive human freedom, mobile and acquisitive, fails to achieve his ends because, in the course of his efforts to possess first Zenocrate and then obtain control of the world's wealth, Tamburlaine loses that freedom and autonomy.

The anti-providentialist message of Marlowe's *Tamburlaine, I and II* implies that there is no metaphysical, divine will that controls events or causes Tamburlaine's death. Finally, there is no motive for Tamburlaine beyond the possession and control of a global network that would funnel wealth and commodities back to him. His success is measured by what Marx called "primitive accumulation."[29] That becomes the definition of his power and his final cause. Tamburlaine becomes attached to the material world and its wealth and, at the same time, he dies a material death, desperately trying to express his dying will on a map that measures only earthly possession. Marlowe gives his audience a picture of an empire created by individual will, by a single, unchanging, unrelenting leader whose burning drive for possession burns out. This model stands in contrast to the adaptability and changeability that we will see in the drama of conversion.

CHAPTER 4

OTHELLO TURNS TURK

Are we turned Turks, and to ourselves do that
Which heaven hath forbid the Ottomites?

—*William Shakespeare*, Othello (*2.3.153–54*)

The tragedy of Othello is a drama of conversion, in particular a conversion to certain forms of faithlessness deeply feared by Shakespeare's audience. The collective anxiety about religious conversion felt in post-Reformation England focused primarily on Roman Catholic enemies who threatened to convert Protestant England by the sword, but the English also had reason to feel trepidation about the imperial power of the Ottoman Turks, who were conquering and colonizing Christian territories in Europe and the Mediterranean. English Protestant texts, both popular and learned, conflated the political/external and the demonic/internal enemies, associating both the pope and the Ottoman sultan with Satan or the Antichrist. According to Protestant ideology, the Devil, the pope, and the Turk all desired to "convert" good Protestant souls to a state of damnation, and their desire to do so was frequently figured as a sexual/sensual temptation of virtue, accompanied by a wrathful passion for power. As Virginia Mason Vaughan (1994) has shown in her historicist study of *Othello*, Shakespeare's Mediterranean tragedy, set at the margins of Christendom, but at the center of global civilization, "exploits...perceptions of a global struggle between the forces of good and evil, a seeming binary opposition that in reality is complex and multifaceted" (27).[1]

Shakespeare's play, like the culture that produced it, exhibits a conflation of various tropes of conversion—transformations from Christian to Turk, from virgin to whore, from good to evil, and from gracious virtue to black damnation. These forms of conversion are linked by rhetorical parallelism, but from the perspective of English Protestantism, these correspondences were not merely metaphorical: the Flesh, the Church of Rome, and the Turk were all believed to be material means for the Devil to achieve his ends. Conversion to Islam (or to Roman Catholicism) was considered a kind of sexual transgression or spiritual whoredom, and Protestantism proclaimed the same judgment—eternal damnation—for all those who were seduced by either the pope or the Prophet.

Shakespeare's *Othello* draws on early modern anxieties about Ottoman aggression and links them to a larger network of moral, sexual, and religious uncertainty that touched English Protestants directly. In part, the idea of conversion that terrified and titillated Shakespeare's audience was a fear of the loss of both essence and identity in a world of ontological, ecclesiastical, and political instability. Othello's loss of identity is caused by his misidentifications of Iago, Cassio, and Desdemona, the Moor fails to know Desdemona and she is converted in his mind from virgin to whore. His fear of female sexual instability is linked in the play to racial and cultural anxieties about "turning Turk"—the fear of a "black" planet that gripped the Europeans in the early modern era as they faced the expansion of Ottoman power.

What has often been forgotten is that while Spanish, Portuguese, English, and Dutch ships sailed to the New World and beyond, beginning the exploration and conquest of foreign lands, the Ottoman Turks were rapidly colonizing European territory. Thus, in the sixteenth and seventeenth centuries, the Europeans were both colonizers and colonized, and even the English felt the power of the Turkish threat to Christendom. By the beginning of the seventeenth century, at the same time that they were developing the trade in African slaves, the English faced the problem of their own people—men, women, and children—being captured and enslaved by "Turkish" privateers operating in the Mediterranean and the northeastern Atlantic.[2] This crisis led English writers of the early modern period to produce demonizing representations of "the Turk," not from the perspective of cultural domination but from the fear of being conquered, captured, and converted. As Anglo-Islamic contact increased during the late sixteenth and early seventeenth centuries, the English fascination with Muslim culture, especially the power of Islamic imperialism to convert Christians to Turks, was intensified and recorded in an outpouring of texts that dealt with Islamic societies in North Africa and the Levant. In England the early to mid-seventeenth century was to see an explosion of printed material concerned with the Barbary pirates and the Ottoman Turks, indicating the sharpened interest that accompanied the rise in English commercial activity in the Mediterranean.[3] *Othello* derived much of its anxious suspense and lurid exoticism from the contemporary perception of Turkish might and from the English fascination with the perilous Mediterranean world. The Venetians' anxieties in the first act—the sense of urgency and dread aroused when "The Turk with a most mighty preparation makes for Cyprus" (1.3.220–21)—would have reminded Shakespeare's audience of the Ottoman Turks' waxing power. Rooted in a history of holy wars and crusades, of Islamic conquest and Christian *reconquista*, the fear of the Islamic bogey was well established in the European consciousness. This long-standing fear and animosity reached one of its high points in 1453, when the Turks captured Constantinople. As Ottoman-controlled territory continued to expand during the next two centuries, gathering a momentum that seemed unstoppable, Western Europeans grew increasingly anxious.

One might assume that people in England felt safely removed from any direct Islamic threat, but in fact English authors of the sixteenth and seventeenth centuries frequently refer to the menace of the Ottoman conquerors in terms that express a sense of proximity and immediacy.[4] An illustration of this is the series of common prayers for delivery from Turkish attack that were directed by the English ecclesiastical authorities in the sixteenth century. For example, during the Turkish siege of Malta in 1565, one English diocese established "a form to be used in common prayer," which asked God

> to repress the rage and violence of Infidels, who by all tyranny and cruelty labour utterly to root out not only true Religion, but also the very name and memory of Christ our only Saviour, and all christianity; and if they should prevail against the isle of Malta, it is uncertain what further peril might follow to the rest of Christendom.[5]

When the news reached England that the Turkish siege of Malta had been lifted, the archbishop of Canterbury ordered another form of prayer to be read "through the whole Realm" every Sunday, Wednesday, and Friday.[6] This text refers to "that wicked monster and damned soul Mahumet" and "our sworn and most deadly enemies the Turks, Infidels, and Miscreants," expressing thanks for the defeat of the

invaders at Malta but warning of catastrophic consequences if the
Turkish invasion of Hungary should succeed:

> if the Infidels...should prevail wholly against [the kingdom of
> Hungary] (which God forbid) all the rest of Christendom should lie as
> it were naked and open to the incursions and invasions of the said sav-
> age and most cruel enemies the Turks, to the most dreadful danger of
> whole Christendom; all diligence, heartiness, and fervency is so much
> the more now to be used in our prayers for God's aid, how far greater
> the danger and peril is now, than before it was. (Clay 1847, 527)

These campaigns were largely successful, and the Ottoman armies
advanced until a truce was signed in 1568. During the 1590s, however, the Turks again launched major offensives on the Hungarian
front, and the war was ongoing at the time that *Othello* was written
and performed in London.

Although the naval battle of Lepanto was hailed as a critical setback
for the Turks, it had no lasting impact, and Turkish territorial gains in
the Mediterranean soon resumed.[7] Two years after Lepanto, the
Turks took Cyprus. Nonetheless, the singularity of a Christian force
successfully united against a Turkish armada aroused a strong
response throughout Europe. In distant Scotland, King James himself
wrote a heroic poem celebrating the Christians' triumph at Lepanto.[8]
The opening lines of James's poem describe the "bloodie battell
bolde, /...Which fought was in Lepantoes gulfe / Betwixt the baptiz'd
race, /And circumsised Turband Turkes" (ll.6–11). As Emrys Jones
has demonstrated in his article on "*Othello, Lepanto*, and the Cyprus
Wars," there are verbal echoes of these lines in Othello's suicide
speech.[9]

In limping verse, the king's poem stresses the heroic role of the
Venetians and presents the battle as a divinely inspired mission. God
decides that he has had enough of the "faithles" Turks and sends the
archangel Gabriel to rally the Christians of Venice:

> No more shall now these Christians be
>   With infidels opprest,...
> Go quicklie hence to Venice Towne,
>   And put into their minds
> To take revenge of wrongs the Turks
>   Have done in sundrie kinds. (ll.80–91)

After the victory, a chorus of Venetian citizens gives thanks to God
for having "redeemd" them "From cruell Pagans thrall" (ll.915–16).

Performed several times at the English court during the early years of James's reign, *Othello* was in line with some of the new king's interests.[10] The play also catered to a contemporary fascination with Moors and Turks, piqued by the presence at the English court between August 1600 and February 1601 of a Moroccan embassy of sixteen "noble Moors."[11] We see this fascination manifested again in Ben Jonson and Inigo Jones's *Masque of Blackness*, presented at court on Twelfth Night, 1605, when Queen Anne and other aristocratic women appeared in blackface as "noble Moors." In the 1608 sequel to that masque, the *Masque of Beauty*, the Moorish masquers are "converted" from black to fair by the virtuous power of the monarch.

As the work of Samuel Chew and Nabil Matar has shown, English anxiety about the Turks—and their power to convert Christians—was intense.[12] Richard Knolles's *Generall Historie of the Turkes*, first printed in 1603, refers in its opening pages to "The glorious Empire of the Turkes, the present terrour of the world" (1). During the sixteenth century, a stream of reports had arrived in England from abroad testifying to the success of the Turks' military campaigns in both the Balkans and the Mediterranean. While on a diplomatic mission to Vienna in 1574, Hubert Languet wrote to Sir Philip Sidney on March 26:

> These civil wars which are wearing out the strength of the princes of Christendom are opening a way for the Turk to get possession of Italy; and if Italy alone were in danger, it would be less a subject for sorrow, since it is the forge in which the cause of all these ills are wrought. But there is reason to fear that the flames will not keep themselves within its frontier, but will seize and devour the neighbouring states.[13]

In the following year, in the dedication to his translation of Curio's *Sarracenicae Historiae*, Thomas Newton wrote: "They [the Saracens and Turks] were indeede at the first very far from our Clyme & Region, and therefore the lesse to be feared, but now they are even at our doores and ready to come into our Houses..." (sig.A3v). Curio reacts typically to the Ottoman menace, calling in his preface for a crusade:

> [If the Christians] would joyne in one and live together in Christian league, no doubte, Constantinople might be agayn recovered and annexed to the Romane Empire...that Sathanical crew of Turkish lurdens might be expulsed and driven to trudge out of all Europa.... But beholde, even at our dores and ready to come into our houses, we have this arrogant and bragging helhound, triumphyng over us, laughyng at our misfortunes, rejoycing to see us thus to lye together by the

eares, and gapyng in hope shortlye to enjoy our goods and Seigniories. (sig. B4v–C1r)

Thomas Procter warns, in 1578, that "the Turkes in no longe time, have subdued...kinges and countreyes, and extended their Empyre... into all the three partes of the worlde, & yet prosecuteth and thrusteth the same further daylie" (v). Procter calls on Englishmen to undertake large-scale military training and thus be prepared to meet this growing threat. Ralph Carr, in his 1600 translation, *Mahumetane or Turkish Historie*, sees a kind of Turkish "domino effect" at work:

> We see this dayly increasing flame, catching hould of whatsoever comes next, still to proceed further, nor that the insatiable desire of dominion in these Turkes canne with any riches be content, or with the gayning of many mightie and wealthie Kingdomes be so settled, but of what is this daye gotten, to morrow they build a new ladder whereby to climbe to the obteyning of some newer purchase. (sig. 112r)

The anonymous *Policy of the Turkish Empire* (1600) reports that "...the terrour of their name doth even now make the kings and Princes of the West, with the weake and dismembred reliques of their kingdomes and estates, to tremble and quake through the feare of their victorious forces" (sig. A3v).

Perhaps the authors just quoted speak out of a collective psychology of fear that transcends the rational facticity of geographic distance, but English fears of "the Turk" were not entirely paranoid or hysterical. By 1604, when *Othello* was first performed, there had been extensive, direct contact with Muslim pirates—both in the British Isles and in the Mediterranean, where English merchant ships sailed with greater frequency after trade pacts with both the Barbary principalities and the Ottoman sultanate were signed.[14] *Othello* was written at a time when English commerce in Muslim entrepôts such as Constantinople, Aleppo, Alexandretta, Tunis, Tripoli, and Algiers was expanding rapidly and the threat of Muslim pirates in the Atlantic and the Mediterranean was on the rise.[15] The power of Muslims was brought home when "Turkish" pirates from the North African regencies began to raid the Irish and English coasts in the early seventeenth century. According to one historian's assessment, pirates from the Barbary ports captured, "on average, 70 to 80 Christian vessels a year between 1592 and 1609" (Hebb 15). English captives taken by the Barbary pirates were sold into slavery or held for ransom.

Faced with the growing problem of Christian captives who "turned Turk" in order to gain their freedom, the English authorities adopted a strategy to prevent such conversions, using sermons to condemn the practice of conversion to Islam. Two such sermons, one preached by Edward Kellett on the morning of March 16, 1627, and one that afternoon by Henry Byam, urged the endurance of suffering or even Christian martyrdom rather than conversion: better to die than to turn Turk.[16] In the second sermon, Byam claims that some converts to Islam actually switched back and forth between religious identities:

> ... many, and as I am informed, many hundreds, are Musselmans in Turkie, and Christians at home; doffing their religion, as they doe their clothes, and keeping a conscience for every Harbor wheere they shall put in. And those Apostates and circumcised Renegadoes, thinke they have discharged their Conscience wondrous well, if they can Returne, and (the fact unknowne) make profession of their first faith. (Byam 74)

Such returned renegades were thought to comprise a kind of unseen menace lurking in the ranks of the Christian commonwealth, concealing their double identities. In 1635 a "Form of Penance and Reconciliation of a Renegado" (promulgated by Bishop Hall and Archbishop Laud) was established for those returned renegades who wished to confess their apostasy and be reinstated in the Church of England.[17]

Post-Reformation anxiety about conversion produced a discourse about "renegadoes" and "convertites," which applied to those who converted to Catholicism as well as those who turned Turk, with the interest in Christian–Muslim conversion clearly related to contemporaneous polemical writings about Protestants and Roman Catholics who renounced one brand of Christianity for the other.[18] English Protestant texts associated both the pope and the Ottoman sultan with Satan or the Antichrist. Despite dire warnings from their religious leaders, many Christians converted from their original faith to Protestantism, Roman Catholicism, or Islam for economic reasons. Others converted as a survival strategy—to avoid martyrdom, persecution, or discrimination—and not as a result of heartfelt religious conviction. Still others may have been genuinely attracted to the culture and message of Islam.[19] John Donne, who was himself a "convertite," was sensitive to this issue and mentions it in his "Satire 3" on religion.[20] Donne's poem eroticizes the drama of religious schism and conversion, sexualizing the relationship between Christian worshippers (personified as men) and various branches of Christianity (personified as women). The pursuit of "true religion" becomes a search for the possession of a pure female body in a world full of "whores" and "preachers, vile ambitious bawds" (l.56). Bishop Hall uses similar language to condemn Jesuit priests who were trying to make converts amongst the English: "if this great Courtezan of the World [the Roman Church] had not so cunning panders, I should wonder how she should get any but foolish customers" (Hall 1837–39, 12:124).[21]

Whether lauded or condemned, religious conversion was frequently described in erotic terms: converts to Catholicism were accused of sleeping with the papal "whore of Babylon" and spiritually fornicating with the Devil's minions. This perceived homology between sexual and religious infidelity originates in biblical language, from the Old Testament condemnation of those who go "whoring" after false gods (see e.g. Exodus 34:15–16, Hosea 4:10–18) to the "great whore of Babylon" in Revelation (see 19:2). In the story of the seduction of Redcrosse by Duessa in Spenser's *Faerie Queene*, Book I, the false beauty of Spenser's Duessa represents the allure of Roman Catholic images, and the capture and imprisonment of Redcrosse (signifying the pope's control over British Christians before the Reformation) results from a sexual encounter with Duessa at the Fountain of the Unchaste Nymph. Throughout Spenser's epic, papal power and wealth are figured as "oriental" prostitution.

* * *

The transformation of Othello, the "Moor of Venice," from a virtuous lover and Christian soldier to an enraged murderer may be read in the context of early modern conversion, or "turning," with particular attention to the sense of conversion as a sensual, sexual transgression. Othello's love and his faith in Desdemona are turned to hate because he believes, as he tells Emilia, that "[Desdemona] turned to folly, and she was a whore" (5.2.141). Here Desdemona's alleged infidelity is, for Othello, a "turning," as it is when he says to Lodovico, "she can turn, and turn, and yet go on, / And turn again" (4.1.250–51). Othello seems to be thinking of a physical turning of her body taking place in the imaginary bed where "she with Cassio hath the act of shame / A thousand times committed" (5.2.218–19). To kill Desdemona is to put a stop to this image of perpetual sexual motion: "Ha! No more moving. / Still as the grave" (5.2.102–03), says Othello, satisfied that her adulterous turning has been stopped.

In early modern English "to turn" could mean to change or trans-form, to convert, to pervert, to go back on one's word, or to turn through space. The *OED*, among the many definitions and citations that are pertinent to *Othello*, gives a citation for the transitive verb form of "turn": "To induce or persuade to adopt a (different) religious faith (usually with implication of its truth or excellence), or a religious or godly (instead of an irreligious or ungodly) life; to convert; less commonly in bad sense, to pervert." As an example, the *OED* cites a threat used by Roman Catholic persecutors during the Marian period: "so they would say to all Protestants, ... Turn, or burn."[22]

In the scenes that lead up to Desdemona's murder and Othello's suicide, the trope of turning (in the sense of conversion) occurs frequently as the effects of Iago's evil are felt and Desdemona, once Othello's "soul's joy," becomes a "fair devil." Othello accepts the circumstantial evidence against Desdemona as Iago makes good his boast that he will "turn her [Desdemona's] virtue into pitch" (2.3.334). Converting Desdemona's virtue, Iago "turns" Othello until Othello's "heart is turned to stone" (4.1.175) and his mind is "perplexed in the extreme" (5.2.355). "I see you're moved" (3.3.221), declares Iago; and once Othello is moved, doubt and retreat seem no longer possible.

"[M]y bloody thoughts with violent pace / Shall ne'er look back, ne'er ebb to humble love" (3.3.460–61), says Othello in the Pontic Sea speech, giving rhetorical force to his irreversible turn from love to hate. "Being wrought," Othello cannot stem the tide of his vengeful passion. "It is not words" that shake him but rather the false image in his mind of Cassio making love to Desdemona. Crying "O devil!", he falls, in 4.1, into "*a trance.*" Othello's epileptic fit is a kind of sexual swoon, an impotent mockery of the climax he imagines Cassio experiencing. At the same time, the fit is a libidinous version of the religious ecstasy that would characterize a soul-shaking conversion experience. Othello's perturbed spirit is "o'erwhelmèd" (4.1.74) by the revelation of "honest" Iago's truth about Desdemona. The Moor's ordeal in 4.1 parodies the physical collapse that accompanies an episode of divine or demonic possession—he kneels with Iago, falls down, and then undergoes a seizure like those experienced by other "prophesying" victims of "the falling sickness," a malady associated with both sacred and Satanic inspiration.[23]

Othello's epilepsy recalls that of the ur-Moor, Muhammed. Christian polemics against Islam printed in Shakespeare's time frequently allege that Muhammed was an epileptic who falsely maintained that his seizures were ecstasies brought on by divine possession. According to John Pory's 1600 translation of Leo Africanus's *Geographical Historie of Africa*, a text that Shakespeare seems to have consulted when composing *Othello*, Muhammed claimed that he "conversed with the angell Gabriell, unto whose brightnes he ascribed the falling sicknes, which many times prostrated him upon the earth: dilating and amplifying the same in like sort, by permitting all that which was plausible to sense and the flesh" (381).[24] Anti-Islamic propagandists maintained that Muhammed's need to account for his epileptic seizures was the original motive for what became a claim to divine inspiration.

In an extraordinary passage from Edward Kellett's 1627 sermon against renegades, Muhammed's epilepsy is explained as a divine punishment for lechery:

> The great seducer Mahomet, was a salacious, lustfull *Amoroso*; and his intemperate lasciviousnesse, was wayted on by infirmities and sicknesses correspondent to his lewdnesse.... he, for his lust, and by it, was tormented with the Great falling-sicknesse; and that disease, is a plague of an high-hand; and in him, a testimonie of a very sinfull soule, in a very sinfull body. For, whereas it *is appointed for all men to die once*, Heb. 9.27 for that one first sinne of Adam; Mahomet, who had so many, so great sinnes, was striken also with many deaths. For, what is the Falling-Sicknesse, but a reduplication, a multiplication of death? He fell with paine, looked ugly, with a foming mouth, and wry-distorted countenance in his fits. He rose with horror, like a pale carcase, and lukewarme corpes, betweene the living and the dead. He was the But against which the Almighty shot his arrowes, bearing the image and figure of an Apostata in his body by relapses; and the torments of a vessell of wrath, in his soule, for his Imposturage. (23)[25]

In Western European texts, from the medieval to the early modern period, Islam was nearly always defined as a licentious religion of sensuality and sexuality.[26] A long-standing tradition of anti-Islamic polemic denounced the religion of Mahomet as a system based upon fraud, lust, and violence. Kellett's attack on Islam includes a colorful but commonplace description of Muhammed's "imposture":

> Let Mahomet be branded for a Juggler, a Mount-bank, a bestiall people-pleaser . . . which Mis-beliefe he hath established by the sword, and not by Arguments; upheld by violence and compulsion; or tempting allurements of the world; forcing, or deluding the soules of men, rather than perswading by evidence of veritie. (23)

It is possible to see these highly negative images of Islam reconfigured in the imposture of Iago and the militant fury and frustrated lust of

Othello. The fraudulent persuasions of Iago, whose false revelation deludes Othello's soul "rather than perswading by evidence of veritie," lead the Moor into "Mis-beliefe." In the guise of angelic informer, Iago plants a diabolical sexual fantasy in the mind of the Moor. Iago is a fiend disguised as an angel, describing his own theology as the "Divinity of hell!" and explaining, "When devils will the blackest sins put on, / They do suggest at first with heavenly shows / As I do now" (2.3.325–27). Iago is the evil angel who communicates a false message to Othello, inspiring him with distempered passion, urging and justifying acts of cruelty and violence. Together they kneel in prayer, and Othello makes "a sacred vow" to "heaven" (3.3.462–63), which is really a deal with the Devil, who will possess him eternally. Through false inspiration and "with heavenly shows," Iago brings on the "conversion" of Othello, and that conversion is dramatized as a fall into a bestial, sex-obsessed condition.

Edward Aston, in *The Manners, lawes, and customes of all Nations* (1611), claims that the "incredible allurement" of Islam has been Mahomet's "giving people free liberty and power to pursue their lustes and all other pleasures, for by these meanes, this pestilent religion hath crept into innumerable Nations" (137). One of the "tempting allurements" offered by Mahomet to his followers was an infamous orgiastic paradise in the next world,[27] described sarcastically in Byam's sermon as follows:

> ...[In Mahomet's] Paradise, the ground thereof is gould watered with streames of Milk, Hony and Wine. How there his followers after the day of Judgement, shall have a merry madd world, and shall never make an end of eating, drinking, and colling wenches. And these (if you will beleeve it) are sweete Creatures indeed; for if one of them should spet into the Sea, all the waters thereof would become sweete. (64)[28]

Christian writers not only criticized Islam for offering sensual pleasure to the virtuous as a reward in the next life; they also condemned the sexual freedom allowed in this life under Muslim law. Islamic regulations governing concubinage, marriage, and divorce were misunderstood and reviled by Western Europeans.[29] According to Leo Africanus, the religious law of Muhammed "looseth the bridle to the flesh, which is a thing acceptable to the greatest part of men" (381). Africanus and others claimed that the attraction of conversion to Islam—and the reluctance of Muslims to convert to Christianity—stemmed primarily from the greater sexual freedom allowed under Islamic law.

Given the conventional association made by European Christians between Islam and promiscuity, it is not surprising that the English expression "to turn Turk" carried a sexual connotation.[30] Significantly, we find a series of contemporary uses of this phrase in the English drama of the early seventeenth century, where its meaning is "to become a whore" or "to commit adultery."[31] In Philip Massinger's *The Renegado* (1624), for example, when the Christian heroine Paulina threatens to convert, saying "I will turn Turk," Gazet's bawdy rejoinder makes the usual connection between turning Turk and sexual sin: "Most of your tribe do so, / When they begin in whore" (5.3.152). Another bawdy play on Islamic "turning" occurs in *The Revenger's Tragedy* (1607) when Vindice reports to Lussurioso on his efforts to arrange a sexual encounter with the virgin Castiza, assuring the Duke's son that "The word I brought / Might well have made indifferent honest naught / ...Many a maid has turned to Mahomet / With easier working" (2.2.24–29). In an earlier play, Thomas Dekker's *The Honest Whore* (1604), the man who has inspired Bellafront (the title character) to forgo prostitution warns her not to relapse:

tis damnation,
If you turne turke againe, oh doe it not,
Th[o] heaven cannot allure you to doe well,
From doing ill let hell fright you: and learne this,
The soule whose bosome lust did never touch,
Is Gods faire bride, and maidens soules are such:
The soule that leaving chastities white shore,
Swims in hot sensuall streames, is the divils whore. (4.1.174–81)

A similar usage occurs in John Marston's *The Dutch Courtesan* (1603). When Franceschina, a Dutch prostitute living in London, is abandoned by the man who has "converted" her from a common whore to a loyal mistress, she asks: "Vat sall become of mine por flesh now? Mine body must turn Turk for twopence. O divila, life o' mine art! Ick sall be revenged. Do ten tousand hell damn me, ick sall have the rogue troat cut..." (2.2.51–55).

Writers of the time frequently compared reformed prostitutes to religious "convertites." In fact, there were nunneries on the Continent made up of "converted" whores. Under "convertist," the *OED* cites Randle Cotgrave (1611) "*filles repenties,* an order of Nunnes which have been profest whores; Convertists." And it defines "convertite" as "A reformed Magdalen," quoting Bishop Jewel's 1565 attack on the toleration of whorehouses in Rome, where Jewel links this allowance to the issue of celibacy: "If they turne and repent, there are houses called Monasteries of the Convertites, and special provision and discipline for them, where they are taught how to bewaile their unchaste life so sinfully past over."[32]

Though post-Reformation England lacked nunneries, plays and stories about "converted" prostitutes were popular.[33] At the time of *Othello*'s first performances, there was a contemporaneous fashion for plays that dramatized life in the stews or featured reformed prostitutes.[34] These plays include Thomas Middleton's *Blurt, Master Constable* (1602)—set, like *Othello*, in Venice—*Michaelmas Term* (1607), *Your Five Gallants* (1608), and *A Mad World, My Masters* (1608); Francis Beaumont and John Fletcher's *The Woman Hater* (1607); Edward Sharpham's *The Fleer* (1607); as well as Marston's *Dutch Courtesan* and Dekker's *Honest Whore*. (The latter appeared in its second printed edition under the title *The Converted Courtezan*.) Shakespeare's *Measure for Measure* (1604), written at almost the same time as *Othello*, also refers to scenes of brothel life.

Many of these comedies include plots or subplots in which a penitent whore either falls in love with or is married to one of the male characters. A male "wittol" is sometimes tricked into marrying the "honest whore," and this duped husband thus becomes an instant cuckold. Othello becomes convinced that he is just such a cuckold and dupe, and the conventional elements of the whore–cuckold plot do seem to have been on Shakespeare's mind when he wrote his "domestic tragedy."[35] Both "honest" and "whore" are key signifiers in the text ("honest whore" is the sexual equivalent of Othello's racially oxymoronic epithet "noble Moor"). Cuckoldry and jealousy, basic concerns of comic drama in seventeenth-century England, are central to the action of *Othello*, in which Iago plays the cony-catcher and Othello imagines himself to be a cuckold and duped by a "super-subtle" Venetian courtesan. The case of Desdemona is a tragic inversion or parody of the pattern of the reformed courtesan. Though Othello calls her "that cunning whore of Venice" (4.2.94), she is "honest."

In one of his soliloquies, Iago depicts Othello as a lust-driven dupe, whose idolatrous worship of Desdemona makes him vulnerable to apostatical backsliding or conversion by a courtesan:

> ...for her
> To win the Moor, were't to renounce his baptism,
> All seals and symbols of redeemèd sin,
> His soul is so enfettered to her love,
> That she may make, unmake, do what she list,

Even as her appetite shall play the god
With his weak function. (2.3.316–22)

The same "weak function" that led him to worship Desdemona will
allow him to "renounce his baptism" and convert (or revert) to the
cruel ways of the Turk. Othello's alleged propensity for religious
instability is, at the same time, a libidinal weakness like that attributed
to the Islamic convert.

The alleged sexual excesses of the Muslims were linked to those of
the Moors or black Africans, who are frequently described in the
Western tradition as a people naturally given to promiscuity.[36] Leo
Africanus says of the North African Moors that there is "no nation
under heaven more prone to venerie..." (38). Othello, the noble
Moor of Venice, is not, however, to be identified with a specific, historically accurate racial category; rather, he is a hybrid who might be associated, in the minds of Shakespeare's audience, with a whole set of related
terms—"Moor," "Turk," "Ottomite," "Saracen," "Mahometan,"
"Egyptian," "Judean," "Indian"—all constructed and positioned in
opposition to Christian faith and virtue. More than being identified
with any specific ethnic label, Othello is a theatrical embodiment of the
dark, threatening powers at the edge of Christendom. Othello's identity
is derived from a complex and multilayered tradition of representation
that includes the classical barbarian, the Saracen or "paynim knight" of
medieval romance, the "blackamoor," and (an early modern version of
the medieval types of lust, cruelty, and aggression) the Turk.

For the spectators at the Globe, the stage Moor (a "white" actor in
blackface) was primarily an emblematic figure, not a "naturalistic" portrayal of a particular ethnic type.[37] As John Gillies reminds readers of
Othello, "the sharper, more elaborately differentiated and more hierarchical character of post-Elizabethan constructions of racial difference are
inappropriate to the problems posed by the Elizabethan other" (32).[38]
Nonetheless, a closer analysis of terms such as "Moor" and "Turk" can
help us to reconstruct more fully what "Othello, the Moor of Venice"
signified in the historical, linguistic, and performative context of early
seventeenth-century England.

Looking particularly at the significance of Othello's epithet, "the
Moor," G.K. Hunter describes how this term was understood: "The
word 'Moor' was very vague ethnographically, and very often seems to
have meant little more than 'black-skinned outsider,' but it was not
vague in its antithetical relationship to the European norm of the civilized white Christian" (51).[39] In various texts, early modern Europeans
described the Moors of Iberia and North Africa as a treacherous,

aggressive, and unstable people.[40] Leo Africanus describes the Moor as honest and trusting but jealous and given to passionate, vengeful rage when wronged. In *Gli Hecatommithi* Geraldo Cinthio has Disdemona say "...you Moors are so hot by nature that any little thing moves you to anger and revenge" (Bullough 7:245),[41] and Shakespeare's Iago tells Roderigo, "These Moors are changeable in their wills" (1.3.339–40). Othello's changeability is linked to his "exorbitance" (Gillies's term) and to his ambiguous status as Christian Moor and a mercenary whose loyalty is for hire. He is, in the words of Iago, "an erring barbarian" (1.3.346–47) who has strayed from his natural course into the civilized, super-subtle environment of Venice. It would be natural, according to early modern anthropology, for a Moor to be barbarous and evil, not noble and virtuous. But Othello is a "noble Moor"—a walking paradox, a contradiction in terms. He is a "purified" and Christianized Moor, converted to whiteness, washed clean by the waters of baptism. Or at least it appears so at first. But the play seems to prove the ancient proverb *"abluis Aethiopem, quid frustra,"* as the Moor shows his true color—demonic black, burnt by hellfire and cursed by God.[42]

We may infer from Iago's comment (at 4.2.224) that Othello is a native of Mauritania, but it is clear from the beginning of the play that Othello is or has become a Christian. Shakespeare may have known from Pory's translation of Leo Africanus that some Moors "are Gentiles which worship Idols; others are of the sect of Mahumet; some others Christians; and some Jewish in religion" (6).[43] Popular knowledge of Christian and Jewish minorities under Islamic rule was limited, however, and early modern parlance often demonstrates the English Protestants' misunderstanding of Islam's ethnic and political complexity. The words "Moor" and "Turk," for example, were sometimes used to refer specifically to the people of Morocco or Turkey, but more often they signified a generalized Islamic identity.[44] English popular culture, including drama, rarely distinguished between Muslims: the Moors of Barbary were often called Turks, and, in spite of their iconoclastic monotheism, Muslims were still condemned as "pagan idolaters" by many writers. A few people among the educated classes of Shakespeare's England might have known that not all of the Barbary Moors were unenlightened pagans or even benighted "Mahometans," but most English were unaware of the Muslim rulers' policy of religious tolerance, which allowed Jews, Christians, and Muslims to live together peacefully within the same community. This policy differed radically from that of England, where the norm was religious persecution and where very few Jews or Muslims were permitted to maintain residence.

In Spain, too, persecution and intolerance were the rule. After the *Reconquista*, the Morisco inhabitants of Spain and Portugal provided an example of Muslim Moors who were officially converted and baptized but who engaged in covert Islamic practices and were increasingly regarded with suspicion by the Spanish Church.[45] Because he is a Christianized Moor, a mercenary Morisco, Othello, like the Moors of Spain, is suspect and liable to relapse. His race and his religious identity, his nobility and his Christianity are all questionable. Othello's oxymoronic epithet, "the noble Moor," signifies a split identity, something unstable and unnatural. Othello's religious affiliation at the time of the play is Christian, but his origins are unclear. Indeterminacy and instability of identity form the common denominator for understanding his character. He is a kind of renegade and thus an object of suspicion in a play about suspicion.

When Othello tells "Of being taken by the insolent foe / and sold to slavery; of my redemption thence" (1.3.136–37), are we to understand that he was a Christian Moor taken captive by Islamic corsairs, perhaps the renegades of Barbary, and then "redeemed" by Christians? Or did his "redemption" involve a conversion from Islam to Christianity? The text does not answer this question, but the text does identify Othello with the renegades themselves. On several occasions Iago associates Othello with renegade pirates, calling him a "Barbary horse" and referring to his elopement as an act of piracy: "he tonight hath boarded a land carrack; / If it prove lawful prize, he's made forever" (1.2.50–51). Like a "Barbarian" pirate or a lusty Turk, Othello has secretly and suddenly deceived Brabantio and stolen away with Desdemona, Brabantio's prized possession.

The play's first act presents a clear analogy between Othello's successful theft of Desdemona and the Turks' equally treacherous attempt to steal Cyprus: "So let the Turk of Cyprus us beguile, / We lose it not so long as we can smile" (1.3.209–10), says Brabantio, equating Othello with "the Turk," and protesting that "if such actions" as Othello's stolen marriage "may have passage free, / Bondslaves and pagans shall our statesman be" (1.2.99–100). Brabantio exaggerates for effect, but his fear that "Bondslaves and pagans" might beguile their way to power, command, and possession refers to a real concern about the growing strength of Islamic sea power, much of that power based on galleys manned by slaves or renegades and sometimes commanded by renegade captains or admirals.[46]

In fact, the Venetians' willingness during the sixteenth and seventeenth centuries to allow free passage in the Adriatic to the Turks, in exchange for trade concessions and access to Ottoman ports, had placed them in a controversial position in the eyes of their Christian co-religionists, especially those who heeded the pope's call for a general crusade against the infidel. At the time that Shakespeare was writing *Othello*, the Venetians were enjoying a period of peace and good relations with the Ottoman sultanate, while the Hapsburgs were engaged in a long, exhausting war against the Turks (1593–1606). Throughout this period the English government was on friendly terms with the Ottomans.[47]

The peace treaty that Venice concluded with the Turks in 1573 relinquished Cyprus, and, in 1595, the Venetians reaffirmed and expanded their friendly commercial alliance with the Ottomans in another treaty. These agreements were partly the result of Venetian resistance to papal pressures. (The quarrel between Venice and the pope was observed with great interest by the English, who expressed strong support for the Venetians.[48]) From the English Protestant point of view, Venice was a sphere of tolerance and rationality located between the twin tyrannies of papal superstition on one hand and Islamic "paganism" on the other.[49] During the late sixteenth and early seventeenth centuries, the English foes of Spanish/papal hegemony looked favorably on Venice because of its strong resistance to Counter-Reformation papism and the power of the Jesuits. In the imaginative geography of early modern England, Venice stood for wealth, commerce, multicultural exchange, political stability, wisdom and justice, tolerance, neutrality, rationality, republicanism, pragmatism, and openness.[50] In fact, Venice was attempting to carry out a peaceable yet profitable trade in an economic sphere that was ruled by violence.[51] The English, like the Venetians, were eager to establish and sustain trade links with areas under Islamic rule. Nonetheless, most Londoners would have thought of the Ottoman sultan or "Grand Seigneur" not as a commercial partner but as the absolute ruler of an empire that menaced all Christendom.

As the Ottomans began to dominate the eastern Mediterranean, the traditional notion of a marriage between Venice and the sea led to jokes about the Turk cuckolding the impotent Venetian patriarchs or raping the Venetian virgin. A 1538 sonnet by Guillaume DuBellay makes this point:

> Mais ce que l'on en doit le meilleur estimer
> C'est quand ces vieux coquz vont espouser la mer,
> Dont ilz sont les maris, et le Turc l'adultere
>
>> (But that which you must find does best adorn her
>> Is when those cuckolds old go wed the sea.
>> Venetians husbands then, the Turk the horner)[52]

The longevity and supposed civic virtue of Venice's republican government led to a conventional personification of Venice as an undefiled virgin. David McPherson, in his study of the English "myth of Venice," shows that "writer after writer identifies her preservation of her liberty (freedom from domination by a foreign power) with sexual chastity" (33).[53] But this virgin bride of the Mediterranean needed the protection of virile foreigners. According to Fynes Moryson,

> the Gentlemen of Venice are trayned upp in pleasure and wantonnes, which must needes abase and effeminate their myndes. Besides that this State is not sufficiently furnished with men and more specially with native Commaunders and Generalls, nor yet with victualls, to undertake (of their owne power without assistance) a warr against the Sultane of Turky. This want of Courage, & especially the feare lest any Citizen becoming a great and popular Commaunder in the Warrs, might thereby have means to usurpe uppon the liberty of their State, seeme to be the Causes that for their Land forces they seldome have any native Commaunders, and alwayes use a forrayne Generall. (139)

The desperate lack of manly leadership in Venice is dramatized in the first act of *Othello*, when an alien is given charge of the protection of the Venetian empire against the Turk. To the English audience this reliance on a Moorish renegade-type like Othello would have been almost as shocking as the elopement and miscegenation permitted by the Venetian senate.

After the first act, the rest of *Othello* takes place in Cyprus. The choice of this island as a setting for much of the play is Shakespeare's (Cinthio's text does not refer to such a locale), and there are particular features of the island that make it well suited for Shakespeare's imaginative geography. The voyage from Venice to Venetian Cyprus constituted a journey from the margins of Christendom to a surrounded and besieged outpost. According to Knolles, "The Venetians had ever great care of the island of Cyprus, as lying farre from them, in the middest of the sworne enemies of the Christian religion, and had therefore oftentimes determined to have fortified the same ... " (847). On sixteenth-century English maps of the Mediterranean world, Cyprus appears in the extreme southeastern corner, encircled by Egypt, Syria, and Turkey.

Shakespeare's play does not provide a historically accurate representation of the real invasion of Cyprus by the Turks in 1571 or of any other Ottoman attempt to conquer the island.[54] As noted earlier, Cyprus was formally ceded by Venice to the Turks in 1573, after three years of futile resistance, including bloody sieges at Nicosia and

Famagusta.[55] This was thirty years before *Othello* was first performed in London.[56] Thus English audiences watching a play set in Cyprus under Venetian rule would have interpreted this setting as a vulnerable outpost that was destined to be swallowed up by the Turks and converted to Islamic rule.[57] "Our wars are done" and "the Turkish fleet . . . are drowned" (2.1.20, 18–19) would have had an ironic ring for an English audience that knew of the Turks' victory over the Venetians and the long-standing Ottoman possession of Cyprus.

The sensational context of military conflict between Christians and Muslims, Italians and Turks, is dramatized in the first scene of the play when Iago tells Roderigo that Othello has fought with Iago "At Rhodes, at Cyprus, and on other grounds / Christian and heathen" (1.1.28–29). The sense of urgency in Venice, the fears of its leaders faced with the Turkish threat, is the force that sets the breathless action of the plot in motion. It is as if Othello has already left Venice before we meet him:

> . . . for he's embarked
> With such loud reason to the Cyprus wars,
> Which even now stands in act, that, for their souls
> Another of his fathom they have none
> To lead their business (1.1.150–53)

When we do meet Othello in the second scene, we see the duke's messengers finding him even more swiftly than do Brabantio's urgently roused forces. The Turkish threat to Cyprus is "a business of some heat" (1.2.40), and the third scene continues to emphasize a sense of impending invasion as the duke calls for immediate mobilization: "Valiant Othello, we must straight employ you / Against the general enemy Ottoman" (1.3.48–49). Othello and the Christian Venetians are described as moving instantly in a direct line to the defense of Cyprus, while the treacherously shifting Turks resist interpretation by moving in a "backward course," which then turns from Rhodes toward Cyprus: "now they do restem / Their backward course, bearing with frank appearance / Their purposes toward Cyprus" (1.3.38–40). The syntax makes their movements unstable and contradictory, implying the retention of a morally questionable backwardness even as they redirect their course "toward Cyprus."

The absent Turks, who never appear on stage but are defined as a powerfully menacing threat just beyond the boundaries of the action, surround the play with their unseen presence. The urgent preparation for war presented in the first act sets up the expectation of a heroic confrontation between Othello's army and the treacherous Ottoman horde. This dramatization of Venetian panic played on the widespread fears about Turkish expansion and conversion: the specific uncertainties felt by the Venetians in the play (where will they attack? Rhodes or Cyprus?) convey a sense of dread that was felt even in England.[58]

The first act of *Othello* thus prepares the audience for a dramatic blockbuster of global scope (like Marlowe's *Tamburlaine* plays), involving one of the greatest oriental despots of all time, the Turk of Istanbul.[59] The play then begins to build frustration by violating the generic expectations raised in act 1. James Calderwood points to the link between *coitus interruptus* and the *miles interruptus* in act 2:

> [the audience is] led to expect a battle, to look forward to experiencing some measure of the pomp and glory and the downright violence that Othello speaks of later. But then, inexplicably, the Turks vanish in an off-stage tempest, the battle comes to nought, and we must content ourselves with this weak piping time of peace.
>
> ...the impulse to battle is displaced onto sex, issues of state divert into domestic channels, and violence to others turns reflexive.... The fatal bedding of Desdemona consummates the marriage and our aesthetic expectations at once. With Othello standing in for the Turk, and Desdemona for Cyprus, everyone rests content in the perfection of form. (126–27)

The frustrated male violence that was initially directed at the Islamic Other is turned on the feminine Other, forming a link between military aggression and sexual transgression, between the Turkish threat to Christian power and the contamination of female sexual purity.

In *Othello* the fantasy of divine protection keeps the Turks from encircling Cyprus. The storm that prevents the Turkish fleet from invading Cyprus in the play is a fictional version of the providential storms that protected the English from Spanish armadas in 1588, 1596, 1597, and 1598.[60] ("'God breathed, and they were scattered'" was a motto inscribed on one of Elizabeth's Armada medals.[61]) The idea of a tempest sent by God against the invading fleet of an evil empire is found in providentialist propaganda directed against the Spanish and the Turkish powers (who were often associated in a Protestant historiography that found causal connections between the rise of papal tyranny or corruption and the coming of Islam as a divine scourge). Cyprus was like England in being a "beleaguered isle," victimized by an "Eastern" foe bent on the extirpation of Christian rule.[62]

But the Turkish demon is not so easily exorcised from Shakespeare's play, and the destructive energy and cruelty of the Turk is repressed only temporarily and soon returns, appearing within the Christian community. The reappearance of the evil empire's threat, in the form of a secret conspiracy concocted by traitors and turncoats, is analogous, perhaps, to the fears of covert Spanish-papal plots and Jesuitical conspiracies that continued to haunt English Protestants, long after the Armada was scattered in 1588. As soon as Othello has arrived safely in Famagusta, Iago identifies himself as "a Turk" (2.1.112), indicating the continued presence of "Turkish" malevolence in a more subtle form. Lazaro Saranzo's description of Turkish power, which was translated in 1601 by Abraham Hartwell and then printed in 1603, tells of how

> The Turkes...do use to mingle deceite with force...neither do they want meanes and ministers, that are cunning and skilfull to practice the same, both because all such, as among them do attend the Arte of warrefare, do endeavor themselves to learne and knowe whatsoever is necessarre for the good managing of an exployte, and also because fraud and deceite is a thing most proper to a Turke. (32)

Soon after Iago affiliates himself with the Turks, the drunken affray instigated by Iago disturbs Othello's "balmy slumbers," and he emerges from his nuptial bed to speak these lines:

> Are we turned Turks, and to ourselves do that
> Which heaven hath forbid the Ottomites?
> For Christian shame, put by this barbarous brawl. (2.3.153–55)

These words imply, first, that "heaven" has providentially intervened on the side of the Venetian navy, preserving their ships while dispersing and perhaps destroying the Turkish fleet; second, that the Turk's own religion prohibits drinking and brawling; and, third, that Christian order has been converted to Islamic violence. Multiple ironies here point to the conversion that Othello is about to undergo.

This conversion occurs in a text that relentlessly employs the Christian language of damnation and salvation, and in which "diabolical imagery" is used in almost every scene.[63] This is part of the play's rootedness in the morality-play tradition, though the morality play of *Othello* (like that of *Doctor Faustus*) is a tragedy of damnation, not a divine comedy, and it ends with the triumph of the Vice, that "demi-devil" Iago, who has won another soul for Satan.[64]

In the speeches that immediately precede the killing of Desdemona, the Moor's references to Christian mercy and to the salvation of his wife's soul are highly ironic, given his own lack of mercy. Othello

enters professing a pious concern and attempting to confer the
sanction of divine justice on the act of murder. "It is the cause, it is the
cause" (5.2.1), he intones, in an effort to justify the execution of an
accused adulteress.[65] Othello presents himself as an agent of divine
retribution and male honor who is forced to enact a terrible but righteous punishment—"else she'll betray more men" (5.2.6). Presuming
an absolutist infallibility, Othello tries to play the priest and asks for
Desdemona's confession. Despite his efforts to maintain calm and
control, the scene ends in jealous rage, with Othello hastily stifling
Desdemona's last request to pray.

As he finishes the murder, Othello again takes up the pose of divine
agent and minister, declaring, "I that am cruel am yet merciful"
(5.2.96). These words allude to attributes of both the Old Testment
and New Testament deity. The Moor sees himself as a "scourge of
God," come to mete out cruel but necessary punishment for
Desdemona's "sin" (5.2.58). His appropriation and perversion of
Christian ritual may be seen as a horribly misguided attempt to ration-
alize and sanctify his bloody deed in the name of religion. Here,
Othello's religious rhetoric reminds us of the allegations against
Muhammed, who was accused of perverting religious doctrine to
justify his own violent and lustful ways.

The word "lord" occurs repeatedly in this scene, with Desdemona
referring to Othello as her lord and husband in the quarto text and
calling on the Lord God. Just before her death, Desdemona addresses
Othello as "my lord" five times, and Emilia refers to him by this title
more than ten times. In the quarto text Desdemona cries "O, Lord,
Lord, Lord" as she is smothered, and her final words are "Commend
me to my kind lord. O farewell!" (5.2.133). Her desperate appeals for
mercy point ironically to the blasphemous nature of Othello's crime:
his imitation of divine lordship is a heathen error made in wrath. His
killing of Desdemona is a parody and a profanation of Christian rite,
just as the Moorish faith, Islam, was described by European Christians
as a bloodthirsty, lascivious perversion of true religion. While Othello
attempts to play the Christian priest and make the murder a sacrament, his mistaken presumption of ministry is damnable blasphemy.
The murder of Desdemona is the pagan "sacrifice" of a pure virgin,
the action of the stereotypically cruel Moor or Turk.

Othello's irreligious assumption—or presumption—of an absolute
power over life and death demonstrates his conversion to a kind of
oriental despotism or tyrannical lordship. In this, the character of
Othello partakes of a stereotype developed by Western authors—the
representation of the "cruel Moor" (5.2.256), bloody Turk, or

"Grand Seigneur," especially the sultan or slavemaster who hastily enacts a violent, arbitrary, and merciless "justice." The Islamic prince is frequently represented in early modern texts as a tyrant who rules by will and appetite, committing rash acts of cruelty and injustice in the name of honor or false religion.[66] This sort of stock character has a long history, going back to the Moorish villains of the romance tradition and the stage tyrants of medieval drama. Once Othello gives way to his jealous will and "tyrannous hate" (3.3.453), the audience sees him transformed into a version of the Islamic tyrant.

Shakespeare's portrayal of a powerful Moorish lord and commander who kills the innocent white woman he loves in order to demonstrate his ability to master his passions is a scene from the seraglio. In particular, the murder of Desdemona by the Moor would have reminded audiences of the story of the Sultan and the Fair Greek, an exemplary tale of Islamic cruelty that features an Ottoman emperor (usually Amurath I or Mahomet II) who must choose between masculine, military "honor" and his attachment to a Christian slave, Irene with whom he has fallen in love. This story was dramatized on the London stage in at least four different versions during the sixteenth and seventeenth centuries. It was printed in both prose and verse forms and was widely disseminated.[67] One version of this tale is staged in Thomas Goffe's *The Couragious Turke, or Amurath the First*, written circa 1613–18 for performance by Oxford University students. Goffe's play follows the standard plot but changes the name of Irene to Eumorphe.[68] Though *The Couragious Turke* was written after, and influenced by, Shakespeare's *Othello*, the story it tells was well known long before Shakespeare wrote his play. Significant to my argument are the correspondences between Amurath and Othello, and between Irene/Eumorphe and Desdemona, correspondences that demonstrate the "Turkish" character of Othello and allow us to see how Desdemona would have been recognized as the victim of Islamic-erotic tyranny.

The Couragious Turke includes several scenes that imitate and parody the tragic action of *Othello*. Most notably, in act 2, scenes 3–5, of Goffe's tragedy, the action closely follows the events and imagery of the bedroom scenes at the beginning of the fifth act in *Othello*. Act 2, scene 3, begins with a dialogue between Eumorphe and her maidservant, Menthe. As in Shakespeare's play, the tragic heroine appears on stage "*as to Bed in her Night-robes attended with Tapers and Ladies.*" After an ominous musical interlude much like the willow song, Amurath enters, also "*in his Night robes*" and carrying "*a Taper in his hand.*" Like Othello, Amurath "*seemes much disturbed*" at this point.

He draws back the curtain over the bed in which Eumorphe is asleep,
and then delivers a long soliloquy. During this speech, he kisses the
sleeping Eumorphe and is tempted by her beauty, but he is worried
that "The Christians now will scoffe at Mahomet" (2.3.50) if he allows
his "manly government" (2.3.6) to be weakened by his infatuation for
her. Urged on by his tutor (who appears disguised as the ghost of
Amurath's father), Amurath persuades himself to kill Eumorphe by
imagining that she will cuckold him:

> For thinke this (Amurath) this woman may
> Prostrate her delicate and Ivory limbes,
> To some base Page, or Scul, or shrunk up Dwarf:
> Or let some Groome lye feeding on her lips,
> She may devise some mishapen trick,
> To satiate her goatish Amurath,
> And from her bended knees at Meditation,
> Be taken by some slave to th' deepe of Hell! (2.4.59–65)

He then calls in his captains and nobles to have them witness the
"spectacle" (2.5.2) of his masculine strength and untempted honor,
which enable him to resist "intemperate Lust" (2.4.4.) by killing the
woman on whom he dotes. Before slaying her, however, he asks his
witnesses if they, too, are not tempted by her beauty:

> Now, which of you all is so temperate;
> That, did he find this Jewel in his Bed
> (Unlesse an Eunuch) could refraine to grapple,
> And dally with her? (2.5.34–37)

They all confess their attraction to her and agree that nothing could
make them destroy such beauty, were she theirs. Hearing this, the
sultan, in a rage, grabs a sword and swiftly cuts off the head of
the sleeping Eumorphe. He then holds up her bleeding head while
saying to his men, "There, kisse now (Captaines) doe! and clap her
cheeks" (2.5.73). "Now," announces Amurath, "shall our swords be
exercised, / In ripping up the breasts of Christians. . . . for he surely
shall / That conquers first himselfe, soone conquer all" (2.5.80–85).
Despite this prediction, Amurath's beheading of Eumorphe leads, not
to a long and glorious career, but to his imminent death and eternal
damnation. Soon after the decapitation of the Fair Greek, the sultan
is fatally stabbed on the battlefield by a wounded Christian soldier,
Cobelitz, who then dies and is escorted, Hamlet-like, to heaven by
"a guard of Saints" and angels (5.4.70).

The Couragious Turke suggests that when English readers and spectators thought of Moors and Turks, they imagined them as rash and violent oppressors who made it a point of religious and military honor to kill innocent women. Both Amurath, "the courageous Turk," and Othello, the "noble Moor," exhibit a masculine "courage," which they direct against a demonized femininity. Both believe that they are nobly resisting the temptation of a "damned whore" whose feminine charms and wiles will supposedly contaminate and weaken their military "virtue." Both Othello and Amurath believe that a higher principle has forced them to harden their hearts and minds against soft, feminine enticements that would master them. "Thinke you my minde is waxie to be wrought [?]" (2.5.67), asks Amurath, as he prepares to decapitate Eumorphe. The irony is that Amurath, like Othello, has been "wrought" upon by a male follower who succeeds in turning him against the virtuous woman he loves and in bringing on his death and damnation. In both cases, dramatic irony exposes the murderer's misogynist code as damnable and deadly to himself. Both of these Islamic woman-killers have names that deploy onomastic quibbles, a common device in the drama of Shakespeare and his contemporaries. Amurath's name suggests both "amour-wrath" and "a-Moor-wrath" while Othello's name, which would have been pronounced in Shakespeare's day with a hard "t" sound for "th," is a compression of "O to hell O!"[69]

The two plays also share an obsession with damnation and devils. In *The Couragious Turke*, between the murder of Eumorphe and the death of Amurath, a strange scene takes place in which "*foure Fiends, framed like Turkish Kings, but blacke,* [Amurath's] *supposed Predecessors...*" arise from the "hell" under the stage. They "dance about [Amurath] to a kind of hideous noyse" (5.3.25), singing a song about how he will soon join them in perdition. This prophecy is later fulfilled, and in the closing lines of Goffe's epilogue, the audience is asked to applaud and thereby help assure the damnation of the infernal Turks, who are crossing to the underworld over the river Acheron:

And as they pass with ioynd streing[th] sink the barge
Which have receav'd the Turkes blacke soule in charge
All heer wish turkes destruction[;] our hope stands
That to their ruine you'le all set your hands.

The Great Turk joins his "Predecessors," and the audience participates in sending Amurath and the other Turks to hell.

Early in Shakespeare's *Othello*, the conventional association of black skin with damnation is established by Brabantio when he refers to Othello, saying "Damned as thou art" (1.2.64). According to the early modern sign system of Christian theology, white is the color of salvation, blackness the mark of damnation. In medieval miracle plays (as in Goffe's tragedy), damned souls were represented by actors painted black or in black costumes.[70] The conventional significance given to theatrical blackface is invoked in Dekker, Day, and Haughton's *Lust's Dominion* (1600), a play, like *Othello*, that features a Moorish warrior, Eleazar, as its tragic protagonist and villain. He is called "That mold of hell" (5.2.38) and repeatedly described as a "devil." In 2.2, when two cowardly friars are suddenly confronted by Eleazar, the bold Moor "*Comes forward*" and says, "Why start you back and stare? Ha? Are you afraid?" One of the friars answers, "Oh! No Sir, no, but truth to tell; / Seeing your face, we thought of hell" (2.2.122–24). Like Shakespeare's Aaron in *Titus Andronicus*, Eleazar is loved by a lustful queen and uses that love to further his own plots. Eleazar is closer in type to Aaron than Othello, but as Othello falls into error and sin, he becomes much like the villainous Aaron or the irascible Eleazar.

The blackness of the Moors, who were supposedly the descendants of Ham (or Cham), Noah's son, was understood by the "white" Europeans as the mark of God's curse. This racist myth was widely disseminated and was recounted, for example, in George Best's *Discourse* (1578), a text that was reprinted in Hakluyt's *Principall Navigations* in 1600. Best rejects the climatic theory, common in the early modern period, that would attribute black skin color to "the parching heat of the Sunne," and argues instead that it is a "natural infection of the first inhabitants of that Countrey, and so all the whole progenie of them descended, are still polluted with the same blot of infection" (Hakluyt 7:261–62). To support this notion, Best draws upon the legend of Ham, who was punished for breaking his father Noah's command that "during the time of the floud while they remained in the Arke, they should use continencie, and abstaine from carnall copulation with their wives" (7:263). Best describes the motives and consequences of this sexual transgression:

> being perswaded that the first childe borne after the flood (by right and Lawe of nature) should inherite and possesse all the dominions of the earth, hee contrary to his fathers commandement while they were yet in the Arke, used company with his wife, and craftily went about thereby to dis-inherite the off-spring of his other two brethren: for the which wicked and detestable fact, as an example for contempt of Almightie

God, and disobedience of parents, God would a sonne should bee borne whose name was Chus, who not onely it selfe, but all his posteritie after him should be so blacke and lothsome, that it might remaine a spectacle of disobedience to all the worlde. And of this blacke and cursed Chus came all these blacke Moores which are in Africa.... (7:263–64)

Jack D'Amico points out that in Best's version of this myth, "sexual transgression and a crafty desire to disinherit his brothers are combined" (65) to explain the origin of blackness.[71] Blackness, according to Best, functions as "a spectacle of disobedience to all the worlde." For Best and for other early modern Europeans, black skin color was believed to be an outward sign of ignorance, sin, and rejection by God: "Blackness suggested monstrosity because the black race, deprived of light, alienated from God's order, merged facilely with the inhuman, bestial world..." (D'Amico 180).[72] Blackness was demonized, but it was also exoticized: Dympna Callaghan has argued that in the early modern period "The capacity of blackness simultaneously to intensify, subsume and absorb all aspects of otherness is a specifically Renaissance configuration of othering" (*Shakespeare Without Women* 79).

In the first two acts of the play, Othello's words and behavior belie this conventional reading of black skin color, but by the end of Shakespeare's tragedy, the Moor is thoroughly blackened—inside and out. His external blackness is confirmed and internalized by the conversion of his soul to "Turkish" infidelity and violence. Othello's damnation is explicitly announced in the final scene. According to Emilia, for example, Othello's blackness (contrasted with Desdemona's white innocence) is the mark of a devil damned: "O, the more angel she, and you the blacker devil!" (5.2.140). According to the Renaissance theory of mind–body relations, the heat and smoke of Othello's passionate jealousy tarnish the mirror of his rational soul. This clouding of his judgment begins in act 2 when his nuptial slumbers are interrupted by the brawl and Othello declares, "My blood begins my safer guides to rule, / And passion having my best judgment collied, / Essays to lead the way" (2.3.188–90). This "collying"—or blackening—continues, and by the end of Shakespeare's tragedy, Othello's skin color has become the external, carnal sign of an internal, spiritual condition—just as it is for Eleazar in *Lust's Dominion*.

* * *

In his final speeches, Othello turns away, first from the divine judge toward his adversary, Iago; then, when that adversary is revealed to be the Devil, Othello turns to his auditors, onstage and in the audience, to persuade them of his honorable intentions. This "turning" is a form of apostrophe, addressing the enemy he has become:

> ...in Aleppo once,
> Where a malignant and a turbaned Turk
> Beat a Venetian and traduced the state,
> I took by th' throat the circumcisèd dog
> And smote him thus. (5.2.361–52)

The language here suggests a circular cutting, as Othello turns on himself and plunges the sword into his own bowels, forming a circle with body and weapon.[73]

Circumcision, according to Christian theology, is an Abrahamic practice, abrogated by the coming of Christ and the new covenant:

> ...as the Jewes have shewed themselves most obstinate in the blind-nesse of their hearts by the retaining of this ceremonie and their olde traditions: so the Turkes likewise, no lesse vaine in the idlenesse of their own imaginations, have and do use Circumcision, as a special token or marke of their fond and superstitious sect.... (*The Policy* 22)

Seventeenth-century English Christians believed that adult-male con-version to Islam required circumcision.[74] In their minds, circumcision emphasized the sexual significance of the change in faith, imagined both as a kind of castration or emasculation and as a sign of the Muslims' sexual excess—the reduction of the phallus signifying the need to cur-tail raging lust.[75] For Othello to cut himself reiterates the ritual cutting of his foreskin, which was the sign of his belonging to the community of stubborn misbelievers, the Muslims. To smite "the circumcisèd dog" is at once to kill the "turbaned Turk" and to reenact a version of his own circumcision, signifying his return to the "malignant" sect of the Turks and his reunion with the misbelieving devils.[76]

The play's recurrent references to hell and damnation lead the audi-ence to consider the eternal consequences of Othello's suicide for his soul. Self-slaughter, for a Christian, is a faithless act of despair, bring-ing certain damnation. Having told Desdemona, "I would not kill thy soul" (5.2.34), Othello goes on to kill his own soul by taking his own life, once again usurping God's power over life and death. Taken out of context, Othello's suicide might be interpreted as a noble act in the tradition of pagan heroes like Antony; but read in the context of the play's persistently Christian language of divine judgment, it merely confirms his identity as an infidel—an irascible creature whose reckless violence leads him to be "damned beneath all depth in hell" (5.2.146).

The desperate grief that Othello expresses just before he kills himself may be called a "Judas repentance." And indeed, in his despair Othello compares himself to that circumcised renegade and suicide, "the base Judean" (if we follow the Folio text [TLN 3658]).[77] Judas's suicide, according to Byam's sermon, was prompted by the Devil's eagerness to see Judas damned: "Yea I know some that tell us how for this very cause [fear of a last-minute repentance leading to salvation] the Devill hasted to take Judas out of this life, least knowing that there was a way to turne to Salvation, He might by pennance recover his fall" (68).

The English Protestant "Homily of repentance and true reconciliation unto God" (printed in *The Seconde Tome of Homilies* [1595]) warns that those who "onely allowe these three parts of repentance, the contrition of the heart, the confession of the mouth, and the satisfaction of the worke," will not receive divine mercy (sig.Kk6v). In the homily, repentance is repeatedly figured as a turning. True repentance is defined as "the conversion or turning again of the whol man unto God, from whome wee goe away by sinne" (sig.Kk2v). The opening sentences of the homily declare that repentance is essential to prevent "eternall damnation" (sig.Ii3r). There are "foure principall pointes, that is, from what we must returne, to whome wee must returne, by whome wee maye bee able to convert, and the manner howe for to turn unto GOD.... *revertimini usque ad me*, saith the Lord" (sig.Ii4v–Ii5r). Rather than turning to God and asking for His mercy, Othello disregards the words of the homily: "they doe greatly erre, which do not turne unto God, but unto the creatures, or unto the inventions of men, or unto theyr owne merites" (sig.Ii6v). Like Judas, Othello exhibits a self-destructive *remorse* (as opposed to true *repentance* and humble submission to God's will); like Judas, Othello is damned for his betrayal of innocence.

Damnation is the fate Christians liked to imagine for all those who followed the path of Islam. Ralph Carr's comments in *The Mahumetane or Turkish Historie* typify English beliefs about how God will judge the Muslims: "the Mahumetans, who[,] misled by the lyes of that wicked Impostor, and following his damned positions, diverting from the eternall path of salvation, are carryed headlong in theyr misbeliefe to hell torments, and everlasting damnation..." (113v). According to Knolles, the religion of "the false Prophet Mahomet, borne in an unhappie houre, to the great destruction of mankind" had not only "desolat[ed]" the Christian Church but had created a vast population of Muslims who would all be damned, "millions of soules cast headlong into eternall destruction" (sig. A4r). Part of Western Europeans' fascination with Islam and the Turks was a feeling that their awesome power, raised by the wrath of God, would experience an equally awesome punishment in the form of mass damnation. In Kellett's view, the same fate awaited the renegade: "By not adhering to Christ, by waiving thy beliefe, by disclayming thy vow in Baptisme, by professing Turcisme, thou hast sold heaven, art initiated into hell, and hast purchased onely a conscience, frighted with horror..." (16).[78]

A baptized Moor turned Turk, Othello is "double-damned" (4.2.39) for backsliding. Sent out to lead a crusade against Islamic imperialism, he turns Turk and becomes the enemy within. He has "traduced" the state of Venice and converted to a black, Muslim identity, an embodiment of the Europeans' phobic fantasy: Othello has become the ugly stereotype. His identity as "the noble Moor of Venice" dissolves as he reverts to the identity of the black devil and exhibits the worst features of the stereotypical "cruel Moor" or Turk—jealousy, frustrated lust, violence, mercilessness, faithlessness, lawlessness, despair. Faced with this terrible identity, one that "shows horrible and grim" (5.2.210), Othello enacts his own punishment and damns himself by killing the Turk he has become.

CHAPTER 5

SCENES OF CONVERSION: PIRACY, APOSTASY, AND THE SULTAN'S SERAGLIO

'Tis the custom of the whole world: the greater thief preys upon the less still.

—*Robert Daborne*, A Christian Turned Turk (*6.132–33*)

Already we have seen in Shakespeare's *Othello* and Marlowe's *Tamburlaine* a pattern of conversion or transformation that can lead to tragedy (Othello's case) or to worldly wealth and conquest (Tamburlaine's). In both of these plays, religious affiliation is unstable, and both texts play upon and respond to English anxieties about violent cross-cultural encounters in the Mediterranean. In this chapter, I will trace this anxiety and the trope of conversion it produces in a group of five English plays set in the Mediterranean. Each of these texts represents a confrontation with religious difference, and each play highlights the conversion or potential conversion of Christians who encounter Islamic culture. The plays that I will analyze here use "turning" as a trope that refers to a variety of transformations, including the shifting of political, religious, sexual, and moral identities. In addition to staging figurative and sometimes overdetermined versions of conversion, these texts also represent religious turning in ways that refer specifically to Christian–Muslim relations in the Mediterranean. In Thomas Kyd's *The Tragedye of Soliman and Perseda* (1592), Thomas Heywood's *The Fair Maid of the West, or A Girl Worth Gold,*

Part I (1602) and Part II (1630), Robert Daborne's *A Christian Turned Turk* (1610), and Philip Massinger's *The Renegado* (1624), religious conversion is dramatized in the multicultural Mediterranean context where characters of various faiths encounter one another in scenes of war, piracy, and commerce—on the high seas, in prison cells, in the public marketplace, on the field of battle, and in intimate, eroticized spaces. In these plays, as in *Tamburlaine* and *Othello*, audiences witnessed a drama of anxiety that works through some of the issues with which a commercially expanding English culture was contending as it confronted religious and cultural difference in the Mediterranean.

Each of these plays represents Islamic culture as powerful, wealthy, and erotically alluring. For these playwrights, Islam is a religion of temptation. In the first part of this chapter, I want to investigate further the English understanding of conversion to Islam. Why did Christians convert? What was the appeal of Islam? What were renegades like? How did the Ottoman empire function as a kind of multi-ethnic nation of converts? After answering these questions, this chapter will move on to analyze the larger, more figurative sense of an English cultural "turning" that was impelled by interaction with the multicultural Mediterranean.

* * *

In his *Geographical Historie of Africa* Leo Africanus, an Andalusian "Moor" who converted to Christianity, offers a detailed account of Muslim success in converting Christians to Islam. He maintains,

> there is nothing that hath greatlier furthered the progression of the Mahumetan sect than perpetuity of victory and the greatness of conquests....I that the greatest part of men, yea, and in a manner all (except such as have fastened their confidence upon the cross of Christ and settled their hope in eternity) follow that which best agreeth with sense, and measure the grace of God by worldly prosperity. (381)

He then remarks at the Muslims' startling accomplishments in spreading their religion far and wide over the course of many centuries, and he describes how in more recent times Islamic missionaries came into competition and conflict with Christian missionaries and colonizers: "and if the Portugals in India and the Malucos, and afterwards the Spaniards in the Philipinas had not met them on the way, and with the gospell and armes, interrupted their course, they would at this instant have possessed infinite kingdomes of the east" (385).[1] Christianity and Islam are imagined here as engaging in a "clash of civilizations"—a competition for imperial power and control over the riches and territories of the East Indies. This is one of those moments, in a text sponsored by the pope and translated by John Pory, a disciple of Hakluyt, when "the common corps of Christendom" comes together to form one half of a binary opposition. The historical reality, of course, was one of violent conflict and competition between Spanish, Portuguese, Dutch, and English merchants in South Asia and the East Indies.

In trying to account, at the level of the specific convert, for why Christians in the Mediterranean were so frequently turning Turk, Leo Africanus offers this explanation:

> the Christians become Turkes, partly upon some extreme & violent passion. ... [others] abjure the faith to release themselves of torments and cruelties; others for hope of honors and temporall greatnes: and of these two sorts there are a great number in Constantinople, being thought to be Christians in hart: and yet through slothfulnes, or first to gather together more wealth, or expecting opportunitie to carry with them, their wives and children, or for fear of being discovered in their departure and voiage, or else through sensualitie, and for that they would not be deprived of the licentiousnes and libertie of the life they lead, resolve not to performe that they are bound unto; deferring thus from moneth to moneth & from yeere to yeere, to leave theis Babylon & sinke of sin. (386)

There is some irony in this account, given Africanus's own position at the papal court in Rome. He speaks from the extraordinary position of a former Muslim who, after he had been "taken by certaine [Christian] pirates, and presented unto pope Leo the tenth," (60) accepted Christianity. The precise circumstances of his conversion are not known, but presumably he was faced with an offer he could not refuse, after which he became a client of papal patronage. His English translator, Pory, is somewhat anxious about the Moorish provenance of his source, but at the same time he presents his author as especially reliable because Africanus is a firsthand, "inside" source. Africanus's brilliant ventriloquism of early modern anti-Islamism testifies to his strategic adaptivity.

Leo Africanus was a very rare example of a Muslim who converted to Christianity. It was much more common for Christians to turn Turk, and by the early seventeenth century, many English subjects had become renegadoes in North Africa and the Middle East. Nabil Matar has claimed that "Thousands of European Christians converted to Islam in the Renaissance and the seventeenth century, either because their poor social conditions forced them toward such a choice, or because they sought to identify with a powerful empire, much like the converts to Christianity in nineteenth-century Africa or the proselytes to . . . Protestantism in the second half of the twentieth century in South America" (Matar 1998, 15).[2] These were not the only factors, however, that encouraged English subjects to take on a new religion, one that had been described to them since birth as damnable and utterly false. I have already mentioned the economic motives for conversion, but it was not only the promise of plunder that tempted Christians to "turn Turk." English Protestants were also attracted to Islam because of the openness and freedom that Islamic culture allowed to its converts and adherents. If we consider the social, religious, economic—even the physical—circumstances in which a typical seaman from London or the West Country lived, and then we contrast those circumstances with the conditions of an English "Turk" living in North Africa or under Ottoman sovereignty, it is possible to understand the appeal of Islam as an alternative way of life. In England the period under study, 1570–1630, was one marked by repeated episodes of famine, plague, and economic depression. Conditions for laborers and seamen were particularly difficult, and after James I made peace with Spain the number of unemployed sailors and soldiers in England grew. It was also a time and place that was defined by a violent, sometimes paranoid, religious sectarianism. Post-Reformation England was marked by a relentless anxiety about the precise nature of the true faith, and this anxiety was expressed in debates that intruded into every aspect of daily life and demanded that worshippers commit themselves to a particular Christian sect and its theology. Early modern England was a culture with a religious climate marked by intrusion, surveillance, and controversy. Constantly bombarded with references to sin and damnation, and caught between various religious factions who competed for followers, English subjects under Elizabeth I, James I, and Charles I lived in an era of ideological discomfort, and many of them, like the Puritans described by William Haller, were "Uprooted and swept this way and that by the confused forces of their age, plucked at on every side by contending interests cloaked in puzzling dialectic and cloudy image" (260). All of this stands in marked contrast with the relative ease, simplicity, and openness that characterized quotidian religious life in the Islamic Mediterranean during the same period. English renegades no longer had to cope with the ceaseless attempts of the ecclesiastical authorities to impose uniformity, or the general atmosphere of struggle and discontent, that afflicted their homeland.

Islam must have appealed greatly, offering conversion through an extremely simple ritual, and once that rite was performed, very few formal practices or demonstrations of faith were required of English converts who were willing to serve under Islamic rule. New converts to Islam were not rigorously catechized—instead they were introduced to a few basic principles (the five "pillars" of Islam) and taught to pray and recite the *shehadeh*. For renegades, there was little stigma attached to their status as new Muslims, and though Islamic society was hierarchical, it was highly absorptive at its margins. On the whole, social mobility was greater than at home, especially for English renegades with valuable skills to offer to their new communities. It also bears mentioning that Muslims bathed more often than the English, who lacked the institution of the public bath (the Muslim practices of head-shaving and ritual ablution also encouraged a level of personal hygiene unknown in England). Adult conversion to Islam was only rarely coerced or forced (despite the claims to the contrary that were voiced in propagandistic Christian writings, including Barbary captivity narratives printed in England) and yet many hundreds, perhaps thousands, of English subjects willingly converted to Islam and took their places within the hetero-ethnic religious communities of the Muslim Mediterranean.

Faced with the worrying reality that Islam strongly appealed to many Christians, English readers turned for comfort to a series of captivity narratives that testified against the allure of Islam and promised that the Protestant deity would deliver English slaves from bondage, if only they kept the faith. Some English captives returned to England and became the authors of printed texts that detailed their experiences. There were more than a dozen of these captivity narratives written between 1570 and 1630, and each of them grapples with the issue of apostasy, a temptation that the narrators claim they faced and rejected.[3] One of these texts, titled *The Famous and Wonderful Recovery of a Ship of Bristol, Called the Exchange, from the Turkish Pirates of Argier, with the Unmatchable Attempts and Good Success of John Rawlins, Pilot in Her, and Other Slaves* (1622), recounts the adventures of John Rawlins and his shipmates, who departed from Plymouth in a merchant vessel that was captured near the Straits of Gibraltar by corsairs from Algiers. At the slave market, "The bashaw had the overseeing of all prisoners, who were presented unto him at their first coming into the harbor, and so chose one out of every eight for a present or a fee to himself" (*Piracy, Slavery and Redemption* 102). Rawlins reports that before he was sold he was informed that the Algerian Muslims would force the newly arrived slaves "either to turn Turk or to attend their filthiness and impieties" (102). The text claims,

> They commonly lay them on their naked backs or bellies, beating them so long till they bleed at the nose and mouth, and if yet they continue constant, then they strike the teeth out of their heads, pinch them by their tongues, and use many other sorts of tortures to convert them.... And so many, even for fear of torment and death, make their tongues betray their hearts to a most fearful wickedness and so are circumcised with new names and brought to confess a new religion. Others again, I must confess, who never knew any god but their own sensual lusts and pleasures, thought that any religion would serve their turns and so for preferment or wealth very voluntarily renounced their faith and became renegadoes. (102–03)

Rawlins was taken to the market, where, he reports, "many came to behold us, sometimes taking us by the hand, sometimes turning us round about, sometimes feeling our brawns and naked arms, and so beholding our prices written in our breasts, they bargained for us accordingly, and at last we were all sold" (103). Rawlins is eventually purchased by a pair of English renegades, "both English Turks," who had also procured a ship and rigged it for a freebooting voyage. They assembled a multicultural crew composed of "sixty-three Turks and Moors, nine English slaves and one French, four Hollanders that were free men...And for their gunners...one English and one Dutch renegado" (*Piracy, Slavery and Redemption* 105). During the course of this ship's voyage, Rawlins leads an alliance of slaves and free European members of the crew in a successful mutiny. The narrative describes how they take over the ship, slaughtering all the Turks and Moors, and bringing the renegade captain and five other English renegades back to England. The narrator gives the credit for his delivery to "the power and goodness of God" (118), providing a conventional providentialist framework to explain the events. His text, like the other Barbary captivity narratives from this period, functions as propaganda for English Protestantism, but it also testifies to the power of Muslims in the Mediterranean where, in order to make a profit, English vessels had to risk capture by pirates. Although English ships were trading in Muslim ports, and Christian pirates were also capturing and enslaving both Muslims and Christians, the Rawlins narrative responds to the converting power of Islam with demonization and condemnation. At the end of the text, the narrator addresses the reader: "Nor do I think you will be startled at anything in the discourse touching the cruelty and inhumanity of Turks and Moors themselves, who from a native barbarousness do hate all Christians and Christianity, especially if they grow into the violent rages of piracy or fall into that exorbitant course of selling slaves or enforcing of men to be Mahometans" (*Piracy, Slavery and Redemption* 119). In spite of the narrator's attempts to present events as part of a Manichean struggle, the details of the story indicate a more complex matrix in which "turning" was common and in which Christians, Muslims, and renegades worked cooperatively and shifted identities as they negotiated for places in the multicultural Mediterranean's violent marketplace.[4] The distinctions between loyal English merchantmen, murderous privateers, pirates, and renegade apostates were blurred.

The English experience of captivity in the Mediterranean, and the representation and interpretation of that experience in texts like *The Famous and Wonderful Recovery*, refers to mobile and peripheral elements like the Barbary pirates, and to their operations in Algiers, Tunis, and other North African ports, but texts describing the multicultural Mediterranean also refer to a centralized, metropolitan power that enabled and reinforced these marginal renegades through its political and military network. The Barbary pirates captured slaves, but in the eyes of the English, the ultimate slavemaster was the Ottoman sultan who commanded the powerful janissary corps and was head of a body politic that systematically incorporated slaves and converts through the *devshirme* (child levy) system. The janissaries themselves were known to be the products of this system whereby Christian children were taken from their families and brought up as Muslims and soldiers who then fought against Christians in order to expand the Ottoman empire through conquest. According to European accounts, the various bashas, viceroys, governors, princes, and kings were simulacra modeled on "The Great Turk" or "Grand Seigneur," and these little sultans allegedly embodied and enacted the same principles of lust, tyranny, and power through enslavement.

The conventional figure of the despotic sultan, as he is depicted in Western writings, derives in large part from the romance tradition, rooted in medieval texts and stimulated by the experiences of crusade and *Reconquista*. That romance tradition features Muslim warriors as "paynim" or "Saracen" knights who worshipped Mahound and served the sultan. This stock cast of characters is adapted in early modern texts, and the conventional pattern remains clear: each "Turkish" court is ruled by a powerful Muslim ruler who insatiably gathers and hoards women, wealth, and warriors. This court, with its sultan and seraglio, is a site where conversion is offered and staged. It is the metropolitan center from which an empire of conversion is administered. English paranoia at the insatiable sultanic will that allegedly drove the Islamic engine of conquest is described in texts like *The Policy of the Turkish Empire* (1597), in which the introductory epistle "To the reader" includes this description of a nation and a religion that is said to be profoundly expansionist in its essential nature:

> For by discovering the nature and the state of their religion, and their immoderate zeale in affecting it, by shewing their inveterate hatred against Christians and christianitie, by making known their Barbarous customes and most cruell disposition, by observing their politique and advised course of proceedings, in all their affaires both Civill and Militarie: we shall easily discerne: That the whole Policie of the Turkishe estate both for their religion, life, and customes, as also for their civil government and Martiall discipline: and that all their actions Counsailes, studies, labours and endevours have beene ever framed and directed, and wholy bent and intended to the enlarging and amplifying of their Empire and Religion, with the dayly accesse of new and continuall conquests by the ruine and subversion of all such kingdomes, provinces, estates and professions, as are any way estranged from them either in name, nation or religion. (sig.A3v-A4r)

Like the "universal wolf" described by Shakespeare's Ulysses, the Turkish sultan was thought to reject all orderly limits to his power, so that "everything includes itself in power, / Power into will, will into appetite; / And appetite, an universal wolf, / So doubly seconded with will and power, / Must make perforce an universal prey, / And last eat up himself" (1.3.119–24). According to this view, Turkish expansionism seeks to devour all difference, digesting other nations and absorbing them into its omnivorous empire. (Ironically, this desire to conquer mirrors English imperial desire.) Pursuing and directing this aggressive agenda is the sultan, a figure who appears in each of the five dramatic texts that were mentioned at the beginning of this chapter. At the center of each play stands an Islamic tyrant, a sultan or basha who conforms to the type of the wrathful, lustful despot. These tyrannical characters are Solyman, emperor of the Turks, in *Soliman and Perseda*; Mullisheg, king of Fez, in *The Fair Maid of the West*; the Governor (or viceroy of Tunis) in *A Christian Turned Turk*; and Asambeg (also viceroy of Tunis) in *The Renegado*. All five plays include scenes in which Christian men are drawn into Islamic temptation, but these plays also present the reverse: the conversion (or reversion) of Muslims and renegadoes to Christianity. In each text, religious and erotic motives are interrelated.

Before these plays were written, a conventional set of characteristics for describing Islamic power had already been established: first, there is a sultan who exercises absolute power over his enslaved subjects. This sultan is imagined as the One who absolutely, arbitrarily, and mercilessly exercises all the power, while all others merely obey. This sultan, in order to feed his passions, is bent on possession and domination. He desires to increase the physical boundaries of his realm and also to obtain women for his harem and capture souls for his religion. Those who resist are killed, enslaved, or converted. Christians are forced or tempted to turn Turk. Because he has absolute power, he rules everyone but himself: his own passions are uncontrollable. This archetypal sultan is depicted as fickle and given to extreme, unstable desires, whims, and sudden fits of irrational anger. He perverts justice, enforcing Islamic law and all codes of honor to suit his whims and lusts.

English descriptions that fixate on the sultan's seraglio are symptomatic of English anxieties about foreign imperial power. The sultan's harem was the hub of the world's greatest empire, an empire whose power, discipline and masculine order were said to be enforced by extreme cruelty; but at the same time, the sultan's palace was allegedly the *locus classicus* for effeminate luxury, hidden sensuality, and sexual excess. Alain Grosrichard, in his analysis of "European Fantasies of the East," claims that Western descriptions of the seraglio comprise "the obligatory *topos* of all the accounts of travel in the Orient" (125). According to Grosrichard, the seraglio is a "phantasmic place, whose power is to fascinate" (143), and the women who inhabit it form an "always incomplete catalogue" of desired objects in contrast to the sultan, who is "The incomparable and absolute Other" (128), the libidinal "One-All." Grosrichard sees in the Western representation of the harem an allegorization of patriarchy that marks the ontological difference between Man and Woman according to the patriarchal regime of Western metaphysics. But the Western account of the seraglio is also a writing of power: this connection between Western representations of oriental power and sexuality is apparent in the opening passage of Michel de Baudier's *Histoire generalle du serrail et de la cour du Grand Seigneur, Empereur des Turcs* (1624), which was translated by Edward Grimestone and printed in English in 1635:

> I have conceived, that having given you the History of the Turkish Empire, from its beginning unto our times, it would not be unprofitable to let you see what their manners are, their kind of living, their conversation, and the order of their governement, which so powerfull

and redoubted a Conquerour doth observe. To do it safely wee must enter into the serrail, where the secret of all these things is carefully shut up. (2).

The sultan's seraglio was a particular obsession with Western describers of Turkish culture, and the early modern reports and translations that depict the Turks and their customs dwell voyeuristically in the forbidden space of the sultan's harem. In Robert Withers's 1625 translation of Ottaviano Bon, for example, the reader is tantalized by the secrets of the seraglio: "for there may none come near, nor be in sight of [the sultan and his women], but himself and his black eunuchs: nay if any other should but attempt, by some trick in creeping into some private corner, to see the women, and should be discovered, he should be put to death immediately" (65).[5] The women never leave the precincts of the seraglio, and the eunuchs who return from the city are routinely searched. This is explained in a description of the Ottoman court from Grimestone's translation of Baudier:

> They doe not only search the women which enter, and the Eunuches at thir returne from the Citie: But moreover they have a care of beasts: They will not allow the Sultanaes to keepe any Apes, nor Dogges of any stature. Fruits are sent unto them with circumspection: If their appetites demand any pompeons which are somewhat long, or cow-cumbers, and such other fruits, they cut them at the Gate in slices, not suffering to passe among them any slight occasion of doing evill, so bad an opinion they have of their continencie. It is (without doubt) a signe of the Turks violent jealousie: for who can in the like case hinder a vicious woman from doing evill? She is too industrious in her designs; and he which had his body covered with eyes always watching was deceived. In the meanetime if any woman in the Serrail be discovered in the effects of her lasciviousnesse, the Law long since established for them by the Sultan, condemnes her to die, the which is executed without remission: she is put into a sack, and in the night cast into the Sea, where she doth quench her flames with her life. (65)

This passage, with its emphasis on both sexual control and tyrannical cruelty, is typical of early modern representations of the sultan and his court.

The paranoid, phallocentric gaze of the male, Western narrator also operates in the case of English eyewitnesses like Thomas Dallam, an organmaker who traveled to Istanbul in 1599 to present an organ as a gift from a group of English merchants to the Sultan.

Dallam's first-person account of his journey to Turkey is preserved in manuscript. While visiting the sultan's palace, Dallam is given a tour of "the Grand Sinyors privie Chamberes" (74). His Turkish escort provides the English visitor with an unexpected opportunity:

> When he had showed me many other thinges which I wondered at,...
> he poynted me to goo to a graite in a wale, but made me a sine that he
> myghte not goo thether him self. When I came to the grait the wale
> was verrie thicke, and graited on both sides with iron verrie strongly;
> but though that graite I did se thirtie of the Grand Sinyor's
> Concobines that weare playinge with a bale in another courte. (74)

Dallam praises their beauty, and describes the women's fine linen clothing, noting "I could desarne the skin of their thies throughe it." Then he writes,

> I stood so longe loukinge upon them that he which had showed me all
> this kindnes began to be verrie angrie with me. He made a wrye
> mouthe, and stamped with his foute to make me give over looking; the
> which I was verrie lothe to dow, for that sighte did please me wondrous
> well. (75)

After telling his interpreter what he had seen, Dallam is advised not to "speake of it, whereby any Turke myghte hear of it; for if it weare knowne to som Turks, it would [be] present deathe to him that showed me them" (75).

Dallam's story is typical of Western representations in the way that the threat of death frames the fantasmic vision of the harem. In European accounts of the seraglio, the libidinal regime at the center of Ottoman power is imagined as the secret core from which the merciless, masculine aggression of Turkish military power emanates. To peep into the seraglio is to penetrate with an intruder's gaze the hidden mechanisms of confinement and slavery that sustain and explain both the private and political success of the empire. Some European authors openly admired Ottoman power as a virile force capable of maintaining a strict discipline and order, but often they argued that such extreme discipline was only possible where relentless cruelty, confinement, and fear produce a slavish obedience. Spectacular punishment and assassination are often emphasized in early modern accounts of Turkish society and government: Sir Henry Blount, for example, describes in his *Voyage into the Levant* (1636) the "horrid executions" such as "...Empaling, Gaunching, Flaying alive, cutting off by the Waste with a red hot iron, [An]Ointing with honey in the Sunne, hanging by the Foot, planting in burning Lime, and the like" (52). Such extreme measures were said to be the key to the Ottomans' success as conquerors and rulers. At the same time, this Turkish cruelty was also linked to sensuality, as European authors sought to effeminate the masculine power they feared and envied. Again Blount: "... for hee [the Prophet Muhammed] finding the Sword to be the foundation of Empires, and that to manage the Sword, the rude and sensuall are more vigorous, then wits softned in a mild rationall way of civilitie; did first frame his institutions to a rude insolent sensualitie..." (78). Islam itself was described by Christian writers as a religion based on sexual license, and permitting polygamy and instant divorce. Furthermore, Turks or Muslims are represented as practitioners of "sodomy": Blount reports that beside their wives, "...each Basha hath as many, or likely more, Catamites, which are their serious loves; for their wives are used (as the Turkes themselves told me) but to dresse their meat, to Launderesse, and for reputation..." (14).

Another English writer who describes the Great Turk and his court is George Sandys. Sandys is best known to scholars of literature as a poet and translator of Ovid. He left England for the Levant in 1610 and returned in 1611, and his travel narrative, *A Relation of a Journey... Containing a description of the Turkish Empire* was first printed in 1615. In Sandys's description of Ahmet I and his seraglio, the sultan himself becomes an embodiment of the contradictions in the English construction of Islamic power: he is "strongly limd, & of a just stature, yet greatly inclining to be fat: insomuch as sometimes he is ready to choke as he feeds" (73). "His aspect is as hauty as his Empire is large," and he is "...an unrelenting punisher of offences, even in his owne household: having caused eight of his Pages...to be throwne into the Sea for Sodomy (an ordinary crime, if esteemed a crime, in that nation)..." (73). Thus, the imperial household is represented as a microcosm of the empire, where both extreme cruelty and sexual excess are exercised. The sultan's sexual prodigiousness stands in contrast to the castrated eunuchs that surround him. Military order and hierarchy dominate Sandys's account of the male inhabitants of Topkapi palace, while the description of the sultan's women is a male fantasy, transgressive in its excess (Sandys's sultan possesses five hundred beautiful virgin slaves, "the choisest beauties of the Empire" [74]). Sexual supply and demand comprise a paradoxical economy by which the excess of bodies provided for the sultan's pleasure also produces his procreative weakness or lack: "But for all his multitude of women, he hath yet begotten but two sonnes and three daughters, though he be that way unsatiatably given, (perhaps the cause he hath so few) and vieth all sorts of foods that may inable performance" (75). Though the harem is secret and off limits to all men but the sultan himself and his imperial eunuchs, Sandys's narrative intrudes voyeuristically in the seraglio by offering a physical description of the imperial concubines, and an engraved image of a Turkish woman is included with Sandys's text.

Sandys's description of the Ottoman sultan's court provides a paradigmatic encapsulation of the contradictions typically found in Western representations of the Turks.[6] The Turks are both immoderate and disciplined, excessively masculine and perversely unmasculine. Military discipline is contrasted with moral misrule. They are both virile and impotent, procreative and self-destructive: the sultan produces many potential heirs by impregnating a large number of wives and concubines, but then the sultan and his only male heir slaughter their own family, strangling their brothers and sons. According to Western, Christian writers, the Turks' immoderate sexuality is demonstrated through multiplicity, excess, and unnaturalness—polygamy, sexual liberty, and sodomy. Libidinal excess is counterbalanced by castration and the seclusion of women. At a time when Christians were not circumcised, circumcision was thought of as a physical marker referring to the sexual significance of Muslim status. At the same time, the descriptions of Islamic culture also recount a pattern of order, centralization, and singularity. The Ottoman empire is a super-civilization, a frighteningly all-inclusive and all-absorbing system (in contrast to a divided Christendom, crisscrossed with borders). All revolves around the sultan—the One—surrounded by his women and his eunuchs: all others—the Many—are his subjects and his slaves. Thus sultanic excess is both sexual and political. Power, wealth, sex, and violence are used to make converts. The Turkish empire increases its population, not by internal procreation alone, but by abducting Christian children and raising them as Muslims and training them as janissaries. Captives are adopted or eliminated: they are offered luxurious, sinful rewards that would indulge the body and its sensual desires, or the body was destroyed, consumed—adopt the prisoner or kill the prisoner, the old myth about the barbarian, but here attributed to a paradoxically barbarous civilization.

* * *

There are two basic narratives from the romance tradition that underlie the dramatic plots of Mediterranean conversion drama. In both, the sultan's seraglio is the setting for a kind of primal scene that is witnessed through Western eyes. First, there is the tale of "The Sultan and the Fair Greek," and second, "The Abduction from the Seraglio." The first involves Islamic masculinity and Christian femininity; the second involves Christian masculinity and Islamic femininity. In the first narrative, the Christian woman is enslaved by the lustful Muslim; in the second, the heroic Christian rescues (and converts) the virtuous Muslim woman—or—in a variation of this second paradigm—is ensnared and destroyed by the lustful Muslim temptress.

Many of the essential ingredients for developing the plots of these conversion plays were taken from the same romance tradition that, as I demonstrated in chapter 4, underlay the plots of both Shakespeare's *Othello* and Goffe's *Courageous Turk*. For example, the principal narrative source of Thomas Kyd's *Soliman and Perseda* is Henry Wotton's translation of a story from Jacques Yver's popular French collection, *Le Printemps d'Yver*, which was printed in *A Courtlie Controversie of Cupids Cautels. Conteyning Five Tragicall Histories* (1578). Yver's tale was a variation on the basic pattern of "The Sultan and the Fair Greek," the traditional romance narrative that influenced Shakespeare and Goffe. The tale of "The Sultan and the Fair Greek" functions as a kind of ur-narrative, which is drawn upon in a variety of early modern texts that represent the passions of powerful Islamic warriors or rulers. *Soliman and Perseda* is one of the texts that rewrites this tale for performance in the English theater.

In *Soliman and Perseda*, Kyd took Wotton's text, which had served as the source for the plot of Hieronomo's deadly masque in *The Spanish Tragedy*, and expanded it to produce an entire play, a spin-off sequel that sought to capitalize on the success of the earlier play.[7] *Soliman and Perseda* begins with a tournament held to honor the wedding of the prince of Cyprus. This tournament is in part a neo-medieval fantasy from the romance tradition, but it also suggests a contemporaneous international community made up of those who interacted or traded within the Mediterranean and met in places like Cyprus: it includes knights from Turkey, Rhodes, Malta, Spain, France, Denmark, England, as well as a "Turke of Tripolis" (1.1.53), "The Moore upon his hot Barbarian horse" (l.56), and an Italianate braggadoccio named Basilisco. The latter, though a fool, is a comic version of the new type of border-crossing European, ready to adapt to the diasporic flow and instability of the multicultural scene. He exhibits a mobility of identity that characterizes the adaptive behavior of those who sought power and profit in this kind of competitive, heterogeneous context. When the prince of Cyprus asks the knights to identify themselves by speaking their national battle cry or native

"woord of courage" (1.3.38), the English knight invokes Saint
George and the French knight Saint Denis, but Basilisco says, "I have
no word, because no countrey; each place is my habitation; therefore
each countries word mine to pronounce" (ll.104–06).

Erastus, a young knight of Rhodes, wins the tournament and the
love of Perseda, but he loses the valuable "carcanet" or "chain" that
Perseda gives him as a love token. Like Portia's ring in *The Merchant
of Venice* or the "chain" in *The Comedy of Errors*, this object circulates
within the erotic economy of the play and its fetishization brings dangerous consequences. The lost object is found by Ferdinando, kinsman
to the Governor of Rhodes, who gives it in turn to his love, Lucina.
When Erastus hears that Lucina is wearing the carcanet, he recovers it
by trickery, but later Ferdinando sees him wearing it. They fight and
Erastus slays Ferdinando. Erastus is then forced to flee to save his life.
He seeks refuge at the Ottoman court, where, upon arrival, he bursts
into the imperial presence and begs for the sultan's protection.

Kyd's "Soliman," the Ottoman sultan, would be identified with
Suleiman I (the Magnificent). The historical Suleiman reigned from
1520 to 1566 and captured Rhodes in 1522, expelling the Knights
Hospitalers who then went on to occupy Malta. In act 1, Soliman is
introduced to the audience in a scene in which one of his brothers,
Amurath, kills the other, Haleb. Soliman then kills Amurath in
revenge for the murder of Haleb, whom he loved dearly. This action
establishes the inseparability of the twin passions of Islamic tyranny—
love (or lust) and wrath—which move Soliman to kill one brother
because he loved the other. It is a typical English representation of the
Ottoman royal house as a dysfunctional family that is power hungry
and unnaturally murderous.

When Erastus arrives in Constantinople and pleads for aid, the sultan
is impressed by the reports of Brusor, a Turk who was bested by Erastus
in the tournament on Cyprus. Soliman agrees to harbor Erastus and
even favors him, granting two requests. Erastus asks, first, "That, being
banisht from my native soile, / I may have libertie to live a Christian"
(3.1.94–95); and second, he asks not to be employed in any action that
would require him to "sheath my slaughtering blade / In the deere
bowels of my countrimen" (ll.123–24). Despite these conditions, it is
clear that Erastus, though he has not formally converted to Islam, has,
in some sense, "turned Turk": he has become a "runagate," leaving his
homeland in order to serve his nation's great enemy. By asking to live as
a Christian, Erastus avoids the choice of death or conversion that his
countrymen face when Rhodes is subsequently conquered by the Turks.
The implication is that normally a turncoat like Erastus would change

religion, but Soliman allows this exception because he wants such a powerful warrior on his side, and because he seems to fall in love with Erastus at first sight. Soliman is happy to send Brusor instead of Erastus to invade Rhodes while he and Erastus go off to share the pleasures of the seraglio together. "Erastus," says Soliman, "come and follow me, / Where thou shalt see what pleasures and what sports / My Minions and my Euenukes can devise, / To drive away this melancholly mood" (ll.146–49).

At Rhodes, Brusor and his army deliver the same ultimatum used by Tamburlaine in Marlowe's plays. When the Rhodians defy the Turkish demands, they are utterly defeated. The governor and his son are killed, and the surviving male prisoners are asked if they will turn Turk. When they refuse, Brusor orders his men to "stab the slaves, and send their soules to hell" (3.5.9). Only Basilisco takes up the offer to convert and live, crying "I turne, I turne; oh, save my life I turne" (l.10). He gives this rationale for doing so: "Think you I turne Turque for feare of servile death that's but a sport? I' faith, sir, no; / Tis for Perseda, whom I love so well / That I would follow her though she went to hell" (ll.13–16). Again, religious conversion is given an erotic motive, though here with derisive irony, but Basilisco is a parodic, degraded version of the Christian hero (like Ward in *A Christian Turned Turk* or Vitelli in *The Renegado*) who turns for love of a Muslim woman.[8]

While the male prisoners are forced to choose between death and conversion, the women are taken to join the sultan's seraglio, where they must decide between death and sexual dishonor. Male captives, if they convert, are potential servants and abettors of Islamic power; the female captives are taken to serve the sexual needs of the same masculine force. When Erastus predicts the fall of Rhodes, his words associate the captive body of Perseda with the captive island: "And Rhodes it selfe is lost, or els destroyde; / If not destroide, yet bound and captivate; / If captivate, then forst from holy faith" (4.1.17–19). When Perseda and Lucina arrive as captives at the sultan's court, Soliman greets them lecherously, asking "what two Christian Virgins have we here?" (4.1.63). Christian purity is gendered as a feminine virtue, embodied by Perseda. She is threatened by an eroticized Islamic empire that is able to capture, possess, convert, and contaminate by means of its potent, masculine capability. At the same time, Kyd's play gives us a Turkish potentate whose extreme masculinity produces its own fear of contamination. The sultan can vent his excess of lust through the many partners of the harem, but to love one other becomes a sign of weakness.

Like Shakespeare's Othello and Goffe's Amurath, Kyd's Soliman exhibits the standard "Turkish" qualities of jealousy and lust. Following the conventional story of "The Sultan and the Fair Greek," Soliman falls in love with Perseda, a beautiful Christian captive. Like Amurath, Soliman feels weakened and effeminated by his feelings for her: "Love never tainted Solyman till now" (4.1.87), he admits. Soliman pressures her to "turn" sexually, and when Perseda rebuffs his offers of pleasure and favor, Soliman threatens her with death, telling Perseda to "kneele thou downe, / And at my hands receive the stroake of death" (ll.109–10). Soliman's masculine resolve is sorely tested, and he is not able to do what Goffe's Amurath did. He asks Brusor to cover Perseda with a cloth of fine lawn, so that her beauty will not deter him from executing her, but the sultan is unable to go through with the killing. "Love would not let me kill thee" (l.131) he confesses, and then grants Perseda's request to "live a Christian virgin still" (l.140). Having exhibited the precipitation of his dual passion (lascivious and murderous), Soliman berates himself: "What should he do with crowne and Emperie / That cannot governe private fond affections?" (ll.143–44). Here, Christian resistance to Islamic power is figured in Perseda's refusal to submit to the sultan's sexual aggression. In the Mediterranean along the unstable border between Islam and Christendom, in places like Cyprus or Rhodes, erotic infidelity is linked to religious conversion. According to this logic, the enduring love of Erastus and Perseda represents a model of resistance to Islamic tyranny.

After Soliman decides not to execute Perseda, Erastus enters and is recognized by Perseda. Just as Soliman determines to "spare" Rhodes "From spoile, pillage, and oppression" (4.1.53–54) for Erastus's sake, so does he agree to let Erastus marry Perseda, sparing her from his aroused lust. The sultan's unruly and omnivorous desire does not distinguish between genders: Soliman says that Erastus is his "other best beloved" (l.153) and declares "I love them both, I know not which the better" (l.169). The sultan represses his passion for both Erastus and Perseda and sends them away immediately to rule as governor and governor's wife in the island of Rhodes. When the Cypriot knight marries Perseda and the couple departs for Rhodes, Soliman is left among his eunuchs and "minions." In public, Soliman behaves honorably, but later he cannot endure "That I shall love her still, and lack her still, / Like ever thirsting, wretched Tantalus" (ll.215–16). Soliman plots privately with Brusor to bring Erastus back from Rhodes and have him killed. Until the arrival of Perseda at the Ottoman court, Soliman had seemed to be a noble, virtuous Muslim (like Othello, "the noble Moor"), but after his passions are inflamed by Perseda, Soliman "turns Turk." Moved by a lustful, jealous nature, he reveals his true colors (like Othello). Again, we witness the emblematic scene of the conqueror conquered by his own passion, a lust that can never be satisfied.

Erastus is summoned back to Constantinople, where the sultan and Brusor stage a false trial and have Erastus executed on trumped up charges of treason. Though "I deerely love" Erastus, says Soliman, "Yet must his bloud be spilt" (5.2.12–13). Two false witnesses swear on the Koran and then deliver their concocted tale to the court while Soliman watches unseen from above. Erastus assumes that his friend the sultan will clear him of the accusation and save his life with a last-minute reprieve, and in this regard the scene resembles the execution of Pedringano in Kyd's other surviving play, *The Spanish Tragedy*. The sultan speaks an aside, "O unjust Soliman; O wicked time, / Where filthie lust must murther honest love" (ll.84–85), and then Erastus is strangled onstage by two janissaries.

The irrational excess and emotional instability of the sultan is confirmed yet again when, immediately after ordering Erastus's execution, Soliman regrets doing so and commands the death of the two janissaries who strangled him, the two witnesses he hired to testify falsely against Erastus, and the Lord Marshall who sat in judgment at the trial. This, the play shows its audience, is what it means to deal with the Great Turk. These scenes function, at one level, as warnings about the English alliance with the Turkish sultanate. Just as Erastus was forced to join the Ottoman court because he was threatened at home by his fellow Christians, so Elizabeth I was obliged to seek an alliance with the Ottoman Turks when she was under the threat of invasion by Spanish power. Although the exact dating of *Soliman and Perseda* is uncertain, I concur with John J. Murray's estimate, which places its original composition in the period 1585–89, precisely the period when Elizabeth was allying herself most closely with the Ottoman empire and the Moroccan sultanate, in her effort to find partners in the struggle against Spanish-Catholic hegemony.[9]

Soliman's excessive passions are as inconstant as the changing allegiances of the braggart Italian knight Basilisco, who turns Turk to save his life and then returns to the Christian fold in order to gain the favor of Perseda, whom he foolishly follows and hopelessly woos. Jonathan Burton (2002) has argued that in the deployment of stage clowns like Basilisco (or Clem in *The Fair Maid of the West* and Gazet in *The Renegado*) the authors of English conversion plays "used comedy... to mediate what was arguably the most disturbing aspect of Anglo-Islamic relations, the threat of 'turning Turk'" (52). "In the

case of 'turning Turk,'" argues Burton (2002), "the comic is a transformative mechanism by which apostasy itself is converted" (51).
Playwrights like Kyd, Heywood, and Massinger stimulated audience
anxiety about conversion to Islam but then offered relief from that
threat by making conversion the choice of a fool who then becomes
the object of laughter and ridicule.

Basilisco undergoes his rite of conversion in Constantinople, the
center of Ottoman power. He boasts that "The Turkes...in procession bare me to the Church, as I had beene a second Mahomet"
(4.2.8–11) and here, in a comic vein, the text deploys various
European myths about Islam, including the charge of euhemerism
that Christian polemicists raised against Muslims who were said to
have deified Muhammed:

> I, fearing they would adore me for a God, wisely informd them that I was
> but man, although in time perhaps I might aspire to purchase God head,
> as did Hercules; I meane by doing wonders in the world. Amidst their
> Church they bound me to a piller, and to make triall of my valiancie, they
> lopt a collop of my tendrest member. That doone, they set me on a milke
> white Asse, compasing me with goodly ceremonies. (4.2.8–17)

Basilisco's ridiculous pride is associated with the supposed absurdities
of Islamic practice and belief, and the audience is invited to laugh
away their fear of being converted and (for the male members of the
audience) circumcised or even castrated.

After he has turned Turk, Basilisco is asked if he prefers his new
status to the old:

> Perseda. Now, signior Basilisco, which like you, the
>   Turkish or our nation best?
> Basilisco. That which your ladiship will have me like.
> Perseda. I am deceived but you were circumcised.
> Basilisco. Indeed I was a little cut in the porpuse. (5.3.1–5)[10]

Perseda draws attention to the fact that circumcision is a permanent
step, and that it will continue to mark Basilisco's body with the act of
apostasy, even if the renegade wishes to be reinstated as a Christian.
Through wordplay about circumcision, religious conversion is linked
to an erotic "porpuse" (meaning both "prepuce" and "purpose").
Lucina (who plays the "bad girl" to the chaste and virtuous Perseda)
continues the bawdy badinage by equating Basilisco's loss of his foreskin with his missing turban: "...how chance your turkish bonnet is
not on your head?" (ll.12–13). The fastidious Basilisco answers,

"Because I now am Christian againe, and by that naturall meanes; for as the old Cannon saies verie pretily: *Nihil est tam naturale, quod eo modo colligatum est*, and so foorth; so I became a Turke to follow her; to follow her, am now returnd a Christian" (5.3.14–18). Here, and in the later conversion plays, exotic apparel, which was certainly part of the outlandish appeal of these plays when performed, is a prominent outward sign of one who has turned Turk (corresponding to the hidden mark of the missing foreskin). Converts traded a "collop" of their "tendrest member" for Turkish garb, which would include a turban and a robe.[11] On the London stage, these costumes would be made from expensive fabric, perhaps using imported silks obtained in the Levant trade.

After Basilisco has shed both his foreskin and his turban, the scene suddenly turns serious as the news of Erastus's unjust execution reaches Rhodes. Perseda, like Bel-Imperia (who played the part of Perseda in *The Spanish Tragedy*'s masque), calls for revenge, asking the emasculated Basilisco to stab Lucina, and when he demurs she grabs the dagger and kills Lucina for her part in the fatal plot against Erastus.

In the play's final scene, Soliman comes to Rhodes to take possession of the city and of Perseda, who has rallied the citizens against the invading Ottoman force. Again, when Soliman sets out to conquer Perseda at Rhodes, military violence and masculine lust are combined. "The gates are shut; which prooves that Rhodes revolts" (5.4.1), grumbles Soliman in a line that equates Perseda's chaste body with the walled city, closed off from Turkish-sexual violation and penetration. When Soliman sounds a parley, Perseda "*comes upon the walles in mans apparell*" (5.4.15) where she hears Soliman declare himself "Lord of all the world" (5.4.19). The play implies that when venturing Christian knights like Erastus or Basilisco turn and serve Islamic masters, it is a virtuous woman like Perseda who must take on a masculine role in order to defend Christendom. Thus, Perseda's sexual purity figures the religious and political independence of the Christian polity, when it is threatened by Islamic power. Since she will not willingly give herself or the city to Soliman, the Turks must undertake a rape. This symbolic rape is represented when the cross-dressed Perseda challenges Soliman to personal combat and taunts him from above, calling him "wicked tirant," and "accursed homicide, / For whome hell gapes" (ll.36–38). Perseda's diatribe against Soliman is an attack on patriarchal rule, its hypocrisies and double standards. This sort of speech, targeting powerful men who betray virtuous men and women in order to serve their own sexual passions, appears in several of these Islamic conversion plays: Emilia to the

Moor in *Othello*, Alizia to Ward in *A Christian Turned Turk*, and Donusa to Asambeg in *The Renegado*. These Christian women speak truth to patriarchal power, targeting an "Islamic" form of the raging male libido. In *Othello* and *A Christian Turned Turk*, frustrated misogyny is given a "Turkish" identity. These two plays provide an onstage suicide as the last desperate act of their protagonists, Ward and Othello, renegade figures whose unstable apostatical identity marks them as suitable scapegoats for the more generalized target of the plays' critique, which is patriarchal oppression. In *The Renegado*, Asembeg does not kill himself on stage, but his acceptance of the Ottoman sultan's inevitable death sentence is tantamount to suicide. Asembeg's final speech announces his own death wish and predicts his imminent demise, either at the hands of his "incensed master" (5.8.34), the Ottoman sultan, or after his withdrawal to "the deserts, or some cave filled with my shame and me, where I alone / May die without a partner in my moan" (5.8.37–39).

In Kyd's play the central exotic figure does not kill himself, but Soliman does suffer a death that he acknowledges to be deserved. Provoked to fury by her accusations, Soliman slays Perseda, completing the symbolic murder/rape of the woman he loves (compare Othello's murder of Desdemona, and Ward's murder of Agar). Like Othello, Soliman then kisses the woman he has loved and killed, but in this case, she has prepared her lips with poison and so Soliman dies, too. Before he expires, Soliman (again, sounding much like Othello) employs imagery of deflowering in order to describe Perseda's death at his hands: "Faire springing rose, ill pluckt before thy time" (l.81), and like the Moor he regrets his actions: "the heavens did never more accurse me / Then when they made me Butcher of my love" (ll.90–91). Finally, Brusor, who like Iago conspires falsely against his trusty, virtuous comrade, is taken away to be beheaded. Soliman's parting words to Brusor sound like Othello's final questioning of Iago: "How durst thou then, ungratious Counseller, / First cause me murther such a worthy man, / And after tempt so vertuous a woman?" (ll.107–09). In this regard, Othello's victims, Cassio and Desdemona, fit the mold of Erastus and Perseda. All of these connections between *Soliman and Perseda* and *Othello* indicate, if not the direct influence of Kyd's earlier play on Shakespeare's later one, then at least that both playwrights drew upon a common model, a basic anti-Islamic narrative in which Islamic cruelty and masculine tyranny destroy Christian virtue and feminine innocence.

In the final scene of Kyd's play, the Turkish emperor calls for a general slaughter of the defeated Rhodians and then expires, killed by the poison on Perseda's lips. Soliman commands that he be buried together in a common grave with Perseda and Erastus, and then begs forgiveness just before he succumbs, burning up like Tamburlaine:

> The poison is disperst through every vaine,
> And boiles, like Etna, in my frying guts.
> Forgive me, deere Erastus, my unkindnes.
> I have revenged thy death with many deaths; (ll.143–46)

Conquered at last by his own lust, Kyd's Soliman is, in many ways, a typical example of the Islamic tyrant, as that figure was described in the Western anti-Islamic tradition that goes back to the medieval period.[12] This stereotypical portrayal of Muslim despotism is given new meaning, however, by the multicultural milieu that provides the setting for *Soliman and Perseda*. The old, demonized tyrant figure is still there at the center of the drama, but a new sense of instability and convertibility places the old polar oppositions of East and West into question as characters like Erastus and Basilisco move back and forth through a Mediterranean border zone that includes Rhodes and Cyprus. These transcultural characters take on a new identity that is mixed and mobile rather than fixed and stable.

* * *

In his book *The Sultan's Court*, Alain Grosrichard claims that the seraglio is "the supreme tragic site," and "the site of absolute power... invested with sexuality" (124), and in many texts it functions as a deadly place. Othello and Desdemona's bedchamber in Cyprus is one version of this tragic site; Soliman's court is another. But it is not always represented as a fatal trap from which there is no escape. In Thomas Heywood's *Fair Maid of the West, Part I*, the seraglio is the place that the play's protagonists, Bess and Spencer, reach at the furthest extent of their adventures. In Heywood's first *Fair Maid* play, nationalistic, commercial energies carry the play's heroes out of harm's way; and in the sequel, Bess and Spencer escape from the clutches of the Moroccan sultan, Mullisheg.

The Fair Maid of the West, Part I, moves from Plymouth and the maritime coast of England's West Country, into Spanish territory and the Azores, and on to Mamorah in "Barbary." The play was first performed at the end of a long period of war with Spain, and its action makes reference to the post-Armada raids on Spanish targets, especially the English attack on Cadiz led by Essex in 1596. At this time of Anglo-Spanish conflict, the English traded diplomatic missions with the Moroccan court and allied themselves with the Moroccan kings (who were Muslim but ruled independently, outside of Ottoman sovereignty). Atlantic and Mediterranean piracy is also an important context for this play, and the text clearly represents the way that piracy, privateering, and warfare were combined in the economic expansion of England's overseas trade to the violent context of the Mediterranean, where Spanish ships, Moorish courtiers, and Italian banditti all posed threats.

The Fair Maid of the West retains some elements of the neo-chivalric romance form that defines *Soliman and Perseda*, but its comic adventure genre and its deployment of commercial and nationalistic discourses reveal new signs of England's changing identity at the turn of the century. Jean E. Howard's analysis of *Fair Maid* takes the play as a case study that demonstrates "how gender, race, sexuality, and national identity were interarticulated in productions of the public playhouse in the twilight years of Elizabeth's reign or shortly thereafter" (102). Howard is interested in how the play's "English-Spanish binarism" is complicated by "a third term—the Moor" in order "to construct a field of racial and sexual difference which at once situates the Moors as subordinate to their English trading partners and allays the anxieties about castration, female power, and female sexuality occasioned by Bess Bridges..." (102).

As Howard's remarks indicate, Heywood's *Fair Maid* complicates the binary opposition between Englishness and foreign identity by creating an imaginary space that is inhabited by a variety of shifting, competing cultures. These commercial and erotic competitors (English, Spanish, Moorish, Italian) learn from each other, and by cooperating with and emulating each other, they sometimes come to resemble one another. This process of imitation or "cultural mimesis," which affected profoundly the formation of English national identity, is explored by Barbara Fuchs in *Mimesis and Empire: The New World, Islam and European Identities.*[13] Fuchs claims, "it was not always easy to distinguish Islamic other from Christian self" (3), but the binary framework in which she presents the issue of an unstable Christian identity is perhaps an inadequate paradigm for properly understanding this cultural exchange. Fuchs effectively demonstrates that this confusion of "Islamic other" and "Christian self" often begins with a mimetic, symmetrical reversal—pirate for privateer, Christian for Muslim, English for Turk—but Fuchs's analysis stops there. English identity was not simply a matter of looking in the strange mirror of the Other and seeing its Self reflected there. Rather, its speculation in Mediterranean affairs and commodities was prismatic, split into multiple identities, images, and representations that comprise a bewildering play of similarity and difference. Islam cannot be singled out or treated in our historical analysis as a monolithic entity. As I have been arguing, "Islam" or "Turkishness" was a layered conglomeration that enfolded Christians, Jews, Muslims, and renegades within a sprawling and expanding cultural mix. Though many English descriptions of Islam do employ binary, Manichean terms to contrast Christian virtue with alleged Muslim evil, these binaries do not remain stable and there are many English representations that depicted early modern Islam as a heterogeneous culture. When, on the other hand, Fuchs refers to "mimesis" as "the deliberate representation of sameness" (3) or "the intentionality, the power dynamics, and the political consequences of pointed imitation" in "the culture at large" (3), and when she recounts how "the very distinctions on which imperial ideology depends are trumped by the production of simulacra, facsimiles, or counterfeits within the text of colonial culture" (3), then Fuchs provides a useful account of how English texts that represented foreign culture could challenge and disrupt the purity or coherence of English identity through a disorienting play of sameness and difference that was not restricted to a binary identity formation. Fuchs's application of Taussig's concept of "cultural mimesis" moves from a polarized duality toward a dialectic relation of self and other (Fuchs cites Taussig: "The self enters into the alter against which the self is defined and sustained." [5]), but this psychological structuralism remains limited by its dualism.

Pursuing the notion of cultural mimesis, Fuchs comments on "the odd closeness between the English and the Moors, a proximity that corresponds not only to the historical contacts between England and Morocco in the period but, more significantly, to the text's othering of the English themselves" (132). This "closeness" is another representation of how the English were "turning Turk." This is seen in the way that Bess, cross-dressed as a male sailor, recruits a crew and equips a pitch-blackened vessel called the *Negro* as a privateer that sails the Mediterranean and "makes spoil / Of the rich Spaniard and the barbarous Turk" (4.5.7–8). After all, the maritime economy represented in the play includes ports in southwest England where men made a living in the same manner as the Muslim and renegade corsairs of North Africa: they "seek abroad for pillage" (1.2.8).

At the beginning of the play, Bess Bridges's employment as a tavern maid in Plymouth allows for a series of scenes in which Bess's virtue is put to the test because her job in the tavern puts her reputation, and at times her virginity, in danger. In the play's early scenes, she is put on public display in an English marketplace where imported goods, brought from the Mediterranean, are also bought and sold. The Windmill, a tavern in the Cornish harbor town of Foy, is owned by Bess's love, Spencer, who places her in charge when he joins an English expedition against the port of Fayal in the Spanish Azores. The Windmill is a place where, according to Bess, "they vent many brave commodities by which some gain accrues. Th'are my good customers, and still return me profit" (2.1.54–56). In these early tavern scenes featuring Bess, the implication of prostitution is ever-present. When Roughman threatens to accost Bess, he compares her to a ship that he will plunder, employing an analogy that likens her body to a ship full of cargo: "I must know of what burden this vessel is. I shall not bear with her till she bear with me" (2.1.19–20). Roughman hopes that Bess is for sale, or at least subject to plunder, but what is for sale is imported, not English. Bess's apprentice tapster, Clem, offers his customers a long list of wines obtained from Spain, Madeira, Bordeaux, and Greece. These imported commodities are fetishized, and the play makes clear that England's domestic economy relies on trade and plunder abroad. Spencer's profitable tavern business, which the aldermen and mayor of Foy eye greedily, depends on spoil, and in this context piracy, trade, and prostitution are linked through a shared sense of cultural openness to foreign goods and influences.

A character called Goodlack tests Bess's patience by calling her a "whore" and pretending to believe this must be the case because of her free and open behavior among her customers at the tavern. Bess's public identity, potentially tainted by the promiscuity necessary for trade, stands for the virtue of the English nation. National purity is threatened with contamination by the intrusion of imported goods, and by the behavior of pillaging sailors who are drunk on imported wine. In a series of scenes that follow, Bess is repeatedly subject to foreign threats: by contact with foreign men on a Spanish ship, then at the Moorish court in Mamorah, and finally in Italy where a bandit attempts to rape her and a Florentine nobleman attempts to seduce her.

When Bess is told that her love Spencer has been killed by Spanish enemies, she becomes a privateer in order to avenge his death. After defeating a Spanish "man-of-war," Bess discovers that this ship had previously "surpris'd, / Pillag'd, and captiv'd" an English merchant vessel of London, "bound for Barbary" (4.4.125–27). When the English captives from this ship are freed by Bess, Spencer is among them. A reunion is foiled, however, when a series of misfortunes prevents Bess from confirming that it is Spencer, and not, as she initially thinks, Spencer's ghost. The English merchant sails immediately for Mamorah in Morocco, and later Bess and the *Negro* also go there,

"forc'd for want of water / To put into Mamorah in Barbary"
(4.5.10–11). There they are finally reunited, but Bess's virtue is
tested again at the court of the Moroccan sultan, Mullisheg.

In Mamorah, Bess is received hospitably by Mullisheg, who has
already been introduced to the audience in a scene that shows him to
be the stereotypical Islamic ruler, one who has taken absolute control
over his slave-like subjects after a bloody civil war. Speaking to his
assembled court, Mullisheg announces:

> Upon the slaughtered bodies of our foes,
> We mount out high tribunal, and being sole,
> Without competitor, we now have leisure
> To 'stablish laws, first for our kingdom's safety,
> The enriching of our public treasury,
> And last our state and pleasure. (4.3.11–15)

It is the last of these, his "pleasure," that overrides all other motives.
Mullisheg plans to stock his harem with a variety of female commodities, and Christian women are at the top of his wish list:

> 　　　　　　　　　Find us concubines,
> The fairest Christian damsels you can hire
> Or buy for gold, the loveliest of the Moors
> We can command, and Negroes everywhere.
> Italians, French, and Dutch, choice Turkish girls...(4.3.28–32)

He also decrees that "all such Christian merchants as have traffic /
And freedom in our country, that conceal / The least part of our custom due to us, / Shall forfeit ship and goods" (4.3.16–19). These
lines refer to the very real economic superiority and political power
that Muslim port authorities wielded when dealing with English merchants who traded in North Africa. English traders were in no position to intimidate the officials with whom they dealt in places like
Mamorah. Instead they had to negotiate.

Bess arrives in Mamorah, and when Mullisheg, "That ne'er before
had English lady seen" (4.5.15), is informed that she is aboard the
Negro, he expresses his hope that "she in a *Negro* / Hath sail'd thus
far to bosom with a Moor" (5.1.8–9). When he asks her to attend his
royal presence, she accepts but appears at first in a veil. When she
unveils, Mullisheg is ravished by her exotic beauty:

> 　　　　　　　I am amaz'd!
> This is no mortal creature I behold,

But some bright angel dropped from heaven,
Sent by our prophet. (5.1.33–36)

He then orders gold to be given to Goodlack, Spenser's friend and now the captain of Bess's ship, mistakenly believing that Goodlack is selling Bess to him. Bess speaks up, claiming that her "followers want no gold" (l.39), showing that she is in charge, and telling the king, when he asks to touch her, to "Keep off; for till thou swear'st to my demands, / I will have no commerce with Mullisheg" (ll.46–47). He agrees to her conditions; a contract is negotiated. This negotiation between a Moroccan prince and a masculinized Englishwoman named Bess offers an imaginary version of the Anglo-Moroccan and Anglo-Ottoman trade agreements. Mullisheg compares her to Elizabeth I, "the virgin queen, so famous throughout the world, / The mighty empress of the maiden isle" (5.1.89–90). Bess, like Queen Elizabeth, is trafficking with the Turk, and this commercial contact, which is given sexual significance, seems almost to convince Bess to "turn Turk." She agrees to kiss Mullisheg and then after doing so joins him "in state" on his throne, risking contamination in order to gain his favor, just as she risked reputation by serving wine and kissing men in the tavern in Plymouth.

The message is the same in both the West Country and the East Country—morally questionable forms of foreign exchange become acceptable when profits can be made. Turning Turk means selling oneself, and Bess, the "girl worth gold," knows how to display her goods to her financial advantage without giving up her virginity. Whether trading with the lustful Muslim rulers or selling wine to horny sailors, Bess preserves her chastity. Her exchange with Mullisheg is a microcosmic version of England's trade in Barbary and with Muslims, and thus the text indicates England's newly promiscuous status in the Mediterranean economy.

Bess's relationship with Mullisheg, and the influence she exercises over the king, benefits the Christians at the Moroccan court. Because of the king's favor, Bess is also able to empower Clem, who enters the Moorish court. He is cross-culturally dressed, like the converted Basilisco, in what must have been a comically overdone "Moorish" costume. Clem's first words are a version of the opening lines of Kyd's *Spanish Tragedy*. He says, " 'It is not now as Andrea liv'd,'—or rather Andrew, our elder journeyman. What, drawers become courtiers?" (5.1.110–11). Clem's hospitable reception at the Moorish court mocks the ability of English nouveau riche merchants to get rich quick by trading with infidels in the Mediterranean. Like Simon Eyre in Dekker's

The Shoemaker's Holiday, who claims to know "how to speak to a Pope, to Sultan Soliman, to Tamburlaine, an he were here" (5.4.90–91), Clem represents the transgressive social-climbing accomplished by middle-class merchants who traded in foreign luxury goods. In an absurd variation on the theme of performative self-fashioning, Clem realizes, through theatrical role-playing, the fantasy of becoming a wealthy courtier. His new status is laughable, and his pretensions are comic, but he is a degraded version of the real English factors, agents, and go-betweens (like the Sherley brothers) who tried to make a career for themselves in Mediterranean courts. Clem himself expresses some anxiety about the potential dangers of going native: he knows that the other Christians may suspect him of converting to Islam, and so he tells them, "Nay, for mine own part, I hold myself as good a Christian in these clothes as the proudest infidel of them all" (5.1.118–19).

With Bess on his side, Clem is able to act as agent for two merchants, a Frenchman and an Italian. He helps the one to regain a ship and goods that were confiscated by Mullisheg, and the other to obtain the release of his men, whom the Moorish king had sentenced to serve as galley slaves. These are exactly the sort of transactions that were nego-tiated by English ambassadors and agents like William Harborne in Constantinople and John Harrison in Morocco.[14]

Clem is too simple to distinguish the Italians from the Moors—they are all exotic to him. When he asks the Italian, "What are you, sir?" the answer is "A Florentine merchant," to which Clem replies with another question: "Then you are, as they say, a Christian?" (l.150). "Heaven forbid else" (l.151), responds the merchant. Clem's confusion parodies the perplexity experienced by Englishmen who were faced, during voyages overseas and in the theater, with a variety of alien peoples whose differences they could not easily identify or distinguish, and with a Mediterranean culture where Italians and Moors might have more in common than an English Protestant tap-ster from Plymouth and a Roman Catholic merchant from Florence.

In the final scene of *The Fair Maid of the West, Part I*, Spencer arrives at the Moorish court because the English merchant with whom he was sailing, "Hath by a cunning quiddit in the law / Both ship and goods made forfeit to the king" (5.2.3–4). Spencer appears at a royal audience, hoping to gain redress for this injustice. Mullisheg, who at this point has come to exemplify the conventional type of the doting sultan, ruled by his love for a beautiful Christian woman, grants, at Bess's behest, the petition of Clem for his merchants' causes. Clem then brings in "A Christian preacher, one that would convert / Your Moors and turn them to a new belief" (5.2.73–74), whom Mullisheg immediately condemns to death. Bess kneels and begs his pardon, and the king says "we can deny thee nothing, beauteous maid. / A kiss shall be his pardon" (ll.78–79). Spencer enters at this point, just as Mullisheg declares, "That kiss was worth the ransom of a king" (l.86). At this point, it appears to Spencer that Bess has turned Turk and become the Moorish king's minion in exchange for a life of power, wealth, and luxury. Mullisheg then sees Spencer enter, and when Bess introduces him as "a gentlemen of England and my friend" (5.2.88), the jealous Mullisheg accedes to Bess's request to "do him some grace" (l.89) by giving an order to "see him gelded to attend on us. He shall be our chief eunuch" (ll.92–93). Bess cries, "Not for ten worlds!" (l.94), and then Clem offers to take on the honor that Bess has refused for Spencer. "Go, bear him hence," says Mullisheg, "Honor him, / And let him taste the razor" (ll.102–03). Clem soon returns, running from a razor-wielding Moor. "Is this your Moorish preferment," he cries, "to rob a man of his best jewels?" (ll.126–27). The kiss that Bess receives from Mullisheg is juxtaposed with the cut that Clem is given at Mullisheg's behest.

Like Basilisco's conversion at the court of Soliman, Clem's effort to obtain preferment from a Muslim ruler gets him into trouble. But Clem is not merely circumcised—the Muslims get more than just a "collop" from him. Thinking that being "gelded" implies an offer of gold, wealth, and preferment, Clem goes off to be castrated. Howard reads this as "a grotesquely hideous warning of the dangers of going native" (115). It is a comic moment that literalizes English anxieties about the effemination that would allegedly result from contact with Islamic culture. If he becomes too much like a Turk or Moor, Heywood's play suggests, the English venturer will lose his English, masculine identity. When Clem laments that his castrators have "tickled" his "current commodity" (l.130), the phrase refers to currants, a commodity imported to England in large quantities from the Mediterranean. At the same time, Clem puns on the meaning of "current" as testicle, and the line also refers to the rapid circulation or exchange of highly salable goods. In this comic incident, and in various ways throughout the play, the commercial continues to be associated with the erotic or the sexual.

Clem's cross-cultural experience is a painful one, but the play ends more happily for Bess and Spencer. They appeal to Mullisheg's mercy, and much like the scene in which Soliman allows Erastus to marry Perseda, the Muslim tyrant relents and allows the couple to be united. Clem's comic castration becomes the object of laughter that works to dissolve some of the anxiety and tension raised by the possibility of Bess's turning Turk.

Twenty-five years after the first *Fair Maid* play was composed, Heywood wrote a sequel in which he returned to the moment when Mullisheg was convinced, by the virtue of the young English couple, Bess and Spencer, to allow for their marriage. At the beginning of the sequel, however, Mullisheg reverts to his stereotypical identity, returning to his essential nature and demonstrating the unstable and arbitrary passion of the demonized Muslim ruler. The fantasy of the Islamic king's willing subordination to those who represent Christian honor and virtue is replaced by the fantasy of the jealous, lustful sultan who always puts passion before reason, honor, or the law. In a soliloquy at the beginning of the sequel, Mullisheg redefines himself according to the logic of the seraglio. He declares, "I should commit high treason against myself / Not to do that might give my soul content / And satisfy my soul with fulness" (1.1.237–39). Just as Kyd's Soliman regrets allowing Perseda and Erastus to marry, Mullisheg wishes that he had not permitted the marriage of Bess and Spencer. Both Muslim monarchs decide that, in spite of honor or justice, they must have the play's central objects of desire, Perseda and Bess, for themselves. The European representation of Islamic power nearly always depicts the sultan or basha as one who directs matters of state according to the priorities of personal passion, and not for the good of his subjects. This is the point of vulnerability that, in many fictional narratives, Christians can exploit. By playing on the uncontrollable passions of the "Great Turk," the European who is at his mercy can find ways to outwit him and escape his clutches. This is precisely what happens in Heywood's sequel.

The Fair Maid of the West, Part II, begins with the entrance of a Black Queen of the East—Tota, queen of Fez. Played by a boy actor in blackface make-up, Tota enters solus, raging about how Mullisheg has neglected her since the advent of Bess at the Moorish court. She plots her revenge with Roughman, one of Bess's swaggering followers, and arranges a sexual tryst with Spencer that she hopes will cuckold Mullisheg and spoil the marriage before it is consummated. Tota offers to "crown" Roughman "with excess" (1.1.182), and when he agrees to help her, she bribes him with gold. After Tota and Roughman seal their bargain, Mullisheg singles out Goodlack and asks him to help bring Bess to his bed. The sultan of Mamorah offers to make Goodlack "a viceroy / And a king's minion" (1.1.335–36) if he will assist in this scheme. Goodlack's initial reaction to this proposed plot is disgust: he asks, "Who but a Moor, / Of all that bears man's shape likest a devil, / Could have devis'd this horror?" (ll.328–30), but he is tempted and soon agrees to aid Mullisheg. Both Roughman and Goodlack are threatened with death if they do not cooperate. It appears that these two Englishmen, fearing the sultan's threats and tempted by the offer of wealth and power, are about to turn Turk. In the end, the two Englishmen confer and then collaborate in planning a bed-trick whereby Tota and Mullisheg are led separately into a dark room where they have sex, each thinking that they are enjoying an exotic English lover. Part of the joke here is that the two dark-skinned Moors cannot see, in the dark, that their sexual partner is as black as they are.

Believing that she has satisfied her desire for an English lover, Tota declares,

> Were I again to match, I'd marry one
> Of this brave nation, if a gentleman,
> Before the greatest monarch of the world,
> They are such sweet and loving bedfellows. (3.1.5–8)

And the dramatic irony continues in Mullisheg's praise for his partner:

> Venetian ladies, nor the Persian girls,
> The French, the Spanish, not the Turkish dames,
> Ethiope, nor Greece can kiss with half that art
> These English can ... (ll.13–16)

The scene advertises the omnivorous libido of the seraglio, but gives the English the last laugh, as they escape from Mamorah. The trick played on the royal couple develops further the theme of cultural competition, which here is put in terms of sexual performance.

In the rest of the play, it is the performance of cultural competition that holds the episodic plot together. Goodlack remarks on this cross-cultural contact: " 'Tis the greatest benefits of all our travels / To see foreign courts and to discourse their fashions" (4.5.22–23). The English characters are repeatedly tested by foreign powers. In most cases the test functions to define English virtue in contrast to the others, but interestingly in the intense rivalry between Spencer and a Moroccan courtier named Joffer, the Moor and the Englishman end up as homologous rivals, and not as the exemplars of opposing codes.

When Bess and the other English characters slip away from Mamorah in the *Negro*, Spencer arranges to join them later, and he tells Bess that if he does not make it, she can assume that he died in the attempt. After a courageous single-handed fight, Spencer is caught while escaping from the city by the Moorish basha Joffer, but the Moor allows Spencer to row out to the ship to tell Bess that he is still alive on the condition that he will return immediately and face the wrath of

Mullisheg. Once Spencer is on board the *Negro*, he tells his countrymen that Joffer "left himself in hostage / To give me my desires"
(3.2.118–19), and Goodlack responds, " 'Twas nobly done. / But
what's the lives of twenty thousand Moors / To one that's Christian?"
(ll.119–21). Bess begs him to stay and save his life, but Spencer
refuses, asking her, "Shall Fez report / Unto our country's shame and
to the scandal / Of our religion that a barbarous Moor / Can exceed
us in nobleness?" (ll.132–35). Later, Spencer calls this potential
shame a "black dishonor," but Joffer, for his part, tells the king that
"If [Spencer] comes not, / Be this mine honor, King: that though I
bleed, / A Moor a Christian thus far did exceed" (3.3.32–34). When
Spencer keeps his word and arrives at the court in time to save Joffer
from execution, Mullisheg marvels at Spencer's chivalric one-upman-
ship, and at the fact that the English, scorning the gifts obtained earlier from Mullisheg, left the gold and jewels they had received behind.
Spencer defies the king and tells him,

> Wert thou the king of all the kings on earth,
> Couldst thou lay all their scepters, robes, and crowns
> Her at my feet, and hadst power to install me
> Emperor of the universal empery,
> Rather than yield my basest ship boy up
> To become thy slave...[,]
>   know, King
> Of Fez, I'd die a hundred thousand deaths first. (ll.87–94)

When Bess returns and begs Mullisheg for Spencer's life, Mullisheg
refuses to be bested in the honor contest. The king of Fez decides to
match their valor with his own "virtuous deeds" (l.140). "These
English are in all things honorable" (l.151), he marvels. Ironically,
Mullisheg bestows on the English "double the magazine" (l.182) that
they had received before. These representations of Anglo-Moroccan
interaction and negotiation evoke, then deflect, anxieties about trading with foreign powers in the Mediterranean. In *The Fair Maid of the
West*, mercantile gain through trade is represented as feudal largess,
bestowed as a reward in a competition for noble status, not commodities. In 1630, when Heywood composed his sequel, this aristocratic fantasy was further than ever from the real circumstances of
English relations with Mediterranean Muslims. English factors in
places like Tunis and Aleppo were willingly kow-towing to Muslim
officials in order to get their hands on the luxury goods that they
could sell at a profit back home. Spencer's protestations, and his

holier-than-thou rejection of the hypothetical gift of "universal empery," are anxious attempts to conceal or repress an envious English desire for imperial possession. Through his cavalier dismissal of Mullisheg's filthy lucre and expression of scorn for Islamic power, Spencer conveys the attitude that Barbara Fuchs (2001) has seen as central to both *The Fair Maid* and *The Renegado*: "the general English reluctance to abandon the aristocratic masculinity of the privateers in favor of a more fluid and performative mercantile model" (11).

The remainder of the second *Fair Maid* play deploys an episodic adventure narrative that carries the characters through a series of separations and reunions that figure the disorientation experienced by English subjects who traveled to the multicultural Mediterranean. The English characters are separated and scattered, then reunited in Italy, where they hire themselves out, mercenary-like, in the employ of various Italian lords. Bess is taken in by the duke of Florence, who then replays the role of Mullisheg when he relinquishes his lecherous claim to Bess and allows her to be reunited once again with Spencer. Earlier, Goodlack had warned Spencer to "Beware of these Italians. / They are by nature jealous and revengeful, / Not sparing the most basest opportunity / That may procure your danger" (4.6.76–79), and when the play presents the actions of the Italian privateer, Petro Deventuro, who defeats the "fierce and bloody Moors" (5.4.6) at sea, Heywood adds the Italians to the list of violent maritime competitors that already included the English, the Moroccans, and the Spanish.

After the English converge in Florence, the noble Moor Joffer is brought in as a prisoner, captured (much like Leo Africanus) by Italian privateers who present him to the duke of Florence. Just as Clem's conversion and castration provided closure to the first *Fair Maid* play, in the second play another conversion comes at the conclusion. Joffer, who attempts suicide but is prevented by his Italian captors, is recognized by Spencer, who acknowledges him as his "noble friend" (5.4.157) and offers to pay his ransom or "redeem him home" (5.4.174) by placing himself in bondage in Joffer's stead. The Duke agrees to release Joffer without ransom. Inspired by this latest display of Christian "honor" and virtue, Joffer chooses conversion to Christianity. The bashaw declares, "Such honor is not found in Barbary / The virtue in these Christians hath converted me" (5.4.184–85). The play's conclusion suggests that the differences between the honorable Joffer and his competitor in virtue, Spencer, are superficial, residing only in their skin color and outward appearance. In a series of tests, Joffer proves to be just as brave, courteous and honorable as Spencer, the play's paragon, and vice versa.

In Heywood's play, the Muslim nobleman, Joffer, is converted through a series of chivalric gestures that occur within an economy of captivity. The episode involving Joffer's switch to Christianity is a theatrical version of the traditional fantasy about the conversion of Moors, one that harks back to the crusades and the romance tales inspired by the crusades. Joffer conforms to the type of the noble Moor or virtuous pagan knight who was represented as convertible. At the same time, the captivity of Joffer and Spencer refers to the contemporaneous practices of captivity, slavery, and ransom that were prevalent in Barbary and the Mediterranean during the seventeenth century.

European fantasies about converting Muslims to Christianity also took the form of prophecies and rumors that the Great Turk or the Sophy of Persia would themselves "turn Christian."[15] By the early seventeenth century, a new version of these old hopes began to appear. We see this, for example, in Thomas Middleton's 1613 civic entertainment, *The Triumphs of Truth*, dedicated to the Lord Mayor of London. This pageant included a procession down to the shore of the Thames, where a "strange ship" carrying "a King of the Moors, his Queen and two attendants of their own colour" arrived, flying "a white silk streamer" that read in letters of gold, "*Veritate Gubernor*, I am Stee'rd by Truth" (*Jacobean Civic Pageants* 152). The king explains to the onlookers what accounts for "my so strange arrival, in a land / Where true religion and her temple stand: / I being a Moor, then in opinion's lightness / As far from sanctity as my face from whiteness" (153). He understands that the assembled Christians, having never seen "A King so black before" (153), might assume that he is an infidel, and so he is quick to inform them of his conversion:

> My Queen and people all, at one time won
> By the religious conversation
> Of English merchants, factors, travelers,
> Whose truth did with our spirits hold commerce
> As their affairs with us, following their path
> We all were brought to the true Christian faith. (153)

In this case, conversion is effected, not through conquest or through exemplary displays of honor, virtue, or bravery, but by means of commerce, which becomes the bearer of a missionary intent as well as a profit-seeking purpose. In this pageant it is the merchants, not crusaders or maritime knights errant like Spencer, who become the heroic disseminators of Christian "Truth" to those living in "Error."

In the closing lines of the second *Fair Maid* play, the duke of Florence celebrates the conversion of Joffer, another Moorish bashaw. He tells Joffer, "we'll honor your conversion / With all due rites" (5.4.196–97). The duke also celebrates the long-delayed consummation of Spencer and Bess's marriage, praising Bess and describing her as "So fair a virgin and so chaste a wife" (l.200). Rather than turning Turk, Bess will be domesticated. She will cease her wanderings and her cross-dressing adventurism and become Spencer's loyal spouse. There is further fantasy fulfillment here in putting an end to Bess's unruly femininity or "queer virginity," which was part of her association with Queen Bess, the virgin queen, and with the English nation.[16] By losing her virginity and subordinating her will to that of her husband, Bess gives up the transgressive, venturing identity that she had maintained throughout the two plays in order to reassure the audience that she has not been contaminated by her contact with the exotic. The play's movement toward closure is accomplished by two rites of conversion—a Muslim becomes a Christian, and a masculinized woman returns to normative femininity within marriage.

Heywood's *Fair Maid*, along with the other conversion plays, features a Christian woman whose virtue, and especially her virginity, are prized "above gold" or valued "as good as gold." The preservation of Bess's virginity, says the duke of Florence after saving her from a rape, is "A gift above the wealth of Barbary" (4.1.148). Perseda in *Soliman and Perseda*, Alizia in *A Christian Turned Turk*, Paulina in *The Renegado*, and Bess Bridges—these female characters carry out similar roles in the economy of exchange and desire that these plays enact. Their sexual virtue is explicitly commodified, and when exported to the multicultural Mediterranean, its value is measured in gold. This placing of a price on the female body is not only metaphoric: it refers to the real practice of captivity and slavery, and to the high value given to female captives in the slave markets.

The desirability of female captives in the Mediterranean is mentioned in another conversion play, Robert Daborne's *A Christian Turned Turk*. In the second scene of that play, a French ship of Marseilles, bound for Normandy, is attacked and captured by John Ward and his band of pirates. During the assault, a young virgin, Alizia, is told by her brother Lemot to disguise herself as a "sailor's boy," in order to conceal her gender and protect her virginity from the "lust" (2.28) of the pirates.

A Christian Turned Turk promises in its prologue to focus on conversion, not piracy: "What heretofore set others' pens awork, / Was Ward turned pirate; ours is Ward turned Turk" (ll.7–8). Daborne's play does not dramatize the astonishing early phase of Ward's career, his rags-to-riches ascent from a common sailor to a wealthy corsair. The Chorus explains to the audience, "Our Muse doth take / A higher pitch, leaving his piracy / To reach the heart itself of villainy" (ll.12–14). The play's opening scene takes place somewhere off the Irish coast, where Ward has presumably been selling some of the booty he has acquired through piracy. "[W]anting men" (1.18), The pirate captain invites on board his ship a group of merchant sailors. While these guests are distracted by a gambling game, Ward sails off without their knowing, eventually forcing them to join his pirate crew. In the dialogue that follows, a debate is joined between the pirates and the kidnapped merchants. In this discussion, Ward expresses disdain for those who stay at home in order to do business:

> Is't not a shame
> Men of your qualities and personage
> Should live as cankers, eating up the soil
> That gave you being (like beasts that ne'er look further
> Than where they first took food?). That men call "home"
> Which gives them means equal unto their minds,
> Puts them in action. (ll.33–39).

Ward calls on these men to take action beyond the shores of England. Again, we see that pirates and merchants are not very different, though the merchant Ferdinand stresses a distinction between legitimate venturing and an illegitimate piracy that targets its own people:

> For we should call that action
> Which gives unto posterity our name
> Writ in the golden lines of honor; where this brands
> Our foreheads with the hateful name of thieves, of robbers.
> Piracy, its theft most hateful, swallows up
> The estates of orphans, widows, who—born free—
> Are thus made slaves, enthralled to misery
> By those that should defend them at the best.
> You rob the venting merchants, whose manly breast
> (scorning base gain at home) puts to the main
> With hazard of his life and state, from other lands
> To enrich his own, whilst with ungrateful hands
> He thus is overwhelmed. (ll.54–66)

In response, the pirate Gismund calls the merchants unmanly cowards, and a brawl almost begins, but Ward breaks up the fight in time to rally his crew for an attack on an approaching ship. What this opening exchange implies is that pirates differ from merchants only in their willingness to attack vessels from their own country. Otherwise, "hazarding," or bravely risking life and limb in order to gain profits, was an activity that both the pirates and the merchants of Ward's day carried out. This international venturing, undertaken by "the venting merchants" and pirates alike, is emblematically indicated in the gambling game in which both the merchants and the pirates participate during the opening scene of *A Christian Turned Turk*. After all, Ferdinand and Albert were operating on the Irish coast and dealing with Ward, and so it is implied that they were buying commodities that Ward had obtained through piracy. The merchant Albert says to Ward and Gismund, "We came aboard to venture with you: deal merchant-like, put it upon one main and throw at all" (1.6–7). They are all playing the same game, "hazard," in which the players "put it upon one main," where "main" signifies: (1) the open ocean, (2) the principal part (of one's assets), and (3) "in the game of hazard, a number... called by the 'caster' before the dice are thrown" (*OED*). We might well pose a question then (not unlike Portia's question in *The Merchant of Venice*): "Which here is the merchant and which the pirate?"

What this opening scene does, and what the play as a whole does, is to set up a distinction between legitimate and illegitimate maritime aggression, only to collapse or destabilize that distinction.[17] Those who betray and "turn" are, in the end, hard to differentiate from those who present themselves as the representatives of an admirable and heroic masculinity. In *Fair Maid*, Spencer was the object of audience admiration, the heroic fighter and noble sea raider who fought England's foes, and in *A Christian Turned Turk*, it is, to a significant degree, Ward himself who takes on that role. Both Spencer and Ward are obsessed, to the point of folly, with a personal code of honor, and both are able to trick, sabotage, and plunder the Barbary Moors.

Since James I made peace with Spain in 1604, England's former foes were no longer subject to state-sanctioned attack by English privateers. Consequently, Daborne's Ward claims that the only remaining way to put his heroic ambition into action is through piracy. Piracy then leads him toward apostasy. After Ward's conversion to Islam, the other leading pirate of the day, Dansiker, "turns" in the opposite direction and repents. The dumb shows that enact Dansiker's pardon stand in symmetrical contrast to the dumb shows that portray Ward's conversion. After Dansiker receives his pardon in Marseilles, he attempts to take on the mantle of honorable and heroic endeavor, but the French merchants he has robbed will not forgive him until he goes back to Tunis to capture the villainous renegade Jew, Benwash.

In the pirates Ward and Dansiker, Daborne shows his audience two cases that operate differently within the same identifying system of conversion and reversion. The process of "turning" begins with honorable Christian bravery finding an outlet for its heroic energy in piracy. This is the situation for both pirates at the play's outset. Both Ward and Dansiker channel their heroic, centrifugal energy toward Tunis and the service of "Turks." Then, though they have turned against their home culture, they are offered the chance to return home and receive amnesty. Dansiker obtains a pardon from the French king and once he does so, his aggressive energy is redirected at the Turks of Tunis. Ward, by contrast, is drawn further into temptation when he falls in love with Voada, a beautiful Turkish woman. Ward then takes another huge step in the direction of Turkish identity when he converts to Islam in order to marry her. At the beginning of the play, Ward says he is open to the possibility of repentance and reintegration, but love, another aspect of his heroic character, leads him further astray instead. All of this suggests a sliding scale of masculine, venturing identities: from merchant venturer to privateer to pirate to renegade. Barbara Fuchs has discussed the ideological and political consequences of this slippage, arguing that

> The movement from the paradox of privateering, in which supposed private quarrels were harnessed to the service of the state, to the murky lawlessness of piracy, to, finally, the absolute break of the renegadoes, may thus be read as a trajectory of increasing independence of the subject vis-à-vis the English state.... Moreover, this unstable continuum of privateer, pirate, and renegado disrupts the legitimacy of a view of the English nation based in commerce. (124)

Fuchs goes on to claim that, in Daborne's play, Ward's conversion and subsequent death place him "firmly beyond the bounds of a Christian community" (125), but Ward retains a sympathetic position even after his conversion, and he dies expressing a conventional anti-Islamic message and calling for a crusade to recover Jerusalem. His final speech conveys the standard exhortation for Christian unity against the "slaves of Mahomet" (16.296). At the play's end, Ward remains an attractive antihero who leaves the Christian community only because it cannot accommodate his bold spirit or satisfy his appetite for unlimited aggression.

English merchants used the same ships and sometimes employed the same methods as pirates (one reason they needed to do so was in order to protect themselves against pirates), but when a Christian pirate converted to Islam, then the difference became more visible. The stigma of apostasy was sometimes seen as an irremovable source of shame. For example, Baptist Goodall's poem, *The Tryall of Travell* (1630), describes the apostasy of the renegado with a sense of contamination and horror that does not allow for reconciliation:

> No Jew or Turk can prove more ruinous
> Then will a Christian once apostulate thus.
> Avoid as death a reconciled foe,
> Nor ever with him reconciled go.
> The sore smooth'd up not cured out will fly,
> And soon'st infect a careless stander by.
> Man of a cross religion do not trust,
> He hath evasion t'be with thee unjust. (Goodall 12)

Only a few years after Goodall's poem was printed in 1637, an official rite for the "Reconciliation of a Renegado or Apostate from the Christian Religion to Turcisme" would be promulgated. Goodall's poem argues that such reintegration was doomed to fail. The physical "sore" of circumcision is figuratively connected with the transmission of a disease, like syphilis, that may recede and go into remission, but may not be cured and may infect unwitting persons who come into contact with the externally "cured" former renegade. The visible mark of chancres, or syphilitic sores, on the penis is associated, in Goodall's text, with the mark of circumcision. This notion of pirates or renegades as disease-bearing threats to the health of the community is also expressed in *A Christian Turned Turk* by the French sea captain Monsieur Davy, who says that the English pirates "have lain / Upon their country's stomach like a surfeit; / Whence, being vomited, they strive with poisonous breath / To infect the general air" (2.44–47). This analogy differs from Goodall's, though, in imagining that the purgation of the English body politic will infect the "general" maritime sphere beyond England's shores. This refers to the way that English pirates like Ward found bases in the Mediterranean and then preyed upon ships from various countries.

Certainly, Ward's status as both pirate and apostate made him the object of popular fascination in London, and this interest is expressed in the two pamphlets that Daborne used as sources for his play. Both were printed in London in 1609: they are Andrew Barker's *True and Certaine Report of the Beginning, Proceedings, Overthrowes, and now Present Estate of Captaine Ward and Dansiker, the Two Late Famous*

Pirates and the anonymous *Newes from Sea, of Two Notorious Pirates, Ward ... and Dansiker.* Barker's narrative condemns Ward as a rene- gade, a traitor, and a thief. And yet, at the same time, Barker makes Ward into an attractive antihero. We see a positive image conveyed, for example, when Barker's text reports the opinion of another pirate, William Graves, who had served under Ward's command:

> ... these last three years, quoth he, [Ward] is grown the most absolute, the most resolute, and the most undauntedest man in fight, that ever any heart did accompany at sea. And if his actions were as honest as his valor is honorable, his deeds might be dignified in the chronicles with the worthiest. (14)

Along with his bravery and resolution, another part of what made Ward an appealing antihero was his extraordinary ascent from poverty to luxury. In *Newes from Sea* his humble origins are described: "... his parentage was but mean, his estate low, and his hope less" (sig. B3r). Ward was born in Faversham in Kent, but later he settled in Plymouth, where by 1603 he had found employment as a common seaman serving on a royal ship, the *Lion's Whelp*, in the Channel squadron. Within two years he had become a wealthy freebooter cruising the Mediterranean and commanding a powerful ship of two hundred tons with thirty-two guns and a crew of one hundred.

In 1606, Ward reached an agreement with the Ottoman com- mander of the janissaries in Tunis, Cara Osman (this is the "Crosman" of *A Christian turned Turk*) to use Tunis as the base for his piratical operations. There followed a spectacular series of raids on Christian ships, culminating in the capture of the six-hundred-ton Venetian argosy, the *Reniera e Soderina*, near Cyprus in 1607. This great ship was carrying a cargo of cotton, cinnamon, indigo, and silk worth more than £100,000. After each raiding expedition, Ward would return to Tunis and sell his booty to Cara Osman at very low prices. Cara Osman would then resell at a huge profit.

Thomas Mitton, who had spent three years in Tunis and had served under Ward's command, gave this testimony to the admiralty court:

> ... the said Carosman is the only aider, assister and upholder of the said Ward in his piracies and spoils for that he (the said Ward) hath no other place to victual save only at Tunis, and at Tunis he could not victual but by the means of Carosman who graunteth him (the said Ward) war- rants to take up and buy victuals at Tunis and the country thereabouts. And the reason that moveth the said Carosman so to do is because

when Ward taketh any prize Carosman buyeth his goods of him at his own price. (qtd. in Senior 90)[18]

Born and raised as a lowly fisherman, he became a roving king of the sea with his own private navy, beholden to no Christian monarch.

The portrait of Ward in Barker's *True and Certain Report* and *Newes from Sea* can be supplemented by the image of the pirate leader that is conveyed in several popular ballads. These ballads praise Ward's audacity and celebrate his victories over foreign ships, but they also reserve some condemnation for his awesome crimes against God and the English king. Passages such as the following, from a ballad printed in 1609, indicate the popular perception of Ward's accomplishments:

> The riches he hath gained,
> And by bloodshed obtained,
> Well may suffice for to maintain a king;
> His fellows all were valiant wights,
> Fit to be made prince's knights,
> But that their lives do base dishonors bring.[19]

Barker's pamphlet confirms the stories of Ward's "royal" status, reporting that Ward "lives there in Tunis in a most princely and magnificent state. His apparel both curious and costly, his diet sumptuous, and his followers seriously observing and obeying his will" (16). *Newes from the Sea* tells its readers that Ward "...hath built a very stately house, far more fit for a prince, than a pirate," and claims that the Viceroy of Tunis has allowed him a personal guard of twelve Turkish janissaries. Furthermore, "His respect and regard is reported to be such with the Great Turk, as he is made equal in estimate with the Bashaw" (sig.B3r).

The ambivalence in these representations of Ward's exploits is similar to the mixture of acclaim and opprobrium bestowed by English writers upon the "luxurious" Islamic rulers of the Middle East. The renegade captain Ward is "orientalized" in these accounts: he takes on many of the features of the stereotypical oriental despot—wealth, luxury, tyranny, sensual, and sexual vices, and so on. He is an "admirable villain," a paragon of wealth and valor who was a model for the success and autonomy that could be achieved by those who dared to move beyond the boundaries drawn by the religious and social system of early modern England.

The year 1607 was the apogee of Ward's career: in the years that followed, his ships suffered a series of setbacks. These circumstances led the pirate commander to initiate negotiations with various authorities for a formal pardon. The Venetian ambassador to England,

Zorzi Gustinian, reported in October 1607 that Ward had formally applied to James I for a pardon, offering, in exchange for amnesty for himself and three hundred followers, to return ships, guns, and commodities valued at more than 30,000 crowns and to cease all piratical activities.[20] Pirates who asked for pardon often received generous terms, especially if they made the traditional statements of repentance and agreed to pay fines.[21] After several unsuccessful attempts to obtain an amnesty on the terms he desired (first from James I, later from the grand duke of Florence), Ward resumed his piratical operations from his base in Tunis. There he formally converted to Islam and married a second wife, a renegade woman from Palermo (he also had left behind a wife in England, to whom he tried to send money). According to the Scottish traveler William Lithgow, who claims to have visited Tunis in 1616, Ward had built a "fair palace beautified with rich marble and alabaster stones" and lived there with a group of "English runagates, whose lives and countenances were both alike, even as desperate as disdainful."[22] Ward continued to be active as a pirate in subsequent years, but not with the same success or notoriety. He is reported to have ransomed and freed Englishmen who were enslaved in Algiers and Tunis. Apparently, he never returned to England and died in Tunis, probably during an outbreak of the plague in 1623.

Ward was not the only renegade pirate to prosper under Islamic sponsorship. There were other English renegades who went further than Ward and became powerful admirals in the Turkish navy. Most notable is Sampson Denball, another English renegade who, after the assassination of Cara Osman in 1610, took the name Ali Reis and became admiral of the galleons of Youssef Dey, the Tunisian ruler who succeeded Cara Osman.

The period immediately before and after the staging of *A Christian Turned Turk* was one in which piracy strongly affected the English trade that flowed back and forth through the Straits of Gibraltar. It was a commercial crisis that continued throughout the early decades of the seventeenth century. At this time James I issued a series of royal proclamations against piracy, including a proclamation that accuses "Captain John Ward and his adherents, and other English pirates" of "diverse great and enormous spoils and piracies" (Hughes and Larkin 1:108). Andrew Barker wrote in his dedicatory epistle, warning English authorities about the Barbary pirates' increasing "success at sea":

> ...it is most lamentable to report how many ships of London and other parts of England have been taken and made prey unto them, without the help of which English, the Turks by no means could have governed and

conducted them through their unskillfulness and insufficiency in the art of navigation. Yet of late, to my woeful experience, I can witness they have been so readied by the instruction of our apostate countrymen (I mean of Ward and others, who have been their commanders) to tackle their ships, to man and manage a fight, that if it do not please God to move the heart of his Majesty and other Christian princes and states to join together for their speedy suppression and the disjointing of their late strengthened forces, which continually increaseth by the ships of England and Holland, which they daily surprise, it will be discommodious to the state, and so dangerous to the commonwealth, in succeeding times, that Christendom must expect no traffic at sea. (sig.A2r–A2v)

England, France, Holland, and Spain all raised fleets and carried out search-and-destroy missions against the Barbary pirates during the first two decades of the seventeenth century. The targets of those raids, located along the Barbary coast of North Africa, included Tunis, the setting for both *A Christian Turned Turk* And Massinger's *The Renegado*.

English sailors who turned Turk were condemned for their crimes against Christianity, but piracy itself was not necessarily considered an evil pursuit. Many English Protestant pirates saw their activities as a continuation of justifiable hostility against Roman Catholic enemies, even after James had made peace with Spain in 1604. There was an aggressive, patriotic impulse that carried over from an earlier era during which the English crown sponsored and encouraged privateers who preyed upon Spanish shipping.[23] After 1603, unemployment among English seamen put pressure upon them to pursue their living at sea unlawfully, since there were fewer legitimate jobs, and many of those were low-paying and toilsome. According to Barker, it was just this sort of nostalgia for the Elizabethan freebooting days that Ward invoked in his successful mutiny on the Lion's Whelp, the royal vessel he took over when he first turned pirate. He reportedly told the other discontented sailors to recover their former liberties:

'Zblood, what would you have me say? Where are the days that have been, and the seasons that we have seen, when we might sing, swear, drink, drab, and kill men as freely as your cakemakers do flies? When we might do what we list, and the law would bear us out in't? Nay, when when we might lawfully do that we shall be hanged for and we do now? When the whole sea was our empire, when we robbed at will, and the world but our garden where we walked for sport? (4)

In fact, life on a pirate ship, even as a low-ranking crew member, was much freer and more profitable than serving as a seaman on a law-abiding merchantman, and piracy was certainly preferable to life under the miserable conditions that existed on royal ships. According to one historian, "Sailors on merchantmen could not expect [to earn] more than £10 a year, whereas a pirate [crew member] could hope to make as much from one prize..." (Senior 41). Given the difficult circumstances endured by most Englishmen who were employed as sailors, to turn pirate (or even to become a renegade) was a tempting opportunity for many English seamen who were given the chance.

Furthermore, what actually constituted a "criminal" act of piracy on the high seas was not clear in the early modern era. Accusations and counteraccusations of piracy were bandied about by various powers in the Mediterranean and elsewhere, but the norm was a sphere of economic activity in which might made right. Every encounter with another ship or group of ships was potentially dangerous. There were opportunities for the profitable taking of booty, but there was also the danger that a more powerful adversary would come along. Everything depended upon the identity and relative technical advantage of the converging ships. Traders and merchantmen habitually combined commerce and plunder—pillage was a routine, legitimate part of any commercial venture or voyage of "exploration." The Age of Discovery was also the Age of Plunder. A case in point is the famous voyage of Sir Francis Drake. J.M. Keynes has described the way that the plunder taken by Drake helped to support England's commercial expansion in the Mediterranean: "the booty brought back by Drake in the Golden Hind may fairly be considered the foundation and origin of the British Foreign Investment. Elizabeth paid off out of the proceeds the whole of her foreign debt, and invested a part of the balance (about £42,000) in the Levant Company."[24]

If the distinctions between pirate and privateer, outlaw and honorable seaman, renegade and loyal subject, were not at all clear or stable, it also seems that, despite official pronouncements, sailors and pirate captains were not universally stigmatized or condemned. In fact there was clearly a sense of popular admiration for the exploits of some pirate captains. For patriotic Englishmen, piracy was not seen as essentially dishonest, especially if directed against foreigners or Roman Catholics, and larceny on the high seas could receive popular approbation and admiration as a sort of "Robin Hood" activity that did no harm to the commonwealth and brought cheap goods into British markets. Pirates had little difficulty in finding buyers for their stolen goods in the Mediterranean or the British Isles, and they were able to engage in open exchange with merchants in Ireland and the West Country.

The Barbary corsairs roamed the main, but this did not deter English merchants from trading in the Barbary ports themselves, and sometimes merchants from France, England, or other European nations traded directly with pirates like Ward. For example, John King of Limehouse reported that in 1608, while King was trading in Algiers, Ward came into the harbor with two prizes, a French ship laden with oil, cochineal, and hides; and a Spaniard with "alligant wines" (i.e. wines from Alicante). In a case of friendly barter, the homesick English pirate gave the French merchant a tun of red wine in exchange for a tun of beer.[25]

Once a pirate captain had made his fortune, it was tempting to retire—given the risks involved in continued piracy. With some accumulated wealth at his disposal, a pirate captain could easily buy a pardon from a king or an amenable Italian principality such as Savoy and retire to live in a courtly style. When English pirates were offered an amnesty by the king in 1612, they were told that if they surrendered and promised to cease their predations they would be allowed to keep the wealth that they had obtained from plunder.

The other famous pirate featured in Daborne's play, Simon Dansiker, did receive a royal pardon. He is also a real historical figure and, like Ward, was the subject of popular ballads. Dansiker is often identified as a Dutchman, though he was in fact a Fleming from Dordrecht who began his career as a ship's master in Flushing (the Dutch port of Vlissingen).[26] In the Venetian reports, he is often associated or compared to Ward: the two of them were the most effective pirates operating in the Mediterranean–North Atlantic sphere in the first decade of the seventeenth century. An English supercargo reported in October of 1608 that Dansiker was operating just outside the straits of Gibraltar with a fleet of four pirate ships manned by Dutch, English and "Turkish" crews, and that he had captured twenty-nine ships off the coast of Spain near San Lucar in one month's plundering.[27] His base was Algiers, but in 1609, word reached the English court of his pardon by Henry IV, "on the condition that he quits piracy and his quarters in Algiers and goes to Marseilles" (*CSPV* 11:575, p. 312). In October it was reported by Giacomo Vendramin, A Venetian living in Florence, that

> Danziker has revolted against the Algerines and slain one hundred Turks and freed three hundred slaves. He then went to Marseilles where he took booty to the value of 400,000 crowns. He was met by the Duke of Guise with every sign of joy.... There will be trouble. This is expected to be the utter ruin of Ward. God grant it be so. (*CSPV* 11:687, p. 375)

Apparently, in 1609 Dansiker did leave Algiers for Marseilles, where he accepted a French royal pardon, went into French service as a privateer, and continued to attack English and Spanish shipping. Dansiker traveled to the French court with the duke of Guise, who was then the governor of Provence. Dansiker reportedly repaid the duke for his support at court with a large bribe. When the Spanish ambassador to the French court protested the capture of a Spanish galleon by Dansiker, the French king refused to punish Dansiker and "held that he [Henry IV] had rendered a service to Spain and other nations by clearing the sea of such a famous pirate" (*CSPV* 11:724, p. 391). The French king may have been plotting to employ Dansiker in a naval attack on the Genoese, but after Henry IV was assassinated Dansiker returned to Marseilles where, it is reported, he planned to attack Algiers while flying the French flag.[28] The ease with which a pirate like Dansiker could switch sides and suddenly become a legitimate privateer (or vice versa) is indicated in Daborne's play when Dansiker announces to his crew that he has received the French pardon. He says, "let's redeem our honor" (5.13) and suggests that they attack the pirates of Tunis: "with the same weapon we may / Our country cure, with which we wounded her" (5.24–25).

There are conflicting reports about the death of Dansiker, but there is one story that matches, to a limited degree, the version of Dansiker's death that is staged in Daborne's play. In 1609 Antonio Foscarini, the Venetian ambassador in Paris, received letters from Marseilles confirming that Dansiker had indeed led a French fleet against Algiers but when he came ashore to parley with the local bey, "he was deceived by the Bey of the pirates, made prisoner and has paid by his death for his excessive credulity and the thousands of murders he committed in former times" (*CSPV* 12:156, p. 105). It is plausible that the news of Dansiker's death may have reached London just before Daborne's play was first staged.[29]

The historical record confirms what is shown in both *A Christian Turned Turk* and *The Renegado*—that relations between English renegade pirates and their Turkish overlords were not always harmonious. Problems intensified after a series of incidents that occurred during the early seventeenth century. Both *A Christian Turned Turk* and *The Renegado* feature renegade pirates who regret their apostasy and turn against their Muslim masters. These representations of renegades betraying and delivering crippling blows to their Muslim sponsors are imaginative expressions of political, military, and economic ambitions that were achievable only to a limited degree. Christian armies and navies deployed against the Barbary pirates in the seventeenth century scored a few small successes and experienced several large-scale defeats. Occasionally, there were Christian ships that raided North African harbors with an intent to cripple the Muslim maritime economy, but this was contrary to the promotion of peaceable, profitable commerce, and during the Elizabethan and Jacobean periods business was normally carried out in a posture of humble submission to North African port authorities and their policies.

In 1609, however, Don Luis Fajardo, a Spanish admiral, accomplished a mission of sabotage in the harbor at Goletta, where he destroyed much of the Tunis pirate fleet by sending in fireships at night.[30] This attack may be what Daborne had in mind when he has Dansiker and some of the other pirates blow up the pirate ships in the Tunisian harbor. Two years later, in September of 1611, Captain Gifford, an English renegade based in Algiers, offended by the way that the Dey of Algiers had handled the purchase of Gifford's prize, succeeded in setting the harbor on fire and destroying most of the Algerine fleet. This made it difficult for Ward, who arrived in Algiers soon after, at a time when English pirates were no longer trusted. Ward was forced to leave Algiers for Tunis.

In Tunis, and elsewhere under Islamic rule in the Mediterranean, Christian renegades were able to gain considerable freedom, wealth, and authority—to a degree which would have been near impossible for English seamen serving on English merchant vessels. Le Sieur de Brèves, a Frenchman who visited Tunis in 1606, observed:

> The great profit that the English bring to the country, their open-handed ways and the excessive debauches in which they spend their money before leaving town and returning to the war (for that is what brigandage at sea is called), has made them cherished and supported by the janissaries above all nations. No one else is noticed but them; they carry their swords at their sides and run drunk together through the town, without ordinary Christian people, usually outspoken by nature, daring to stand up against them. They sleep with the wives of the Moors and when discovered, buy their way out of being shot; the penalty which others have to suffer without remission. In short, every kind of debauchery is allowed them: even that which is not tolerated among the Turks themselves. (qtd. in Senior 95–96)

In return, English, French, and Dutch renegades helped to teach Moors and Turks about the latest nautical and military technologies. From them, Turkish shipbuilders gained important knowledge about how to build and sail the new "round ships" or "galliots" that were faster and more maneuverable. Renegades living amongst the

Muslims also shared information about how to manufacture guns and cannons used on ships and in the field of battle. Captain John Smith, in the last chapter of his *Travels* describes how "the Moors scarce knew to sail a ship ... those [renegades] were the first that taught the Moors to be men of war" (59) and explains how seamen who had served lawfully against Spain turned renegade after James made peace. Lithgow confirms Smith's assertion:

> For true it is, the natural Turks were never skillful in managing of sea battles, neither were they expert mariners, nor experienced gunners, if it were not for our Christian runnagates, French, English, and Flemings, and they are too subtle, accurate, and desperate fellows; who have taught the Turks the art of navigation, and especially the use of munition, which they both cast to them and then become their chief cannoneers, the Turks would be as weak and ignorant at sea as the silly Ethiopian is unexpert in handling of arms on land. For the private humor of discontented castaways is always an enemy to public good, who from the society of true believers are driven to the servitude of infidels and refusing the bridle of Christian correction, they receive the double yoke of despair and condemnation. Whose terror of a guilty conscience, or rather blazing brand of their vexed souls, in forsaking their Faith, and denying Christ to be their Saviour, ramverts most of them, either in a torment of melancholy, otherwise in the ecstasy of madness: which indeed is a torturing horror that is sooner felt than known and cannot be avoided by the rudeness of nature, but by the saving grace of true felicity. (188–89)

Lithgow's account, like that of Daborne's play, exaggerates in order to demonize the renegades. In fact, many of these pirates who had turned Turk were accepted, contented members of the thriving corsair communities at Tunis, Algiers, Sallee, and other ports. Once they returned home to port with their booty, they usually sold these goods (including captives sold as slaves) to Jewish or Muslim merchants. These merchants often resold these stolen commodities to Christian merchants. Local rulers from Morocco to Egypt tolerated and encouraged the pirates to operate out of their ports because the trade resulting from plunder was good for the local economy. As time went on, some of these ports, including Tunis, came to rely upon freebooting and the slave trade as the mainstay of their economy. These ports not only served as harbors for the corsair community, but they also became trading centers that permitted merchants from all over the Mediterranean to buy and sell. The commodities bought and sold included human beings—captives who were taken and sold in the slave markets. If a merchant ship surrendered peaceably to the Barbary corsairs, the pirates would usually not take the crew captive as part of the spoils, but they would often do so if the ship resisted. This piratical law of the sea, like Tamburlaine's colored tents threatening the besieged city, is recorded in the letter from the masters of the *Charity* and the *Pearl* (two English vessels captured by Ward and his confederates) appended to *Newes from the Sea*:

> For this was a decree amongst them (which they had established should stand irrevocable) that what Christian soever they met (be he of what country soever) if he submitted not upon the first summons or durst be so hardy as to outdare them with the least blast of breath: if he were taken he should be a slave; if not taken, they would sink them in the sea. (C2r)

When pirates like Dansiker or Ward took a prize, the people on board that ship might be taken prisoner and brought back to the corsair's home port. There, ransoms would be arranged for some, while other captives would be sold into slavery. Some of those captives who were enslaved by Muslims would be encouraged to turn Turk. While some English Christians willingly converted to Islam in order to pursue the career of "Turkish" piracy, others converted in order to better their lot after they had lost hope of being ransomed or "redeemed." In addition to the English renegades, there were many English held in North Africa as slaves who remained Christian. By the 1620s, there were thousands of English captives held there.[31] In 1624 a petition was presented to the House of Lords, "the humble and lamentable complaint of above 1,500 poor captive souls, now under the miserable oppression of the Turks in Argier, Tunis, Sally and Tituane" (*Journals of the House of Lords* 3:411–13). Parliament ordered a general collection of monies throughout England for the redemption of the captives, and the King issued letters patent for that purpose.

A Christian Turned Turk stages the spectacle of Christian captives being sold into slavery in Tunis. When a father and his two sons are captured by Ward, he offers them for sale to the "renegado Jew," Benwash, who is an "engrosser" of goods and persons brought by pirates to Tunis. The sons are then separated from their father when Benwash offers to buy all three, but the Jewish merchant only offers thirty crowns for the father, a price that Ward refuses to accept. In a scene of high pathos, the father weeps and laments, and when his sons are hauled away, he dies. All the while, Ward laughs, taunts, and curses his victims, then calls for wine and women.

Ward's attempt to procure a woman leads him to a meeting with Voada, Benwash's Turkish sister-in-law and the sister of Crosman.

In the next scene, Crosman and the Governor of Tunis (who is himself a convert) ask Ward to turn Turk, but the English pirate refuses. It is only when Crosman brings in his sister to tempt Ward further that he is persuaded. The two men leave Ward alone with Voada, while Crosman comments in an aside, "What devils dare not move / Men to accomplish, women work them to" (7.87–88). Ward falls for Voada immediately, but when he woos her, she brings up their religious difference as a barrier to love and marriage. Voada says, "Know then I love, / But not the man...whose religion / Speaks me an infidel" (7.119–22), and then she makes him an offer—"Turn Turk—I am yours" (7.127). Ward succumbs, agreeing to convert immediately. After Voada exits, Ward delivers a soliloquy in which he rationalizes his apostasy and determines that he will only gain by his impending conversion:

> What is't I lose by this my change? My country?
> Already 'tis to me impossible.
> My name is scandalled? What is one island
> Compared to the Eastern monarchy? (7.179–82)

He embraces the unholy trinity of "beauty, command, and riches" (l.193), and heroically but tragically asserts his courageous, defiant, solitary will against god, country, and "the power of kings" (l.192). At this moment in the play, Ward is (like Tamburlaine) a bold overreacher, but since he is English and not Scythian, his aspiring individualism comes closer to home for the English audience. His statement registers the reality of England's marginality and weakness when compared to the Ottoman empire. At this point, Alizia enters and begs Ward not to turn, telling him that conversion is "the denial / Of your redeemer, religion, country, / Of him that gave you being" (7.198–200) and that it is a slavery of the spirit with eternal consequences. When the Turks return to escort him to his conversion ceremony, he tells Crosman that he has reneged on his vow. "I am now myself," he assures them. "Her looks enchanted me" (l.232–33), he explains, and this is confirmed when Voada appears and compels him to keep his promise. Ward changes his mind once more and has Alizia removed. After his conversion Ward's mind is never at peace. Instead he experiences a violent oscillation between irrational love and irrational despair. Once again, we see the conflation of religious conversion with erotic passion, an association that is a crucial pattern of meaning in other conversion plays, including *Soliman and Perseda*, *Othello*, and *The Renegado*.

The next scene features a dumb show in which Ward is formally initiated as a Muslim. The play's representation of this ritual is based on the descriptions of such ceremonies that appeared in contemporary travel narratives.[32] Ward is seated by the Mufti, who, according to the stage directions, "*puts on his turban* and robe, girds his sword, then swears him on the Mahomet's head" (s.d., 8.10). While Ward undergoes circumcision offstage, Dansiker turns away from Islam by burning the Turkish pirate ships in the harbor and then departing for Marseilles. After Dansiker arrives in France, however, his patron, Henry IV, is assassinated, and with his protector dead, Dansiker is accused by the French merchants who were the victims of his past piracies. When Dansiker asks "what act they can desire / Man to accomplish to redeem his peace / And their great losses," the French merchants "with one voice demand Benwash the Jew / As his just ransom" (14.41–45). Dansiker agrees "To bring him prisoner, or in the action die" (l.47). He returns to Tunis on a final mission, but fails to take Benwash alive. After stabbing Benwash, Dansiker is taken by Turkish officers, and then he commits suicide. Dansiker's death is closely followed by that of Ward, who is also arrested after his wife Voada falsely accuses him of attempting to murder her. These dual suicides are a double rewriting of Othello's suicide. Like Othello, both Dansiker and Ward make examples of themselves. The Dutch pirate, when threatened by the Governor with tortures to make Dansiker reveal "what project now / Led you unto this second venture" (16.219–20), confesses that he intended to have kidnapped Benwash and "made a massacre of the whole town, dashed out the miscreant brains of your young infidels" (l.222–24). After hearing this defiant confession, the Governor commands Dansiker's death. Finally the Mufti asks, "Wilt thou turn Turk and save thy soul yet?" (l.231). Dansiker's last lines and his final action, stabbing himself, reiterate the words and actions of Othello. Like Othello's final speech, Dansiker's last words suggest divine retribution and damnation for his crimes— "heaven is just: / Christians did fall by me, by slaves I must" (16.204–05). And yet, what is fascinating about Daborne's rewriting of *Othello* is that Dansiker and Ward also resemble Iago at the conclusion of Shakespeare's play. Trapped by the local authorities, including the Governor, Dansiker and Ward are called "dog! Devil!" (16.214) and "Inhuman dog" (16.290) by those who have caught them, and the Governor threatens Ward with "All the tortures man e'er knew" (16.288). But they both resemble Othello in their suicides, acts that correspond to Othello's because Dansiker and Ward also wish to avoid torture and humiliation at the hands of their captors. For Ward especially, suicide becomes what it was for Othello, the staging of a self-inflicted punishment and the killing of a cruel "Turk."

A Christian Turned Turk ends with a double cautionary lesson for anyone thinking about a career in Barbary. Ward's last words, directed at the Turks on stage, also refer to the audience:

> O may I be the last of my country
> That trust unto your treacheries, seducing
> treacheries, All you that live by theft and piracies,
> That sell your lives and souls to purchase graves,
> That die to hell, and live far worse than slaves,
> Let dying Ward tell you that heaven is just,
> And that despair attends on blood and lust. (ll.315–21)

Ward's reference to "my country," followed by "All you that live by theft and piracies," speaks to both the Turks onstage and to the potential Turks in the London playhouse. It is as if the English spectators are also prone to commit the "theft and piracies" of a Ward, and that they may be ready, in some sense, to turn.

Ward's plea fell on deaf ears. He was certainly not the last of his country to convert or to join the Muslim communities in North Africa and the Levant. As the number of English renegades in Muslim lands increased during the early seventeenth century, the issue of conversion was manifested in yet another drama about renegades in Tunis. Philip Massinger's 1624 play, *The Renegado*, is set, like *A Christian Turned Turk*, in the Barbary pirate community of Tunis. Most of the scenes in Massinger's play occur in the viceregal palace where the lustful and tyrannous Asembeg rules in the name of the Great Turk, but the first scene of *The Renegado* takes place in the common marketplace of Tunis, where Christian merchants are permitted to sell their wares openly and publicly. Within this sphere of commerce and exchange, the desire for profit leads to other lusts and the market becomes a site of temptation and potential contagion.

In *The Renegado*, as in Daborne's play, religious conversion is offered as an erotic temptation. Massinger's play emphasizes the conventional association of Islam and sexual sin and ties that issue to the main action of the drama. Vitelli, the play's young hero, comes from Venice to Tunis to rescue his sister from enslavement, but while in Tunis, Vitelli is seduced by Donusa, a beautiful Turkish princess. Vitelli's priestly mentor, Francisco, warns the young Venetian about the sexual aggression of Muslim women:

> ...these Turkish dames
> (Like English mastiffs that increase their fierceness

> By being chained up), from the restraint of freedom,
> If lust once fire their blood from a fair object,
> Will run a course the fiends themselves would shake at
> To enjoy their wanton ends. (1.3.8–13)

Despite this admonition, when he is put to the test, Vitelli fails. Posing as a merchant selling cheap goods in the Tunisian marketplace, he gains the attention of the Ottoman princess, Donusa. When she unveils herself before him, Vitelli beholds her as a "wonder" (1.3.141). Later, when secretly admitted to her quarters (a "forbidden place / Where Christian yet ne'er trode" [2.4.32–33]), Vitelli is awed by her beauty, power, and wealth. The audience is also allowed a vision of the forbidden palace. The spectators in the theater are permitted to peep into the seraglio and witness a scene of wealth, sensual pleasure, sex, and danger. Donusa's private chamber is a version of the hidden seraglio that was revealed in early modern European representations of the sultan's court. Vitelli gives in to the enticements offered there, and Donusa's exotic charms and social status succeed in reversing the normative gender hierarchy, compelling Vitelli to submit to a woman's will.

At first, Massinger's play seems to offer a rewriting of Ward's eroticized conversion, but (thanks to the interventions of the pious Jesuit, Francisco) Vitelli repents and resists temptation. He regrets his sexual liaison with Donusa, and rather than converting to Islam for love, he eventually succeeds in converting Donusa to Christianity. It is interesting that Massinger's Christian *raisonneur* has the same name as Daborne's—Francisco. This similarity, among others, indicates that Massinger may have been consciously responding to the earlier play, rewriting it with a happier outcome. In *The Renegado*, the destructive, tragic Ward–Voada relationship is reconfigured in the Vitelli–Donusa relationship. Donusa herself resembles a stock figure from the romance tradition—the virtuous Saracen maiden who is converted to Christianity after falling in love with a Christian knight who has been held captive by her father, the sultan.

Even today, Islamic law and custom do not permit a Christian man to marry a Muslim woman until he converts to Islam, while a Muslim man is permitted to marry a woman who remains Christian. This was noted by Harry Cavendish, an Englishman who visited Constantinople in 1589: "No Christian man may have to do with a Turkish woman, but she shall die for it if it be known, but a Turk may have as many Christian women as he will" (17.2:24–25). And Leo Africanus reported, "If the wife of a Christian turneth Turke, and marrieth herselfe with a Turke...the Christian husband by turning

Turke may take her again" (387). This perception of Muslim sexual standards informs Massinger's play, in scenes that emphasize the murderous jealousy of the Islamic potentates, Asembeg and Mustapha, who discover the relationship of Donusa and the Christian Vitelli. They carry out the will of the Great Turk, Amurath, whose commands are conveyed in a sinister "black box" and then publicly read out at the court in Tunis. The Ottoman sultan commands the execution of his own niece because she commits the crime described by Cavendish. Donusa's power and independence as a Muslim woman are contrasted with the confinement imposed on Vitelli's sister, Paulina, who was given to Asembeg to be his slave. She becomes the captive object of Asembeg's raging lust and only a sacred charm with protective powers prevents the viceroy from raping her.

Grimaldi, the play's titular "renegado," is the pirate who has captured Paulina and sold her to Asembeg. He eventually returns to the Christian fold, but only after having his ill-gotten wealth confiscated by the Turks, and not without a harrowing spiritual struggle. Grimaldi, like Ward, is an unruly man of blunt speech who is punished by his Muslim masters for his bitter insolence. Like Dansiker, he repents before it is too late and comes to serve the Christian cause again. His spiritual recovery is preceded, however, by a steep descent into despair. Grimaldi's desperate condition is brought on by a guilty conscience that leads him to believe he deserves damnation. Grimaldi's spiritual roller-coaster ride reflects the seventeenth-century understanding of religious conversion and its psychology. There were extremely well-known cases involving apostates who attempted to rejoin Christianity but were agonized or destroyed by remorse and hopelessness. Most notable was the case of the Italian lawyer, Francis Spira, who publicly renounced his Protestantism in St. Mark's in Venice and then came to believe that God had abandoned him. He threatened suicide and became convinced that he was possessed by the Devil. Finally, despite the ministrations of various priests, he died of starvation.[33] The Spira story was widely disseminated and was certainly known to Massinger, who may have been thinking of Spira's recantation in St. Mark's when he has his apostate, Grimaldi, commit an act of blasphemy in the same church in Venice. Grimaldi experiences the sufferings and near madness of a Spira, but in the end he is rehabilitated and restored to sanity by Francisco. In the character and accomplishments of Francisco, Massinger includes a highly sympathetic portrayal of a Jesuit priest. The play is free of anti-Catholic statements and encourages the notion of Christendom's common cause against Islamic evils and temptations. Massinger seems to stress the role that Catholic priests played in redeeming Christian captives from slavery in North Africa.[34]

Restored to Christian virtue, Grimaldi becomes the successful, surviving hero that Ward, or even Dansiker, could not be. Grimaldi's unruly virtue is recuperated for the service of Christendom, and he aids in the escape plot that concludes the play. Just as Vitelli and Donusa are about to be executed, Paulina suddenly offers herself to Asembeg and by doing so, she is able to delay their execution. The play's conclusion stresses the definitive Turkish vice of lust which proves a weak point for the Christians to exploit. All of the Christians escape with their lives, leaving Asembeg in a state of despair, facing torture and death at the hands of the Ottoman authorities—a fate that in Daborne's play was the lot of Ward and Dansiker. Both Donusa and Grimaldi forsake Islam, escaping from Tunis with their bodies and souls intact. Thus *The Renegado* might have been subtitled "A Turk Turned Christian": Massinger's tragicomedy rewrites *A Christian Turned Turk* to create a plot that reverses the outcome of Daborne's tragedy by affirming the power of Christianity to "redeem" and recover both Muslims and renegades.

* * *

What scholars of English Renaissance drama have yet to recognize is the survival of a tightly knit body of conversion plays, forming a coherent subgenre and linked together by a shared set of references to conventional plots and characters that represent Christian–Islamic relations in the Mediterranean. The relations between these plays exhibit what Linda Hutcheon has called "intertextual bouncing."[35] As each play builds on its predecessors in the subgenre, it produces parodic repetition and enhances the "dual consciousness" that is always a feature of early modern drama written for the London playhouses. This is perhaps true of the early modern theater as a whole, but it is particularly clear that in the plays I have discussed here there is a strong pattern of repetition, rewriting, and sequel. These plays, like a series of merchant voyages to the same destination, follow the basic plot of conversion through exotic, erotic experience. They dramatize various versions of the primal scene at the sultan's court, and they draw their dramatic tension from the fear of conversion. Taken together—Marlowe's two *Tamburlaine* plays, Heywood's two *Fair Maid* plays, the sequence of conversion plays from *Soliman and Perseda* to *Othello* to *A Christian Turned Turk* to *The Renegado*— these texts carry out a series of transactions, each one building on the foundation of the preceding plots. From Kyd's *Soliman and Perseda* to Heywood's *Fair Maid of the West, Part II*, playwrights worked with this shared set of conventions, forming a pattern that owes its persistence to the continued interest and involvement of English subjects in Mediterranean and Islamic affairs, and to the powerful conjunction of sexual, commercial, political, and religious anxieties in early modern English culture.

These plays focus on the temptation and threat of conversion. On the English stage, phobic representations of those who have turned Turk depict converts as villains, dupes, or tragic victims. But even if characters like Erastus, Tamburlaine, or Dansiker do not embrace Islam, they do "turn Turk" in a figurative sense. They are contaminated by their contact with the Turks, they become "Turkish" in their willingness to change identity and serve or emulate Muslim masters, and in the end they pay a price for this affiliation. In my analysis of these plays, conversion is a concept that includes the religious conversion of individuals but also describes a collective cultural and economic transformation that English society was undergoing. English culture was "turning Turk" not only in the sense that some English subjects were converting to Islam, but more broadly and significantly in the sense that English society was adopting new procedures and identities that were based on a Mediterranean experience defined by an instability of identity and a questionable moral and religious status. This anxious new identity for English subjects was expressed in a theater of conversion that featured, not only Turks or Moors, but also Italians, Spaniards, Jews, and other foreigners. And more than any specific racial or national identity, these Mediterranean "ethnics" were defined, from an English point of view, as creatures of hybridity and instability. Chapter 6 will look at theatrical representations of Italians and Jews who figure forth the Machiavellian identity that the English themselves feared to take on.

CHAPTER 6

MACHIAVELLIAN MERCHANTS: ITALIANS, JEWS, AND TURKS

Thus, loving neither, will I live with both,
Making a profit of my policy,
And he from whom my most advantage comes
Shall be my friend.
This is the life we Jews are used to lead,
And reason, too, for Christians do the like.

> —*Christopher Marlowe*, The Jew of Malta (*5.3.111–16*)

So you have profit, all religious laws
Must suffer violence...

> —*Robert Daborne*, A Christian Turned Turk (*6.362–63*)

As we have seen in chapter 5, the temptation of religious conversion and the idea of "turning" is not only a matter of religious identification. "Turning Turk" was associated with a more general sense of cultural transformation that the English were undergoing, beginning in the late sixteenth century. I am referring here to the early modern usage of the phrase, but also to my own argument, based on a cultural analysis of economic and textual evidence, that the English were anxiously "turning" into a more open commercial society, and that in theatrical representations they could observe and reflect upon their new status as merchant adventurers competing for profit. Very often, it was the Mediterranean that functioned as the imaginary site where these changes in identity were acted out in a play of fear and desire. Plays set in the Mediterranean represented and responded to the very real cross-cultural encounters that English subjects experienced in places like Algiers, Aleppo, and Constantinople. But it was not only the Ottoman or Levantine parts of the Mediterranean that English culture identified as the source of this converting power—there were other places and other peoples who were seen as corrupters of English purity, morality, and masculinity. Two non-Muslim groups, in particular, were seen as threats because of their perceived moral and religious difference—Roman Catholics (especially Italians and Spaniards—or the Italianate Spaniards present in places like the kingdom of Naples or Malta) and Jews.[1]

The image of the Machiavellian Jew in Elizabethan drama has an important prehistory in late medieval drama. An awareness of this tradition can inform our readings of the stage Jews that began to appear later in the London playhouses. The image of the Jew in medieval drama is part of a long history of anti-Semitic persecution, demonization, and stereotyping that is well known.[2] One aspect of the European construction of "the Jew," going back to the Middle Ages, is an awareness of Jewish migration and mobility. In *The Jew of Malta*, Barabas comments on the Christian view of his people, making the following statement: "They say we are a scattered nation" (1.1.120). The culture of early modern England describes Jews as parasitical vagabonds, both outcast and invasive. According to the Western European representations of the time, they occupy no stable national or geographical position—they are defined as a kind of "runnagate" people, subversive of both the social and economic order and economically aggressive as well. A typical articulation of this racist stereotype is the reference made in passing by Nicolas de Nicolay, a French traveler in the early modern Mediterranean:

> this detestable nation of the Jews are men full of malice, fraud, deceit and subtle dealing, exercising execrable usuries amongst the Christians and other nations without any consciences or reprehension, but have free licence, paying the tribute: a thing which is so great a ruin onto the country and people whereto they are conversant. (131)

Since the expulsion of the Jews from England by Edward I in 1290, the only people of Jewish origin permitted to reside in England were "conversos" or "marranos" from Spain and Portugal or other Jews who had turned Christian, but even these people were considered by the English to be radically unalterable in their essential Jewishness. An English theologian, Andrew Willet, wrote in 1590: "A Jew...whether he journeys into Spain, or France, or into whatever other place he goes to, declares himself to be not a Spaniard or a Frenchman, but a Jew" (qtd. in Shapiro 168).[3] Like Othello's Islamic identity, Jewishness was not believed to be something that could be washed away by the waters of baptism. In Robert Daborne's *A Christian Turned Turk*, for instance, the merchant Benwash, though he has formally converted to Islam, is still identified as "the Jew" of Tunis.

In England, traditional views of Jewishness focused on biblical and theological notions of Jews as stubborn in their refusal to convert to Christianity or as the killers of Christ, but English Protestants also hoped for the mass conversion of the Jews, an event that they believed would signal the beginning of the end times and prepare the way for the second coming of Christ. At the same time, European writers describe Jews as hoarding usurers and treacherous poisoners, and in the most violently anti-Semitic representations, Jews steal communion bread or collect the blood of Christian babies in order to perform their Satanic rites. In England, these traditional, anti-Semitic images persisted in the fifteenth and sixteenth centuries and after. An interesting example of this kind of demonization, in a text that focuses on the idea of conversion, is *The Croxton Play of the Sacrament*, written in the late fifteenth century (ca. 1461–1500). Already in this play we can see the emergence of an association between Jewish identity and international commerce, and specifically a scenario involving a corruptive trafficking between Christians and Jews. The play's first scene introduces a character named Aristorius Mercator, a merchant of Aragon who introduces himself to the audience by claiming a transcultural status: "Ful wyde in this worlde spryngeth my fame" (l.91). He promptly provides a catalogue of places where his "merchaundyse renneth" (l.94) from Denmark to Turkey. His list of place names includes "Saby" (Saba in Arabia), "Alysander" (Alexandria), "Antyoche" (Antioch), "Jerusalem," "Taryse" (Tarsus in Turkey), "Surrey" (Syria), "Salern" (Salerno), "Rome," and "Naples" (ll.95–114). He concludes by declaring, "thus thorowght all this world sett ys my sale" (l.116), punning on "sail" and "sale." In the opening scene, the play establishes a conflict between the worldly wealth and power of this merchant—who lives "as a lordys pere" (l.119) and whose "curat wayteth upon [him] to know [his] entent" (l.120)—and the priorities of the Christian faith, to which the worldly Aristorius pays only lip service. After Aristorius sends his men off to seek business with other merchants, the Jew Jonathas ("the grettest marchante in all Surre [Syria]," l.251) enters. His opening lines indicate his reverence, not for a Christian or Judaic deity, but for "almyghty Machomet" (l.149), who is the object of his worship and "Whose lawes tendrely I have to fulfyll" (l.150), he says. Jonathas offers a prayer of thanks to Machomet for the "Gold, sylver, and presyous stonys, / And abu[n]ddaunce of spycys thou hast me lent" (ll.158–59) as he launches into a long list of the valuable luxury goods that he possesses. The whole monologue, including its list of precious commodities, resembles the one spoken by Barabas at the moment of his first appearance in *The Jew of Malta*. Both Jonathas and Barabas are identified with an international trade in luxury goods that flowed through the Mediterranean, and they both claim to be a "chefe merchaunte of Jewes" within a transnational network of Jewish traders.

The central events of *The Play of the Sacrament* are first, the purchase of a communion wafer, sold by the Christian Aristorius to the Jewish Jonathas, and the subsequent miracle that inspires Jonathas and the Jews to turn Christian. The Spanish merchant's trafficking with the Jew comes about because of Aristorius's ambition and drive for greater wealth through participation in a specifically international and multicultural marketplace. His search for business partners who can operate at the same level and scope as himself leads him to make a deal with his commercial peer, Jonathas.

The plot thickens when Jonathas and his Jewish partners, Jason and Masphat, determine to obtain some communion bread in order to destroy it and thereby weaken the power of the Christians. This act is presented as an effort to prove that the Christians religion is false and to resist their proselytization. While the priest goes off "to saye myn evynsong" (l.231), Aristorius goes to meet with the Jewish merchants. Jonathas offers to purchase the communion "cake" for twenty pounds, but Aristorius refuses at first, for fear that if "preste or clerke myght me aspye, / To the bysshope thei wolde go tell that dede / And apeche me of eresye" (ll.300–02). But soon it becomes clear that Aristorius's protestations are simply a strategy to drive a hard bargain. When Jonathas offers one hundred pounds and brings out a bag of gold ducats as payment in advance, the Spanish merchant agrees immediately. That night, Aristorius gets the priest drunk, takes the church key, steals the host from the church, and then delivers it secretly to Jonathas. The Jews try to desecrate the host with blows of their daggers, and when it bleeds as a sign that it is the true body of Christ crucified, they attempt to destroy it by throwing it into a cauldron of boiling oil set inside a furnace. This is emblematic of the fiery furnace from which the three Jews who refused to worship the idols of Nebuchadnezzar emerged unscathed in Daniel 3, and also of the boiling cauldrons in hell that were said to await all usurers (like the cauldron in which Barabas is boiled alive at the end of *The Jew of Malta*). When Jonathas tries to throw the host into the boiling oil, it miraculously sticks to his hand. Frantically trying and failing to get it off his hand, the Jewish merchant "*renneth wood*" (l.504) and when his coreligionists attempt to restrain him by tying him up and nailing him to a post (in a parodic reenactment of Christ's crucifixion), the hand that has the host in it comes off (much like Faustus's leg) and remains nailed to the post. The Jews then pull out the nails with a pair of pincers and throw the hand, with the host still stuck to it, into the cauldron, but the boiling oil "waxyth redde as blood, / And owt of the cawdron yt begynnyth to rin" (ll.674–75). Next they stoke the fire and heat the furnace, removing the host with a pair of pincers out of the cauldron and casting it into the oven. After they close the oven doors, when they finally believe that they have burnt up the host once and for all, the oven explodes, blood spewing "owt at the cranys" (l.713), and a wounded, bleeding Jesus appears and chastises the Jews, asking them, "Why do ye thus? / Why put yow me to a newe tormentry, / And I dyed for yow on the crosse?" (ll.731–33). Jesus then instructs Jonathas to put his hand in the cauldron, and it is miraculously made "hole agayn" (l.778). The host, still intact, is returned to the church, where the Jews are baptized by the bishop at the end of the play. Meanwhile, the merchant Aristorius confesses that he has made "An onlefull bargayn ... / For covytyse of good" (ll.852, 854) and "sold owr Lordys body for lucre of mony" (l.902). His penance is pronounced by the bishop:

> Now for thys offence that thou hast donne
> Agens the Kyng of Heaven and Emperowr of Hell,
> Ever whyll thou lyvest good dedys for to done
> And nevermore for to buy nor sell ... (ll.912–15)

Both the "new tormentry" perpetrated by the Jewish merchants who buy the host, and the selling of God's body "for lucre" by the Spanish merchant, Aristorius, dramatize the central, traditional conflict of Christian moral drama—the struggle between the appeal of worldly, material wealth and the welfare of the soul. But this homiletic message is communicated through a new kind of negative model—the foreign, Machiavellian merchant whose wealth comes from international commerce and from trading with infidels in foreign (especially Mediterranean) ports. These are the new men described by Robert Crowley in *The Way to Wealth* (1550): "Men without conscience...."

Men that live as if there were no God at all! Men that would have all in their hands" (132). Already we see in Jonathas and Aristorius two versions of this new, hyper-acquisitive merchant villain, a figure that will appear with increasing frequency on the Elizabethan and Jacobean stage.

By the late fifteenth century, when *The Croxton Play of the Sacrament* was written, English merchants had begun to assert themselves in the sphere of Anglo-Mediterranean commerce. English vessels began to trade directly with Italy when previously commodities had been carried to and from England by Venetian, Genoese, and Florentine vessels. The Levant trade prospered during the early Tudor period, but from the 1530s to the 1570s it dropped off severely because of Turkish domination of the Eastern Mediterranean. English cloth, which had been exported by sea, went overland instead, from the Netherlands to Italy. In the 1570s, however, the Mediterranean trade was redeveloped by English merchants, and in 1579 trade capitulations with the Ottoman sultanate were granted.[4] By 1638, Lewes Roberts, a "husband" of the Levant Company, was able to claim that his joint-stock company "for its height and eminency is now second to none in this land."[5]

During the mid-sixteenth century, Italian merchants were still carrying luxury goods to London, Italian bankers and financial dealers held positions of power in England, and London was absorbing an influx of Italian and Jewish immigrants (though these Jews were "conversos").[6] In 1575, at the urging of the earl of Leicester, Elizabeth granted a monopoly of the Venetian import trade (mainly in oil, currants, and wine) to Acerbo Velutelli, a native of Lucca resident in London and an important figure in London banking and finance. This caused a storm of protest from the English and Venetian merchants involved in the trade, and eventually a compromise was reached whereby Velutelli's license was purchased for one thousand pounds by the merchants.[7] According to R.H. Tawney (1925), whose seminal work on the rise of capitalism in England is still of value, "the most typical and most important of the financial developments" (60) of the Tudor period was the rise of foreign exchange transactions tied to the development of an international money market. Especially in the 1550s and 1560s, Italian merchants conducted much of this business. In 1553, when "Cecil prepared a programme for controlling the exchanges, what he emphasized most was the necessity of keeping a tight hold on the Italians, who 'go to and fro and serve all princes at once…[and] work what they list and lick the fat from our beards'" (Tawney 1925, 64). Italian financiers like Pallavicino, Vellutelli, and Spinola were also employed by the Elizabethan government to raise loans.[8]

As a consequence of English dealings, at home and abroad, with Italian merchants and financial agents, Italians were instrumental in the introduction of new financial practices to England. Many of these alien practices were found objectionable: Italian merchants were described as grasping, exploitative, and un-Christian, and they were compared to the stereotype of the usurious Jew. Italians and Jews were both represented as guilty of carrying immoral financial practices into England, where these aliens and their ways were said to be threatening both the English economy and the moral health of the commonwealth. Many of these new commercial activities were classified as "usury" in the early modern sense of the term. The meaning of "usury" was not limited to the charging of interest at a high rate, but applied to a whole range of supposedly un-Christian and immoral ways of doing business.[9] For example, any kind of economic activity whereby persons parasitically "manage to enrich themselves by lending and dealing in exchange without ever meddling with commodities" (De Roover 1949, 11) was considered to be a form of usury.[10] Commodification was disturbing enough to the common people (and to many members of the upper classes), but this wheeling and dealing that took money without providing any kind of substantial commodity whatsoever was considered shockingly sinful. Thomas Beard, in his *Theatre of Gods Judgements* (1595), provides a definition of usury that indicates how, as capitalism first emerged, many English Protestants saw its exploitative nature quite clearly and deployed a religious discourse to condemn it:

> Usurie consisteth not onely in lending and borrowing, but in buying and selling also, and all unjust and craftie bargaining, yea and it is a kind of Usurie to detaine through too much covetousnesse those commodities from the people which concerne the publicke good, and to hoord them up for their private gaine, till some scarcitie or want arise, and this also hath evermore ben most sharply punished....(413)

One Tudor economist, Miles Mosse, in his *Arraignment and Conviction of Usurie* (1595) describes usurers as masters of financial disguise:

> Some, to cover their sinne, and to upholde their credite, have devised faire cloakes to shroude their ragged garments, and have begotten a more cunning and subtile kinde of trafficke in the worlde....All which cloakes and subtilties, if I would goe about to discover, I should attempt to tread an endles maze....Like are common usurers unto the monster Hydra: for they have many heades, that is, infinite devises.... (Tawney and Power 3:380–81)

These "infinite devises" included practices such as sharp dealing in credit and debt, commodity speculation, currency trading, hoarding of grain, "dry exchange," "fictitious exchange," and other new tricks of the foreign exchange trade.[11] A "Memorandum Prepared for the Royal Commission on the Exchanges, 1564" discusses "howe the sleightes and Cuninges" of bankers and exchange dealers has led to "the greate losse and hinderaunce of the comone wealthe of England" (Tawney and Power 2:346). In the same text, a conspiracy of "cunning" and fraudulent merchantes, and especially "straunge marchantes" dealing in "Strange wares" is held responsible (Tawney and Power 2:358–59). A manuscript authored by Thomas Smith around 1576, the memorandum "For the Understanding of the Exchange," provides a list of twenty-four "feates Marchaunts devise by exchaunge / for their owne gayne."[12] These include the following:

> To live and growe rich withowt travayle and venter of Sea.
> To doo great feates having creditt and yet be nothing worthe.
> To gett a parte or sometyme all his gayne that employeth money taken up by exchaunge on wares and so make others travayle for their gayne.
> To take up money to engrosse a commoditie eyther newe come or whereof they have some store to bryng the whole trade of that commodity into their handes that they may sell the newe bowght and the old store at their pleasure. (300–02)

Smith regarded these manipulations of the market as harmful to the nation's economic well-being.

A wide range of plays from the late Elizabethan and early Stuart period include satirical attacks on usurers and financial tricksters. Often their "feats" were characterized as un-English and anti-Christian: in Marlowe's *Jew of Malta*, these practices are the "extorting, cozening, forfeiting, / And tricks belonging to brokery" (2.3.193–94) that Barabas boasts of carrying out. When illicit dealings, financial swindles, or economic parasitism were represented on the London stage, the largest profits and the most valuable commodities were often said to come from international trade. The exotic, the economic, and the unethical are strongly linked through the activities carried out by stage Jews like Barabas, Shylock, and Benwash in plays by Marlowe, Shakespeare, and others. According to Tawney,

> It was a common impression among observers of economic conditions that more than half the profits of the export trade, and far less than half

the trouble, went to the financier who, "knowing certainly whether and what the merchants gain upon the wares they buy and sell," was able "to get a part and sometimes all his gains that employeth money taken up by exchange on wares, and so make others travell for his gains." The successful trader, while continuing...to be called by the generic term of "merchant," retired from trade and became, in effect, a banker. (Tawney 1925, 66)

Tawney makes these remarks in the introduction to his edition of Thomas Wilson's *Discourse Upon Usury by Way of Dialogue and Orations* (1572), a text that is also worth mentioning here. In Wilson's *Discourse*, the Preacher asks, "What is the matter that Jewes are so universallye hated wheresoever they come?"

The answer follows: "For soothe, usurie is one of the chief causes, for they robbe all men that deale with them, and undoe them in the ende," but in the conclusion of his oration, the Preacher declares that English usurers are worse than Jews:

For go whither you wil throughout Christendom, and deale with them, and you shall have under tenne in the hundreth, yea sometimes for sixe at their handes, whereas englishe usurers exceede all gods mercye, and wil take they care not howe muche, wythout respecte had to the partye that borroweth, what losse, daunger, hinderaunce soever the borrower susteyneth. And howe can these men be of god that are so farre from charitie, that care not howe they get goods so they may have them? (232)

The Lawyer responds immediately to the Preacher, pointing to the gap between Christian teaching and economic practice: "You have sayde muche, and verie godlye; but whether politiquely, and altogether aptly, I cannot constantlye affirme, for that I see all commonweales in the Christiane worlde are governed otherwyse then you preache" (233). And then, when the merchant-usurer Gromel-Gayner attempts to excuse his usurious ways, the Preacher launches into a long rebuttal, asserting that it is "almost impossible for these worldly merchants to be good Christians" (272) and concluding that "a Christian is no Ethnik, Paynim, nor Jew, so is he no usurer" (361–62). Toward the end of the dialogue, at the urging of the Preacher and the others, Gromel-Gayner is "converted" from "Jew" to "Christian."

Because foreign trade was, by definition, conducted through cross-cultural exchange, and because it led to usurious profit-making without the production of goods, it was seen as a threat to England's very identity as a Christian commonwealth. Nonetheless, the process of incorporating this foreign threat continued inexorably, fueled by the rise of capitalism and primitive accumulation. By the time Antwerp surrendered to the Spanish in 1585, putting the international exchange there out of business, the English had already established a Royal Exchange of their own in London (built by Sir Thomas Gresham and completed in 1569). At Gresham's Exchange, the English themselves began to take over the financial operations that were associated with the Italians and other strangers who had initially performed these functions for the English. In the introduction to his edition of Smith's memorandum, Raymond de Roover describes how, during the Elizabethan period, "the English public and the government officials were obsessed with the idea that the exchange was ruled by a sinister conspiracy of continental bankers" (179). Nonetheless, by the 1580s, the English had thoroughly incorporated a set of "foreign" financial practices: a new system of credit and debt used in foreign exchange, involving "invisible" or "dry" credit and using bills of credit for transactions between merchants; and the establishment of joint-stock companies like the Levant Company. And what gave the English a competitive edge as they moved beyond their own shores was their ability, after having experienced and observed the kind of violent competition for goods and bodies that was carried out in the Mediterranean, to build a merchant fleet that was fast, mobile, and heavily armed with the best maritime military technology of the time.

Critics of this new, aggressive commerce felt that the English were undergoing a double conversion that combined "Jewish" finance and "Turkish" force. The old images of Jewish and Italian merchants were not forgotten: they were revived and informed by these new economic developments and influences. English alliances with Islamic princes, mediated by Jews and renegades, and English involvement in piracy and the slave trade, led to the perception that there was a new, Machiavellian commercial mentality during this period, and that English subjects were coming increasingly into contact with an amoral economy of maritime competition that was based on force and fraud. Not only in the Mediterranean, but also in Asia and the New World, English vessels were becoming active, effective participants in a transcultural economic system that depended on a fluid combination of commercial negotiation and commodity exchange, credit financing, privateering, violent exploitation, and slavery.[13]

One of the leading scholars on naval history in the period, Jan Glete, points out that "Cheap cast-iron guns were one of the main instruments for Elizabethan privateering and the British mercantile expansion into... the Levant" (1:25). During the last three decades of the sixteenth century, the English quickly rose to the top of the maritime pecking order in the Mediterranean. In France, the civil wars of the 1560s and 1570s destroyed all permanent French naval forces. According to Glete, "by the early 1590s the French galley fleet had disappeared" (2:513). At this same time, the Venetian empire and its galley fleet declined under the combined pressure of Ottoman power and endemic piracy.[14] In the Mediterranean, where "Expressions such as 'peaceful trade' and 'state monopoly on violence' were bad jokes" (Glete 1:115), English vessels rushed aggressively into the power vacuum.[15]

These corruptive foreign influences were thought to come, not from distinct and coherent groups of foreigners who could be identified by stable religious or national affiliation, but rather the English saw that the agents of this new economic system were highly mobile, adaptive, and hybridized—Portuguese and Spanish Jews or *conversos*, Italianated Spaniards from the Kingdom of Naples, Jewish and Armenian factors in the Levant, Dutch renegades working in the Barbary ports, Venetian or Genoese merchants and bankers who did business with Muslims, Jews, and Christians alike.

Another text that, like *The Croxton Play of the Sacrament*, dramatizes an alliance between Mediterranean Jews and Christian merchants is Robert Wilson's *Three Ladies of London* (ca. 1581). In this play, produced much later in a post-Reformation context, religious identity and interfaith commerce are represented in a way that is even more troubling and unstable. Wilson's morality play begins with the lamentations of Lady Love and Lady Conscience, who bemoan their "fall" and the rise of Lady Lucar (i.e. "Lucre"). Love's opening complaint is directed against the same power that corrupted Aristorius in *The Croxton Play of the Sacrament*:

> For Lucar men come from Italy, Barbary, Turky
> From [Jewry]: nay the Pagan himselfe,
> Indaungers his bodie to gape for her pelfe.
> They forsake mother, Prince, Countrey, Religion, kiffe and kinne,
> Nay men care not what they forsake, so Lady Lucar they winne.
> (ll.14–19)

In the late Elizabethan period, it is not only religion that is for sale: primitive accumulation and commodification, encouraged by Mediterranean models of venture capitalism, have gone much further. Englishmen are prostituting themselves, turning Turk, for the sake of Lady Lucar. Lady Lucar is surrounded by admirers who offer their services: these suitors include Fraud, Dissimulation, Symony, and a character called Usery. Upon meeting Usery, Lucar asks him, "didst thou never knowe my Grandmother the olde Lady Lucar of Venice [?]"

Usery's response, "Yes Madam I was servaunt unto her and lived there
in blisse" (ll.279–81), indicates the English awareness that the Italian
cities were the places where the usurious practices of modern banking,
venture capitalism, and the joint-stock company began and that the
Italian merchants who came to London in the mid-sixteenth century
exported their financial methods to England. The Venetian Usery and
the Roman Symony tell Lucar how they first came to England aboard
the ship of "some English Merchauntes" (l.297). In the next scene, an
Italian merchant named Mercadore enters and is introduced to Lucar by
Davy Dissimulation. The following interview ensues:

> Lucar: Gentleman you are hartly welcome, howe are you called, I
>   pray you tell us?
> Mercadore: Madona, me be a Mershant and be cald Merkadorus.
> Lucar: But I pray you tell me what Countriman.
> Mercadore: Me be Madona an Italian.
> Lucar: Yet let me trouble ye, I beseeche ye whence came ye?
> Mercadore: For sarva voutra boungrace, me come from Turkie.
> (ll.388–93)

Mercadore's Italian accent, his use of French, his being Italian but
coming from Turkey—all these testify to his slippery mobility and
unstable identity. He serves Lucar, not any single nation or faith.
Lucar questions him further on his willingness to serve her in ways
that violate both general moral principles and specific national interests: "Gramerci, but senior Mercadore, dare you not to undertake, /
Secretlie to convey good commodities out of this country for my
sake?" (ll.394–95). Mercadore answers,

> Madona, me doe for love of you tinck no paine to mush,
> And to doe any ting for you me will not grush,
> Mee will a forsake a my Fader, Moder, King, Countrey & more
> den dat.
> Me will lie and forsweare me selfe for a quarter so much as my hat.
> What is dat for love of Lucar me dare or will not doe:
> Me care not for all the world, the great Devill, nay make my God
> angry for you. (ll.396–401)

Lucar then tells him that he must carry grain, leather, tallow, beef,
bacon, and bell metal out of the country, "and for these good commodities, trifles to Englande thou must bryng" (l.411). She informs
Mercadore that "every day Gentlewomen of England doe aske for suche
trifles" (l.413). According to Tudor and Early Stuart commentators on

the balance of trade, these useless baubles threatened to drain, weaken, and effeminate the domestic economy. Mercadore represents the kind of merchant who was the object of criticism for exporting gold and silver currency in order to import luxury goods. His catalogue of commodities includes luxury goods that were shipped from the Mediterranean to England, and his own resources seem to be in the form of coin and jewels. From the mid-sixteenth century on, there were frequent objections, both at the popular and official level, to the importation of expensive foreign commodities. For example, a manuscript from 1549, "Policies to Reduce this Realme of Englande unto a Prosperus Wealthe and Estate," complains, "The onlie meanes to cause mouche Bullione to be broughte oute of other realms unto the kinges mintes is to provide that a great quantitie of our wares maye be carriede yerly into beyonde the Sees and lese quantitie of wares be brought hether a gaine" (Tawney and Power 2:321). This kind of objection to the exchange of gold, silver, or staple commodities for unneeded luxury goods from exotic sources runs through the economic writings of the sixteenth and seventeenth centuries in England. These objections influenced economic policy. The English government "sought to restrain the export of bullion during the Tudor period" (Challis 184).[16] At the time of Wilson's play (in 1582 and 1584), the Muscovy Company had to obtain special permission to export large quantities of bullion, as did the East India Company toward the end of the century. In 1582 the queen lent "members of the Levant Company 10,000 lbs. of silver bullion on the condition that it was repaid in five years at the rate of 2000 lb. per annum" (Challis 185). Piracy and privateering, along with "bi-metallic flow," brought a great deal of gold and silver into England during the Elizabethan period, but according to Challis, "How far the mercantilist ideal of exports consistently exceeding imports, thereby inducing a net inflow of bullion into England, was ever realized in the Tudor period is something of an open question" (185).

Lucar and Mercadore exit the stage together, and as soon as they leave the stage, an unemployed Englishman named "Artifex an Artificer" appears, seeking work. He asks Dissimulation if he can help him to find a job, and then Artifex complains about immigrant laborers:

> There be such a sort of straungers in this cuntry,
> That worke fine to please the eie, though it be deceitfully,
> And that which is slight, and seemes to the eie well,
> Shall sooner then a peece of good worke be proferred to sell. (ll.467–70)

Artifex is turned away, and when Mercadore returns to the stage, he meets his old friend Usery, who has been raising rents and evicting

Lucar's impoverished tenants. When Lucar asks Mercadore if he will "goe amongest the Moores, Turkes, and Pagans for my sake" (l.891), the Italian leaves immediately "to search for some new toyes in Barbary or Turky / Such trifles as...will please wantons best" (ll.898–99).

Later, having arrived in Turkey, Mercadore meets Gerontus, a Jewish moneylender who accuses him of borrowing three thousand ducats two years earlier before fleeing the country without paying. Gerontus's admonishment contrasts Jewish honesty with Christian double-dealing and oath-breaking: "Surely if we that be Jewes should deale so one with an other, / We should not be trusted againe of our owne brother: / But many of you Christians make no conscience to falsifie your fayth and breake your day" (ll.1243–45). Economic immorality and religious imposture are associated in this comment, which is implicitly aimed at the "Christians" in the audience.

Holding out the hope of recovering his money, Gerontus tells Mercadore that if he pays his overdue debt, Gerontus will trade with him. But the Italian merchant fails to discharge his debt, and Gerontus swears "by mightie Mahomet" (l.1545) that he will have Mercadore arrested. When called before a "Judge of Turkie," Mercadore arrives "in Turkish weedes" (l.1710). When the judge declares that "if any man forsake his faith, king, countrie, and become a Mahomet, / All debts are paide, tis the lawe of our Realme" (ll.1712–13), Mercadore announces, "me will be a Turke, and for dat cause me came heere" (l.1720). "[F]or Lucars sake" (l.1725) Mercadore swears to "forsake my Christian faith" (l.1729), but Gerontus attempts to dissuade him and says that he is "loth to heare the people say, it was long of me / Thou foresakest thy faith" (ll.1740–41). The Jewish moneylender then offers to forgo the interest if Mercadore will pay the principal. When this proposition is refused, Gerontus asks for only half the principal. Finally, he agrees to forgive the whole debt if only Mercadore will remain a Christian. Mercadore accepts this last offer, and when the judge asks the Italian if he "will be a Turke for all this" (l.1746), he replies, "not for all da good in da world, me foresake a my Christ" (l.1747). The judge, who can only marvel at this bandying about of religious allegiance, leaves the stage after pronouncing, "One may judge and speake truth, as appeeres by this, / Jewes seeke to excell in Christianitie, and the Christians in Jewisnes" (ll.1753–54). Playing against the old medieval stereotype of the miserly, usurious Jew, Wilson's play violates expectations by showing the moneylending Jew to be charitable in comparison to the new breed of faith-breaking, border-crossing chameleons like Mercadore. These men have no stable religious or cultural affiliation and are willing to turn and turn again for the love of lucre.

* * *

The theatrical representation of Jews on the early modern stage was derived not only from the presence of Jews and other "aliens" on English soil or from the popular beliefs and homegrown anxieties detailed by James Shapiro in his study, *Shakespeare and the Jews*, it was also informed by direct English contact with Jewish merchants in the Mediterranean region, including North Africa and the Ottoman empire.[17] During Shakespeare's lifetime, the frequency of encounters between Jews and Englishmen in the Mediterranean increased rapidly because of two coincidental developments, both taking place during the second half of the sixteenth century: "a significant increase in the involvement of Jewish merchants in eastern Mediterranean trade" (Arbel 3) and the simultaneous resurgence of English trade in the same region.[18] English knowledge of Jewish culture suddenly expanded because it was part of the "intelligence" gathered for the purpose of merchant adventuring in the Levant. One consequence of these economic encounters was the increased production of ethnographic knowledge by Englishmen who had met or observed Mediterranean Jews. Beginning in the 1570s, commercial reports and ethnographic texts appeared in print with increasing frequency. These texts include detailed descriptions of Jewish merchants and Jewish communities in the Mediterranean, and sometimes they describe an alliance between Muslims and Jews, particularly between the Ottoman state and Jewish citizens of the Turkish empire. This renewed contact with Mediterranean cultures helps to account for the appearance on the London stage of Mediterranean scenes featuring Jewish and Islamic characters interacting with Christians.

The remainder of this chapter looks at three plays in the context of English foreign trade and contact with Jews in the multicultural milieu of the early modern Mediterranean: Christopher Marlowe's *Jew of Malta* (1590), William Shakespeare's *Merchant of Venice* (1596) and Robert Daborne's *A Christian Turned Turk* (1612). In each case, the play must work hard to eliminate the threat of contamination posed by non-Christian alterity. If we examine these plays as a group, we can see the emergence of Jewish merchant figures who represent the historically specific conditions of economic interaction and exchange between English and Jewish participants in the Mediterranean economy.

During the late Elizabethan period, international economic competition and proto-colonialist ambition encouraged English elites to invest in international trade, plunder, and settlement. This led to the development of direct trade links with harbor and market towns in the parts of the Mediterranean under Muslim rule, and to increased contact with Jewish communities in Ottoman and Barbary entrepôts. Stage Jews such as Marlowe's Barabas, Shakespeare's Shylock, or Benwash in Daborne's *A Christian Turned Turk* are, in part, representations of the Jewish traders and middlemen that English merchants encountered from Morocco to Istanbul. At the same time, these rapacious characters represent and reconfigure English anxieties about the Machiavellian practices of English merchants themselves. The "pound of flesh" demanded by Shylock is a version of the commodification of human beings that English merchant-privateers began to practice in an era of proto-imperial aggression. Marlowe's Barabas, as the ultimate advocate of foreign trade in luxury commodities, scorns the "vulgar trade" conducted for lesser wares or limited by the borders of a single nation. His desires resemble those of English merchants trading for luxury goods in the Mediterranean. Marlowe's play takes an ambivalent attitude toward the wealth derived from importing exotic commodities as its starting point, and then presents Barabas himself as a demonized version of the Machiavellian merchants who grew rich from foreign trade.

In the Mediterranean market, it was business as usual for Christians to make deals with both Muslims and Jews: commercial partnerships often crossed the boundaries of ethnic or religious difference. English subjects were not always comfortable with this, and the Christian fear of the Jew as ally of the Muslim was partly based on real social and economic circumstances that Englishmen witnessed in the Ottoman territories. When English captives taken by the Barbary pirates were brought to the slave markets of Algiers or Tunis to be sold, Jewish merchants sometimes acted as middlemen and were known to purchase both slaves and other commodities obtained by piracy.[19] These merchants were part of the Jewish communities that thrived under the relatively tolerant rule of the Ottoman empire. During the sixteenth century, the Ottoman Jewish communities emerged as the foremost centers of Jewish culture in the world, rivaled, perhaps, only by those of Poland and Lithuania. The expulsions during the twelfth to sixteenth centuries had forced many Jews to leave Western Europe, and the Ottoman empire appealed to Jewish immigrants because of its religious tolerance, its cultural pluralism, its polyethnic society, as well as the economic opportunities it provided. Jewish citizens of the

Ottoman empire enjoyed much more freedom than their co-religionists did under contemporary Christian rule, and some Jews were even granted a tax-exempt status for their service to the Turkish state, or for performing administrative duties within the Jewish community itself. Turkish custom attached a stigma to many commercial practices that were carried out between foreigners and merchants, and so they usually preferred to leave these transactions in the hands of others.[20] The Ottoman authorities came to regard Jewish residents as economically productive and politically dependable. Their managerial and entrepreneurial skills were employed by the expanding bureaucracy of the Turkish empire, especially in the areas of tax collection, custom farming, banking, and minting. In early modern Istanbul, Jews were the third largest ethnic group, after the Turks and Greeks, and throughout the empire they played a very important role in international trade. Nicolas de Nicolay's *Navigations and Voyages Made into Turkie* (an English translation appeared in 1585) gives a late sixteenth-century Frenchman's view of Jewish merchants in the Levant:

> The number of the Jewes dwelling throughout all the Cities of Turkie and Grecia...is so great that it is a thing marveilous and incredible, for the number of these, using trade and trafique of merchandise, like of money at usurie, doth there multiply so from day too daye, that the great haunt and bringing of merchandises which arrive there of all parts...is such, that it may be said with good reason that at this present day they have in their handes the moste and greatest trafique of merchandize and readie money, that is in al Levant. And lykewise their shops and warehouses the best furnished of all riche sortes of merchandises.... (130)

In Leo Africanus's *Geographical Historie of Africa*, translated by John Pory in 1600, the Jewish diaspora in North Africa is traced from Ethiopia to Timbuktoo to Egypt and the Levant, where "...in all the cities and townes thereof, they exercise mechanicall arts, and use traffick and merchandize, as also take upon them the receit of taxes and customes" (380).

The recent work of scholars interested in the history of Jewish merchants and Mediterranean commerce during the sixteenth and seventeenth centuries confirms these early modern descriptions of Jewish Levantine culture. Bernard Dov Cooperman, for example, declares,

> There can be no doubt that Jews were prominent and active participants in the new Ottoman commercial economy generally, and in the trade between East and West in particular....Ottoman expansion... brought certain new factors into play which served to encourage the

Jewish participation in commerce....Jews also benefited from the renewed religious bifurcation of the Mediterranean into warring Christian and Muslim worlds....this division gave at least some advantage to the religiously "neutral" Jews who could pass between the two worlds with relative ease and who were able to find communities of their co-religionists almost wherever they went. (Cooperman 68–69)

Cooperman and other historians have pointed to an alliance between Muslims and Jews under Ottoman rule that raised many Jewish merchants and dignitaries to positions of power and wealth. Joseph Nasi is perhaps the best-known example of this, and he has often been cited as a model for Barabas as a Jew given the governorship of an Ottoman-controlled island.[21] Nasi was created duke of Naxos by Selim II in 1566, and it was rumored that he would be made Ottoman governor of Cyprus, which was conquered in 1570. Nasi was not an isolated case, though he was unusually close to the sultan himself. When Ottoman officials were sent to administer distant provinces, it was common practice to hire a local Jew who would serve as a private banker, commercial agent, and financial advisor.

Richard Knolles, in *The Generall Historie of the Turkes* (1603), describes an incident that indicates how this relationship sometimes operated in highly visible ways that may remind us of the events in *The Jew of Malta* and other plays. According to Knolles, after a Turkish attack on Corsica in 1556, the pope

exacted of his people a great subsidie, and finely stript the Jews of their money, and seized upon their rich marchants goods in his territorie: at whose earnest sute Solyman writ in their behalf unto the bishop [of Rome] as followeth:...certaine Hebrews have come unto us, complayning that they are oppressed of thee with too greevous exactions, when they come to traffic at Ancona: This burden I request thee to take from them, and to restore againe unto them their goods, that thereby they may be able to pay unto us our tribute: which if thou (as I hope thou wilt) shall doe, thou shalt feel our favour. (766)

The plays by Marlowe and Daborne indicate a consciousness of this kind of special relationship between Ottoman officials and Jewish entrepreneurs. It was the customary practice for a Jew to hold the office of merchant-banker to the janissary corps, and as chief financier and purveyor for the Ottoman military elite, these Jewish officials must have been on close terms with powerful janissary officers.

There was also an awareness that wealthy Jewish merchants were living under Christian rule in cities like Ancona, Genoa, and Venice, where they enjoyed the protection of local authorities. This protection also became available to Jewish émigrés in Elizabethan London (as James Shapiro and C.J. Sisson have shown). But Christian tolerance of Jews in Western Europe was often in tension with tendencies toward religious persecution. In Shakespeare's Venice, Shylock's appeal to the privileges granted under the city charter indicates the sometimes beleaguered position of Jews in places like Venice where they were tolerated but subject to unequal treatment. He defends his right to fair treatment under the law, but he knows that without an economic incentive the Venetians would not grant him even those limited rights and privileges:

> For the commodity that strangers have
> With us in Venice, if it be denied,
> Will much impeach the justice of the state,
> Since that the trade and profit of the city
> consisteth of all nations. (3.3.27–31)

The Christians' need for Jews and other foreigners to help stimulate trade was mirrored and rivaled by the Ottomans' need for skilled go-betweens who could conduct trade and manage their money. The Christian perception of a Muslim–Jewish alliance may be traced back to the era of the Crusades, and for centuries Western European writers confused the two religious systems. We see this confusion still operating in *The Croxton Play of the Sacrament*, when the Jewish Jonathas worships "Machomet" and swears by his laws. This misrepresentation of Muslim and Jewish belief systems was then mapped from this older tradition onto a new set of texts that placed Jewish merchants and Turkish officials or janissaries side-by-side in the early modern Mediterranean.

According to one account, the Turko-Jewish alliance was a relationship that was first fostered at the time of the conquest of Constantinople by Mahomet I. The genesis of this relationship is recounted by an Italian author, Ottaviano Bon, whose description of the Ottoman court was translated into English in the early seventeenth century:

> Mahomet, after hee had thus taken the City, resolving to keepe there the seat of his Empire, caused . . . the wals to be new made, and certaine of the ruinated places to be repaired. And in stead of the great number of the people that were there slaine and carried away as prisoners, he caused to be brought thither, out of all the Provinces and Cities by him conquered, a certaine number of men, women, and children, with their

faculties and riches, whom he permitted there to live according to the institutions and precepts of such Religion as it pleased them to observe, and to exercise with all safety, their handicrafts and merchandises; which ministered an occasion unto an infinite multitude of Jewes and Marannes, driven out of Spaine, for to come and dwell there: By meanes whereof, in very short time the City began to increase in trafficke, riches, and abundance of people. (23)

During the sixteenth and seventeenth centuries, under both Christian and Muslim rule, many Jewish merchants enjoyed special privileges and protection, as well as special vulnerabilities. Under Christian rule, this protection was frequently and arbitrarily dissolved when it served the ideological or financial interests of those in power—and then confiscation, expulsion, or persecution could occur. Under the Ottoman empire, however, the juridical status of Jews as a *dhimmi* minority prevented mass victimization during the early modern period (though the Turks did force the deportation of many Balkan Jews to urban centers like Istanbul).

Scholars have argued that the important role played by Jews in Ottoman empire-building (what Avigdor Levy has termed "the Jewish-Ottoman symbiosis") contributed significantly to Western anti-Semitism. Jews and Muslims were both understood by the early modern English to be "infidels" expelled from Iberia at the same time, and with a similar history of forced and feigned conversion preceding and following their expulsion. Both were circumcised, a practice not used by early modern Christians in Europe, and both practiced a radically iconoclastic form of monotheism. Several long-standing traditions, both learned and popular, linked Muslims and Jews. In the earliest tradition, going back to the seventh century, Christian authors blamed Jews for the victory of Muslims over Byzantine Christians. According to David M. Olster, "they used the Jew as a rhetorical device to personify the doubts within their own community with a recognizable, evil, and most important, eminently defeatable opponent" (3). In a curious way, this "device" continued to operate for many centuries, and what was said of the Arabs was applied later to the Turks and their relationship to Jewish communities.

Alan and Helen Cutler have also argued that during the medieval period "Western European Christians tended, in their own minds, to associate Jew with Muslim, and to consider the Jew an ally of the Muslim as well as an Islamic fifth columnist in Christian territory" (2). "A Jew is not a Jew until he converts to Islam," was a medieval Latin proverb, and the Crusades saw this attitude confirmed when Frankish soldiers slaughtered Jews and Muslims indiscriminately.[22] These medieval conceptions of Jews, Muslims, and their relations with each other form the basis for later representations, but the early modern image of the Jew in England developed new features that emerged in the context of the sixteenth and seventeenth centuries.

English post-Reformation anxieties about religious difference exhibit a fixation on the religious Other (whether Jewish, Muslim, or Roman Catholic), but with the validity of pilgrimage and crusade questioned or rejected by Protestantism, and with the emergence of a new foreign trade in the late sixteenth century, we see an ethnographic turn in English texts about Jews and Muslims that shifts from an interest in the fantastic to the pragmatic. No longer do we find a Jewish Herod swearing by "Mahound," the Saracens' idol, but we observe instead a new economic relationship between Jews and Muslims.

A series of plays written and performed in early modern England dramatizes Jewish–Muslim partnerships: Gerontus and the Turkish judge in Wilson's *The Three Ladies of London*; Barabas, Ithamore, and Selim-Calymath in Marlowe's *Jew of Malta*; Abraham and Selimus in Greene's *Selimus, Emperor of the Turks*; Benwash, Crosman, and the Governor of Tunis in Daborne's *A Christian Turned Turk*; Zeriph and Halibeck in Day, Rowley, and Wilkins's *The Travels of the Three English Brothers*; and Hamon and Bajazet in Goffe's *The Raging Turk*. In all of these texts, Jewish characters seek to gain by doing the bidding of a powerful Muslim figure, and (with the exception of Greene's Abraham) these stage Jews serve as go-betweens or mediators between Muslims and Christians. For Barabas and Benwash, the only Jewish characters in this list who play a central role in the action of the play, their alliance with Muslim officials creates a larger, systematic threat within the political and economic spheres.

In Marlowe's *Jew of Malta*, English anti-Semitism is frequently linked to the fear and awe felt toward Turkish-Islamic wealth and power. In Marlowe's play, anxieties about the acquisition of money and commodities by means of foreign trade produce a new representation of the merchant adventurer, a demonized version of the actual Jewish merchants that English ship masters encountered in Mediterranean ports. With one foot in medieval convention and another straining toward a radically new and modern sense of performativity, Marlowe gives us Barabas, who is not a miserly usurer or a poison-peddling physician, but a merchant adventurer and ship owner accumulating wealth openly in a multicultural environment. He is not confined or contained in a ghetto. Instead Barabas inhabits an imaginary space that is defined by its centrality within the multicultural Mediterranean world. He positions himself at the center of a network where he is best able to connect with various groups. Malta was at the crossroads of the Mediterranean Sea, and in the midst of a turbulent maritime borderland where Christian and Muslim spheres of influence intersected.

In his *Navigations into Turkie*, Nicolas de Nicolay recounts two visits to Malta during the time that he traveled as a member of a French embassy to the Ottoman court of Suleiman. In May of 1551 the ambassador and his entourage left Marseilles in two gallies headed for Constantinople. Nicolay refers to recent Turkish raids on Sicily and Malta, and to the on-going siege of Tripoli (which was held by the Habsburg Emperor Charles V at the time). During the French embassy's stop in Malta, the Maltese Grand Master persuaded the French ambassador to go to Tripoli and attempt to induce the Turks to give up their siege of the city. There, after the conditions of surrender had been negotiated between the Turkish commander "Sinan Bascha" and Governor Vallier, Nicolay witnessed the surrender of the castle of Tripoli to the Turks. Nicolay provides this report of Turkish oath-breaking:

> . . . the Bascha: who being by the knight Vallier admonished of his faith, which he had twice given, answered that there was no promise to be kept with dogges, and that they had first violated their oth with the great Lord, unto whom at the giving over of Rhodes, they had sworn that they never would take on armes agaynst the Turkes. (24–26)

Nicolay then comments on this Turkish perfidy: "they are the most barbarous, covetous & cruel nation of the world, & in whom there is neither truth nor fidelity, never observing the one half of that they promise: and yet men must always be giving to them" (27). Fourteen years later, the Turks would besiege Malta itself, and subsequently Marlowe would present his stage Turks as the least treacherous of the three religious groups that come together in his Maltese meeting ground. Nicolay describes Malta as he saw it in the 1550s: "shee is inhabited and peopled with a great number of Commaunders, Knights and Merchants of all nations: and above all there is great aboundaunce of Curtizans, both Greeke, Italian, Spaniards, Moores, and Maltez" (17). In Nicolay's description, both militarization and prostitution are emphasized, and this combination of power and sex for sale is something that Marlowe also depicts in his dramatization of Malta as a multicultural border zone.

Marlowe's Malta is a place where contact and mixture involving Jews, Muslims, and Christians leads to violent instability. From the start, Barabas's dilemma is that he wishes to hoard and remain separate (accumulating capital and keeping his daughter from marrying a Christian), while at the same time he seeks profit through extensive mixture and exchange. He is happy to have the Turks take Malta, as long as his business interests are not adversely affected. In the play's first scene, Barabas hopes that the Turkish Muslims "combat, conquer, and kill all, / So they spare me, my daughter, and my wealth" (1.1.151–52), and he ends the scene by exclaiming, "Why, let 'em enter, let 'em take the town!" (1.1.189). Soon the audience learns that Barabas is not the sole exemplar of greed, but that all those who conduct business in Malta are ready to sell themselves. Three religious groups are represented: Jews (Barabas and his co-religionists); Muslims (Ithamore the Turk and the Ottoman officials); and the Roman Catholic friars, nuns, whores, and knights of Malta. The play reveals a sort of "triangular trade" between Roman Catholics (including the Maltese and the Spanish), Jewish merchants and middlemen, and Muslims (including both the "Moors" of the Barbary coast cities and the Ottoman Turks). Turks and Moors, captured by the Spanish Vice-Admiral, Martin del Bosco, are enslaved and sold in the Maltese slave market, where the Jewish merchant Barabas arrives to view the wares. Because the Maltese have confiscated most of his property, he is only able to afford one slave, but one of the officers in charge recognizes Barabas as a merchant who was once the principal purchaser of slaves in the Maltese market: "Here comes the Jew; had not his goods been seized, / He'd give us present money for them all" (2.3.5–6). Like Benwash in Daborne's play, Barabas is an "engrosser" of commodities taken in war or by piracy and then sold in the local market. He and Benwash act as middlemen, buying up stolen or forcibly appropriated goods cheaply and then selling them at a profit. In fact, Christian Malta is no different than Muslim Tunis or Algiers in its approach to piracy, captivity, and slavery. According to Fenton's 1618 translation of Guicciardini's *History of Italy*, the Knights Hospitallers of Malta "were not without some note of infamie, for that having a continuall custome, for the better defending of those shores, to spoile the vessels of the infidels, they sometimes forgot themselves so much as to make pillage of the ships of Christians" (595).

The slave that Barabas chooses is Ithamore, a Muslim who may have been the property of a Turkish master before the Spanish captured him. The dialogue exchanged by Barabas and Ithamore in act 2, scene 3, with its catalogue of anti-Jewish myths, has often been read as confirmation that Barabas is a neo-medieval representation of the traditional anti-Semitic stereotype. Ithamore and Barabas, Jew and Turk, introduce themselves to each other, and when Ithamore declares his profession to be "what you please," this indicates to Barabas that he has found a kindred being, another self without a stable identity. When Barabas tells Ithamore that he has been a poisoner of wells, a usurer, an extortionist, a false witness, and so on, he does this not to indicate to the audience a true report about his career as a Jew, but with a wink at the spectators. He uses this catalogue of stereotypical behaviors as an ironical boast, to manipulate the naïve, malleable malevolence he sees in Ithamore. It is a highly exaggerated list of atrocities, and its excess is ridiculous—black humor intended to make the audience laugh. The effect of this speech (2.3.176–202) is to undermine these absurd claims about Jews. Barabas rises above the hackneyed images of Jewish villainy to a more sophisticated level demonstrating his protean meta-villainy. His identity is not fixed in the images of the physician-poisoner, the parasitical usurer, or the hoarding miser. His list of "confessions" indicates that these parts have already been played; they belong to the past, to an earlier form of drama. Barabas the Jew has metamorphosed into a new incarnation: he is a much more slippery, self-fashioning devil, adapted to the conditions of the early modern marketplace. He is a master trickster, a shape-shifter, and a survival strategist (and that is why his sudden demise at the end comes as such an unexpected shock). The very variety and number of roles that he claims to have played make it clear that he is not limited to any one of them—he can be anything, even a French lute-player or a dead body. He is mobile, unstable, improvisational, and adaptive.

By the end of their dialogue, Ithamore and Barabas have become "fellows"—"Jew" and "Turk" are indistinguishable, and their identification seems to have erased, at least temporarily, the master–slave difference. Barabas proclaims, "we are villains both: / Both circumcised, we hate Christians both" (2.3.216–17). And in a more general sense, at the play's conclusion greed obliterates identity because Christians, Muslims, and Jews become homologous rivals operating according to the same Machiavellian principles and venal desires. The more the characters insist on their difference, the more the audience recognizes their similarities. Jew, Turk, Roman Catholic knight of Malta—these identities become interchangeable positions in a nexus of commodity exchange that is both mutually constitutive and aggressively competitive. The audience is made to feel as Abigail does after Ithamore and Barabas succeed in plotting the death of her love,

Don Mathias: "I perceive there is no love on earth, / Pity in Jews, nor piety in Turks" (3.3.50–51).

The context of Malta is such that all alliances, all contracts, are destined to be broken. Ithamore turns against Barabas, his "second self" (3.4.15), in order to buy the love of Bellamira the courtesan. It is at this point that Barabas finds a new and more distinguished Islamic ally, Selim-Calymath, the son of the Great Turk himself. In order to convince Selim-Calymath of his loyalty, he immediately identifies himself as a Jew and offers to betray the besieged city to the Turkish army surrounding it. This establishes his motive for genuine hostility to the Christians of Malta. They have confiscated his property and persecuted him. Such treatment was not the policy of the Ottomans in their dealings with Jewish merchants like Barabas. Selim-Calymath offers to make him governor, and he is good to his word, but Barabas seems unable to stop changing sides. He does not remain fixed in a particular posture of animosity toward any one religious group. Instead Barabas betrays Selim-Calymath and proclaims his loyalty to neither Christians or Turks:

> Thus, loving neither, will I live with both,
> Making a profit of my policy;
> And he from whom my most advantage comes
> Shall be my friend.
> This is the life we Jews are used to lead,
> And reason, too, for Christians do the like. (5.2.111–16)

In the end, he dies cursing them both: "Damned Christian dogs, and Turkish infidels" (5.5.85). Marlowe's Barabas becomes the victim of a savage farce of his own making, and the scaffold that he builds himself, like the apparatus of his mercantile network, collapses under the strain of his furious instability. He is an effigy shaped in the image of the foreign trader, a demonization of the new merchant adventurers who, like Barabas, sought profit through "policy" but also used strong-arm tactics when they could. English merchants in the Mediterranean operated as privateers when they had a chance, and some of them did not hesitate to be involved even in the slave trade there: as Nabil Matar has noted, "only the English and the Maltese used their ships for transporting captives to the slave markets of Constantinople" (Matar 1994, 38). Barabas represents the new venality and commodification that the English themselves were adopting as versatile go-betweens competing aggressively for profit in the Mediterranean marketplace.

* * *

The reports of Jewish wealth and power that reached England were undoubtedly exaggerated, and these descriptions of Jewish culture do not accurately represent the variety of Jewish activities and income levels in the Levant. Nonetheless, tales about influential Jews circulated in England. These stories adapted and reconfigured old stereotypes to form a new image of "the Jew" that still maintained some of its former features, such as usurious lending and transnational conspiracy. As Michael Neill remarks in an essay on early modern constructions of ethnic identity, the Europeans' fear of the Jew had to do with his strategies of mimicry, "with his insidious role as the hidden stranger, the alien whose otherness is the more threatening for its guise of semblance" (272). For Neill, early modern England "was a culture whose own expansionism... generated fears of a hungrily absorptive otherness...; in its fictions the Jew represents the deepest threat of all—that of a *secret* difference, masquerading as likeness, whose presence threatens the surreptitious erosion of identity from within" (272).

Shakespeare's rewriting of Barabas as Shylock in some ways takes a step backward toward the older image of the Jew as usurer, but Shakespeare's problem comedy, like Marlowe's tragic farce, exhibits contemporary anxieties about foreign trade and investment in overseas ventures. *The Merchant of Venice* features a contract between a Jewish merchant banker and a Christian merchant "adventurer," and that relationship represents real tensions and conflicts that were enacted in the Mediterranean marketplace. The dispute between Shylock and Antonio corresponds quite closely to a pattern of social and economic struggle that existed in Venice during the second half of the sixteenth century as the Jewish community in Venice began to shift its most visible economic activities from banking to international trade.[23] Attacks on usury and attempts to convert prominent Jews to Christianity were frequent during this period and it is just these issues that are foregrounded in Shakespeare's play.

As John Gillies and others have shown, Shakespeare's Venice is a site of tremendous uneasiness about "trade, intermixture and miscegenation" (Gillies 136). It is a place where a violent contradiction between "intrusion" and "exorbitance" exists, "as if the dynamic outward thrust of the world-city had imploded, drawing the transgressive and polluting energies of the outside in upon itself" (Gillies 67). Antonio's mysterious melancholy and his virulent hatred of Shylock are indicative of an aristocratic "royal merchant" (3.2.238) who desires profit but feels contaminated by the means necessary to gain that profit. Antonio's status as "royal merchant" implies that he has government sponsorship, through license or monopoly, to import or export a certain quantity of a specific commodity or commodities. In England, real royal merchants included people like the earl of Essex, who received from the monarch the privilege of controlling and collecting customs on the trade of specific commodities. Such men were hated by merchants who accused these royal appointees of economic parasitism. Despite the customs "farm" and monopolies granted to Essex by Elizabeth, by 1600 he was deep in debt and complaining to the queen about losing his pound of flesh and blood to his creditors:

> that farm is both my chiefest maintenance and mine only means of compounding with the merchants to whom I am indebted....If my creditors will take for payment many ounces of my blood, or the taking away of this farm would only for want finish my body, your Majesty would never hear of this suit. (Qtd. in Harrison 271)

Like Essex, Antonio and his Christian friends represent a class of aristocrats who can no longer maintain their wealth and position without becoming deeply involved in foreign trade, debt, and investment. In an important study, *Theatre, Finance and Society in Early Modern England*, Theodore Leinwand argues that Antonio's melancholy is a product of his disgust with these aspects of the early modern economy. In Leinwand's carefully historicized reading of *The Merchant of Venice*, Antonio is revealed as a "privateering merchant" whose hazardous investments and dependency on credit produce "in him a neurotic form of nostalgia, an affect-intensive longing for a self-image untrammeled by exchange values..." (9). Bassanio's complaint to Antonio, and Bassanio's unpaid debts, are symptomatic of cash-poor, credit-dependent aristocratic elites not only on the Rialto, but in Shakespeare's London:

> ...I have disabled mine estate
> By something showing a more swelling port
> Than my faint means would grant continuance.
> Nor do I now make moan to be abridged
> From such a noble rate; but my chief care
> Is to come fairly off from the great debts
> Wherein my time, something too prodigal,
> Hath left me gaged. (1.1.123–30)

In England, aristocrats were becoming increasingly willing to invest in overseas "ventures" (like the Barbary Company or the Levant Company) in order to maintain their income and privileges. At the same time, loans with interest and the extension of credit were becoming necessary for any aristocratic investor who wanted a piece of the action. The Venetian men in *The Merchant of Venice* embody or express many of the anxieties about new economic enterprises that involved them in profit-seeking exchange with foreigners. Their homosocial network of relationships begins to feel new pressures as they become involved in systems of lending, credit, debt, interest, profit-sharing, and profit-taking that conflicted with an older system of class values that disdained forms of prestige or alliances based on cash and credit alone. Antonio's predicament refers to the uneasy sense of financial risk, dependency, and instability that prevailed in the new economy of international trade. For Antonio and his peers, to be in debt is dishonor; it is, as Bassanio puts it, to be "worse than nothing" (3.2.259). Though he desperately wishes to avoid such dishonorable entanglements, Antonio's social status and economic resources are not enough to preserve him from dependency on an alien figure like Shylock, who judges a man's value by his liquid capital and tells Bassanio that "Antonio is a good man" (1.3.11) because he has good credit, and not because of his breeding or moral standing. Though Antonio claims that he is different, the marketplace has a leveling effect. He and Shylock are competitors in the same commercial environment, and Shylock's way of doing business gives the Jew an economic advantage that Antonio resents.

When Antonio's confident prediction that in two months he will possess "thrice three times the value" (1.3.155) of Shylock's loan fails to come true, he is "undone" (3.1.103). Pursued by his creditors, Antonio eventually declares himself unwilling to "outlive his wealth" (4.1.264). The anxious concerns expressed by Salerio and Solanio in the opening lines of the play appear to have been justified: Antonio's reckless investment of all his assets, a move he defends by pointing out that his "ventures are not in one bottom trusted / Nor to one place" (1.1.42–43), leads him to bankruptcy. These are the risks taken by the new investors who send ships away from the safety of the homeland, expecting them to return, full of valuable cargo, "From Tripolis, from Mexico and England, / From Lisbon, Barbary, and India" (3.2.267–68). The reversal of Antonio's fortune at the end of the play, and the sudden return of three richly laden argosies, is another indicator of how money is made in Venice—by good fortune, not good deeds. The defeat of Shylock also demonstrates the arbitrariness of mercantile success, when the law can be twisted to serve the purpose of a judge like Portia, who is anything but unbiased, a judge who will do whatever is necessary to serve the husband that her father's money has bought her. And surely some members of Shakespeare's audience would have been troubled by the cruelty shown toward the Jew (despite Shylock's lack of mercy for Antonio). As Michael Neill points out, "One reason why Shylock remains such a deeply troubling figure at the end of *The Merchant* is the unspoken possibility that his forcible conversion (like that of the Jews in sixteenth-century Spain) will only institutionalize the very uncertainty it is designed to efface" (272). Portia's question, "Which is the merchant here? And which the Jew?" (4.1.169), directs the audience toward an awareness of the similarities between Christians and Jews who participate in the same community of aggressive, commercial competitors operating within the Mediterranean.[24]

Shylock is the internal alien in Venice, a necessary part of the financial system, while the prince of Morocco, a "tawny Moor," is an external alien who embodies the military prowess and imperial success of Islam. He is affiliated with Islamic power and with figures like Othello and Tamburlaine because he speaks their lofty language and boldly claims the same privileges based on his experience as a warrior. Despite the differences in their occupation and linguistic register, Morocco and Shylock are both figures of alterity defined against European, Christian identity. As Alan Rosen (1997) and Geraldo de Sousa (1999) have shown, the humiliation of Shylock is closely paralleled by that of Morocco. According to Rosen, there are clear symmetries that link Shylock and Morocco by means of dramatic structure and rhetorical pattern, and furthermore, "The play promotes this association of Jew and Moor by linking the way they themselves manipulate the discourse of insider/outsider" (75). Both Shylock and Morocco are repulsed by Portia; both "match wits with Venetians in a fierce battle of textual interpretations" (de Sousa 91). Both are purged from the body politic in order to satisfy the economic needs of the debt-ridden Christians of Venice. Morocco's values are not, however, the same as those of Shylock. Morocco articulates the traditional, chivalric values of the old aristocracy, offering to compete for Portia in single combat. When the Moorish prince says, "men that hazard all / Do it in hope of fair advantages. / A golden mind stoops not to shows of dross" (2.7.18–20), this clearly refers to Antonio the overextended investor. Morocco knows that he deserves Portia because of his intrinsic merit; he does not, like Bassanio, seek her hand because he needs money. But in the end he misreads the intended symbolism of the caskets and their inscriptions, and is defeated by an arbitrary contest in which skill, honor, and virtue mean nothing. His defeat and sudden "expulsion" means that the external power of the Islamic alien is eliminated as a threat to Christian Venice, leaving the prize to an inside trader like Bassanio who is favored by Portia.

The symbolic affiliation of Shakespeare's Shylock and Morocco may be contrasted with the more direct connections dramatized in the plays by Marlowe and Daborne. Daborne, in *A Christian Turned Turk*, goes further than Marlowe or Shakespeare in developing a representation of the alliance between Muslims and Jews. An important character in Daborne's play is Benwash, a wealthy Jewish merchant who has converted, at least formally, to Islam (he still attends the synagogue). He reminds his Jewish servant Rabshake of his reasons for converting:

> Thou hast forgot how dear
> I bought my liberty, renounced my law
> (The law of Moses), turned Turk—all to keep
> My bed free from these Mahometan dogs.
> I would not be a monster, Rabshake—a man-beast,
> A cuckold. (6.73–78)

Despite these desperate measures, his conversion (like Ward's) fails to accomplish its objective, and he is cuckolded by his wife, Agar, who is the sister of the Turkish viceroy in Tunis. Benwash's wife is exposed to constant temptation because the Jewish merchant uses her to attract business, and the play repeatedly uses figurative language that compares commercial exchange to sexual intercourse. For example, Gallop, a renegade pirate who has just returned to Tunis with a prize, succeeds in seducing Agar with pick-up lines that are crude but effective: "I am thy merchant, wench," he says, "and will deal with thee by wholesale" (16.40–41). Agar complains that her husband subjects her to the lust of other men: "So you have profit, all religious laws / Must suffer violence, your wife be exposed / Unto all goers" (6.362–64). Rabshake wonders why Benwash uses this strategy when his master is so worried about being cuckolded: "But seeing you fear your vessel hath a leak, wherefore do you put her to sea, man her thus?" Benwash answers, explaining his motive: "For commodity: thou seest rich shopkeepers set their wives at sale to draw in custom, utter their wares, yet keep that gem untouched—all for profit, man" (6.81–85).

Benwash is clearly a rewriting of Barabas and Shylock. Like his dramatic precursors, he uses a woman in his family to promote his financial interests, and since he has no daughter, no Abigail or Jessica with whom he can tempt Christian men, he employs his wife instead.

Daborne's play, like *The Jew of Malta* and *The Merchant of Venice*, represents women as precious commodities who are the objects of bargaining and purchase between men. The influence of Shakespeare is also apparent during the scene in which Benwash discovers that his house is burning. As his men labor to put out the fire, Benwash (having found a ladder of ropes and a pair of men's breeches) realizes that his wife was inside having sex with his new customer, Gallop. Benwash's hysterical reaction and his cries of "My bags, my obligations, my wife!" (11.4) would remind audiences of both Barabas and Shylock, especially Barabas hugging his moneybags and Shylock shouting "O my ducats! O my daughter!" (2.8.15). Benwash is a version of Barabas and Shylock, but with a parodic twist: he is also a cuckold. His Jewish monstrosity is exacerbated by the cuckold's horns that are repeatedly compared to the devil's horns. Benwash is not a harmless comic wittol, though. Once he finds out about his wife's infidelity, he kills both his wife and her lover. Benwash persuades Agar to tempt Gallop to a feast, promising to spare her life if she cooperates with his revenge. But after he stabs Gallop, he orders Rabshake to kill her, too. When Agar protests that he had sworn to show her mercy, Benwash tells her, "I sware as I was a Turk, and I will cut your throat as I am a Jew" (16.75). At the end of the play, Benwash is assassinated by the repentant pirate, Dansiker, who returns to Tunis to kill him. In his death throes, Benwash confesses to the murders he has committed and dies with these words: "Bear witness, though I lived a Turk, I die a Jew" (16.213).

Featuring characters like Benwash and Ward, a Jew and a renegade pirate turned Turk, *A Christian Turned Turk* adds further to the confusion, conflation, and instability of identity that is exhibited in *The Jew of Malta* or *The Merchant of Venice*. In these three plays, the older notion of the postexilic Jews as lawless vagabonds, wandering from nation to nation, is revised in the figure of the Jewish merchant who thrives amidst the marketplace of a heterogeneous Mediterranean port. These Jewish merchants form an international network that belongs to no central homeland, and is loyal to no Christian nation. Barabas, Shylock, and Benwash live and trade with Jews, Christians, and Muslims; they are willing to form profitable relationships that cross the boundaries of religious identity. This construction of Jewishness resembles the situation of the English Protestants in the early modern Mediterranean, people without political power who came to trade and who formed ghetto-like communities of factors and mercantile agents, but who could have no citizenship or shared faith in the region (unless they turned Turk).

Seen through English eyes, the instability of identity and habitation that mark the Mediterranean region made the English presence there a source of paradoxical anxiety: on the one hand, they felt their difference as outsiders acutely, as alienation; on the other hand, the English felt drawn into exchange and relations that threatened to "convert" them to a foreign condition or, at least, contaminate them (again, in this regard, the English in the Mediterranean are situated much like Barabas in Malta or Shylock in Venice). This contradiction is what Stephen Greenblatt (1980) calls, in his analysis of *The Jew of Malta*, "[English] culture's bad faith, its insistence upon the otherness of what is in fact its own essence" (209). The "essence" of Englishness, to the degree that these texts by Marlowe, Shakespeare, or Daborne acknowledge the possibility of such an essence, is revealed as an aggressive, profit-seeking versatility. Free market competition becomes a contest to see who can swindle, confiscate, and accumulate the most, and the contestants shift and trade public roles, morphing and replicating with the force and speed of an invasive, alien monstrosity. Renegades, apostates, and imposters change sides and exchange stolen commodities. Like Marlowe's Machevil, they "weigh not men" (prologue, 8) and "count religion but a childish toy," (prologue, 14). This lesson is learned and passed along. Shylock tells us that he has been taught by example: "The villainy you teach me I will execute, and it shall go hard but I will better the instruction" (3.1.60–61). Christians sell Turks to Jews, Turks sell Christians to Jews, Christians forcibly convert Jews who own Christian flesh. "And thus far roundly goes the business" (5.2.110), says Barabas, a sentiment echoed by Rabshake in *A Christian Turned Turk*, who declares, " 'Tis the custom of the whole world: the greater thief preys upon the less still" (6.133–34). Shylock points out that if the Christians of Venice treat people as property, flesh as commodity, why shouldn't he?

> You have among you many a purchased slave,
> Which like your asses and your dogs and mules
> You use in abject and in slavish parts,
> Because you bought them. Shall I say to you,
> "Let them be free!"?
> 							...You will answer
> "The slaves are ours." (4.1.89–93)

He points out that their dehumanizing treatment of these slaves is a necessary part of the Christians' socioeconomic system, and that his harsh treatment of Antonio is no different from the systemic violation of human freedom and dignity carried out under the rules of their class-based system.

In these three plays, religious and racial affiliations are unstable, giving the audience a sense of Jewish, Muslim, and Christian identities as interchangeable roles in a Machiavellian marketplace where identity was a slippery matter indeed, and where, from an English perspective, various forms of foreignness (or religious difference) were blurred, or in some cases, indistinguishable. In this context, all are "done" and "undone" according to a rapidly changing series of turns. These sudden turns of fortune, conveyed by "the wind that bloweth all the world besides, desire of gold" (3.5.3–4), transform human beings (even kings and sultans) into commodities and can bring unexpected downfall to the wealthiest and most powerful people. And they can induce a religious conversion wherever conversion is motivated by venal or libidinal desires. Thus, the "hempen proverb" of the thief, Pilia-Borza, is the ruling principle in Marlowe's Malta: "*hodie tibi, cras mihi*" (Your turn today, mine tomorrow). Whether Muslim, Jew, or Christian, the profit-seeker must eschew a stable identity in order to cope with this precarious reality and seize commercial advantages or opportunities.

English Renaissance drama constantly refers to the contradictory status of commerce in early modern culture. The theater itself was attacked repeatedly for introducing the commercial production and consumption of "false" and outlandish spectacles.[25] On the London stage, controversial economic activities like slave trading, commodity speculation, or usury were often carried out by foreign characters in Mediterranean settings. In plays like Marlowe's *The Jew of Malta*, Heywood's *The Fair Maid of the West*, or Shakespeare's *The Merchant of Venice*, destabilizing economic activity takes place far away from England, in Malta, Venice, Tunis, or Constantinople, and yet these plays convey something that English audiences greatly feared for themselves—that they would somehow be "converted" or contaminated by the new economic conditions produced by the obsession with "making merchandise." These anxieties were articulated in the theater, but they were also recognized and expressed by the commercial intelligencers and propagandists of the early modern period. The *Treatise of Commerce*, printed in 1601, and written by John Wheeler who worked for the Merchant Adventurers Company, contains a passage that acknowledges the power of the new commodification:

> . . . all the world choppeth and changeth, runneth & raveth after Marts, Markets and Merchandising, so that all thinges come into Commerce,

and pass into traffique (in a manner) in all times, and in all places: not onely that, which nature bringeth forth, as the fruits of the earth, the beasts, and living creatures, with their spoiles, skinnes and cases, the metals, minerals, and such like things, but further also, this man of another man's labor, one selleth words, another maketh traffike of the skins & blood of other men, yea there are some found so subtill and cunning merchants, that they perswade and induce men to suffer themselves to bee bought and sold, and we have seene in one time enow, and too many which have made merchandise of mens soules.

Wheeler writes as an apologist for foreign exchange, and yet in the quoted passage he alludes to two disturbing phenomena that his contemporaries in England would have associated with the Mediterranean economy—the slave trade, which makes traffic of men, and the conversion of Christians who "sold their souls," so to speak, when they "turned Turk" in order to enjoy a prosperous career as a renegade in North Africa or the Ottoman empire. The Mediterranean, with its Barbary pirates, Turkish galleys, and slave markets, must have seemed to Londoners to be a place where everything was up for sale and subject to exchange, a place like Marlowe's Maltese slave market where "Every one's price is written on his back" (2.3.3). Piracy and slavery were the most sensational aspects of this mercenary mercantilism, but in a more general way, what disturbed and titillated English culture was simply the multicultural mixing that any participant in the Mediterranean marketplace was obliged to experience firsthand.

The period covered by this study, 1570–1630, comprised a pivotal moment in the history of English commerce and English relations with the outside world. As Marx points out in volume three of *Capital*, this was a period of primitive accumulation within the domestic economy as well as the "starting-point" of capital in the beginnings of "world trade and the world market" (333 and passim). These economic changes produced shock waves that resonate through the cultural productions of early modern England, and they were strongly registered in the London theater of the time. On stage, various forms of exchange were represented—commercial, sexual, religious—and, as we have seen, the Mediterranean was frequently drawn upon as the setting in which those anxious exchanges took place. The Mediterranean was the place where English subjects went to make a profit by "venturing" capital, and there they learned to conduct a flourishing transnational trade by taking on new, aggressive strategies. Plays like *The Fair Maid of the West, The Merchant of Venice*, and others discussed in this study disclose and convey the exciting possibilities that the Mediterranean model of violent commerce offered to venturing English subjects, but at the same time these plays exhibited a fear that the changes necessary to adopt these new, exotic ways of doing business would "convert" good English Protestants in ways that were worrying.

The new posture required to thrive in the Mediterranean was adaptive, improvisational, and fluent. In an age of economic revolution and religious conflict, with an increasing flow of information and commodities from the world beyond coming into London, with the imperial powers of Spain and Turkey threatening, it seemed as though England might not be able to preserve its traditional identity, its cultural coherence. It was felt that, in the past, trade and conquest were two separate areas of endeavor, but now England was eager to join in the new process of empire-building through trade, plunder, and extra-territorial violence. What was the spiritual or moral price to be paid for this new way of doing business? Were the English becoming like the inhabitants of Venice, a place that Lewes Roberts, in *The Marchants Mappe of Commerce* (1638), called "the onely place where Policie, Warfare and merchandising have kist together" (sig. Ff5)? What was the nature of England's commercial and cultural transformation? Was it not true that Englishmen by the hundreds were literally turning Turk? Charles Fitz-Geffry, in his 1637 sermon, *Compassion Towards Captives*, complained that England was inhabited by "Turkes at home, Land-pyrats, Usurers, Oppressours" (sig. F3), and he cautioned his audience not to turn into domestic Turks: "O that England may be warned by these sad examples. God can turne great Britaine into Barbary" (sig. B). The English drama of this period presents numerous warnings to avoid the damnable course of those who "turn Turk," literally or figuratively. For example, in *The Renegado*, Francisco warns Vitelli, who has just been seduced and enriched by Donusa, the Turkish princess: "They steer not the right course, nor traffic well, / That seek a passage to reach heaven through hell" (2.6.45–46). At the same time, the drama offers, again and again, examples of heroic venturing that promise profit and honor to those who can boldly seize the occasion. Out of this profound ambivalence, in a period when English subjects sorely lacked but desperately desired an empire of their own, came a theater of the exotic that helped to influence the ideological development of English culture. Before the seventeenth century was through, the English nation had turned Turk indeed, and had acquired a mercantile empire that was able, by the end of the century, to do what had seemed impossible for the embattled Elizabethans. The lessons learned in the Mediterranean, through the English engagement with economic and imperial powers there, would be applied in the colonial projects of the future. The Mediterranean was translated and domesticated, made familiar through performances that featured Jewish merchants, renegade pirates, Islamic rulers, Muslim princesses, and the Christian characters who encountered these exotic figures. Theatrical representation, along with other forms of cultural production, helped to introduce a model of contact and engagement with foreign peoples that prepared the way for empire.

NOTES

1 BEFORE EMPIRE: ENGLAND, ALTERITY, AND THE MEDITERRANEAN CONTEXT

1. For a useful survey of approaches to the history of the British empire, see the essays on "Historiography" in volume 5 of *The Oxford History of the British Empire*.

2. See Goffman's chapter "The Proto-Imperialist" 3–12 in *Britons in the Ottoman Empire* and Matar, *Turks, Moors & Englishmen* 8–11.

3. Important studies of English writings that represent the process of "discovery" and nascent colonization include Mary Fuller's *Voyages in Print*, Andrew Hadfield's *Literature, Travel, and Colonial Writing in the English Renaissance*, Thomas Scanlon's *Colonial Writing and the New World*, and Jeffrey Knapp's *An Empire Nowhere*. See also Lesley B. Cormack's *Charting an Empire*, in which she argues, "The study of geography was essential to the creation of an ideology of imperialism in early modern England" (1).

4. On the issue of Ireland as an English (or British) colony during the early modern period, consult Quinn, *The Elizabethans and the Irish*; Canny, *Kingdom and Colony*; Karl S. Bottigheimer's essay, "Kingdom and Colony: Ireland in the Western Enterprise, 1536–1660" in Andrews, Canny, and Hair, 1978; and Jane H. Ohlmeyer's essay, "'Civilizinge of those rude partes': Colonization within Britain and Ireland, 1580s–1640s" in volume 1 of *The Oxford History of the British Empire*, edited by Canny. Canny begins his study, *Kingdom and Colony*, by citing Sir Thomas Smith, a promoter of English settlement in Ulster, in order to suggest that during the Tudor period Ireland "was colonized or perceived as a colony" (13). The bulk of his evidence for this claim is based upon English perceptions and rhetoric expressed in promotional texts.

5. These are the titles of chapters five and six of Lenman's study, *England's Colonial Wars, 1550–1688*.

6. Perhaps the most important essays in setting this trend were Greenblatt's "Invisible Bullets": and his chapter "Marlowe and the

Will to Absolute Play" in *Renaissance Self-Fashioning*. For examples of the scholarship on New World imperialism, see the essays in *New World Encounters*. See also John Beverley's "Marvellous Dispossession: On 1492, Stephen Greenblatt's *Marvelous Possessions*, and the Academic Sublime."

7. The index to Hall's *Things of Darkness* includes twenty-nine references under the heading "Imperialist Expansion" (313–14).

8. In a more recent article, "*Othello* and Africa: Postcolonialism Reconsidered," in *William and Mary Quarterly* 54:1 (January 1997), Bartels seems to have revised this view, arguing that "Readings based implicitly or explicitly on a domination narrative may be problematic even in studies of periods and societies where imperialism has taken hold either as an ideology or as a practice" (47).

9. When discussing "the imperial rivalry between England and Spain" (10), Fuchs wants to make that conflict more symmetrical by referring to "England's own empire" (11)—something that barely existed, if at all. Later, she states that in 1588 "England had not yet managed to acquire its own empire" (118), but a few pages later refers to "The [English] state's imperial sovereignty" (121).

10. There is much of value in Little's book, including some brilliant readings of Shakespeare's black bodies in performance, but in his introduction Little falters in making this generalization.

11. See Foucault, *Power/Knowledge* 78–133 for his theorization of power.

12. For example, after the break with Rome in 1533, Henry VIII began to claim that England was an empire or "imperium," meaning that the kingdom of England was an autonomous polity (an idea that was introduced in the preamble to the 1533 Act in Restraint of Appeals). This definition of "empire" is not the one that is generally used in early modern, colonial, or postcolonial studies today. A kingdom, like Tudor or Early Stuart "Britain," that is free from outside influence, but struggling to maintain its hold on the parts that make up its composite monarchy—that is quite different from a full-fledged empire engaging in successful external expansion and colonization.

13. In an important study of *The Ideological Origins of the British Empire*, David Armitage argues persuasively that "the emergence of the concept of the 'British Empire' as a political community encompassing England and Wales, Scotland, Protestant Ireland, the British islands of the Caribbean and the mainland colonies of North America, was long drawn out, and only achieved by the late seventeenth century at the earliest" (7). Other useful discussions of how early modern nations began to develop colonial theories or make claims to an "imperial" status include Knorr, Pagden, and Armitage (eds.), *Theories of Empire*.

14. For helpful discussions of "Britain" as a self-described empire in the sixteenth and seventeenth centuries, see Armitage, chapters 2–4; and Marshall. Marshall's study, *Theatre and Empire*, deals with the *idea* of empire during the Jacobean period and with what he calls

"the iconography of empire" (31). His book does not explore the huge gap between wishful Jacobean propaganda (or theatrical fantasy) and the material failure of imperial endeavors.

15. For an introduction to this debate on *The Tempest*'s colonialism, consult the articles collected in Graff and Phelan's *William Shakespeare, "The Tempest": A Case Study in Critical Controversy* and in Hulme and Sherman's *"The Tempest" and Its Travels.*

16. See Fuchs 1997 and chapter 10, " 'The Duke of Milan/ And his Brave Son': Old Histories and New in *The Tempest*," in Kastan 1999. Fuchs claims that the "critical privileging of America as the primary context of colonialism for [*The Tempest*] obscures the very real presence of the Ottoman threat in the Mediterranean in the early seventeenth century and elides the violent English colonial adventures in Ireland..." (46).

17. Fanon describes a very different historical context, in which "The colonial world is a world cut in two" (38) and where a violent dualism and a "reciprocal exclusivity" (39) predominate. He goes on to give his account of "A world divided into compartments, a motionless Manicheistic world... a world which is sure of itself, which crushes with its stones the backs flayed by whips..." (51–52).

18. Pratt defines "contact zone" as a colonial space "in which peoples geographically and historically separated come into contact with each other and establish ongoing relations, usually involving conditions of coercion, radical inequality, and intractable contact" (6).

19. Lisa Jardine and Jerry Brotton have pointed out that "We are now in a position to reject the appropriateness to the [sixteenth century] of Said's version of Western Europe's construction of the Orient as an alien, displaced other, positioned in opposition to a confident, imperialist Eurocentrism" (61). Though in *Global Interests* they cling too rigidly to the binarist categories of "East" and "West," Jardine and Brotton do offer a persuasive critique of the notion that during the Renaissance, the "Orient" was understood in direct opposition to "the West." "Just as Renaissance Man turns out," they argue, "to be a retrospective construction of nineteenth-century ideology, so does its alien Other" (61).

20. On Roanoke and the early Massachusetts settlements, see the books by Kupperman and Quinn.

21. At one point, Said goes so far as to say that an early form of Orientalism is present in ancient Greece, "as early as Aeschylus's play *The Persians*" (21), and he claims that a full-blown "Orientalism" began in "the late Renaissance" (7).

22. The incompatibility of Foucault and Gramsci is discussed by Dennis Porter in "Orientalism and Its Problems," and by James Clifford in "On Orientalism" in *The Predicament of Culture*. In his Marxist critique of *Orientalism*, Aijaz Ahmad argues, "Said's procedures of 1978 are radically anti-Foucauldian and are taken directly from the High Humanist traditions of Comparative Literature and Philology" (*In Theory* 167).

23. Braudel's great study, *The Mediterranean and the Mediterranean World in the Age of Philip II*, is an invaluable resource for all scholars studying the early modern Mediterranean. See especially, chapter VI, "Civilizations," a colorful account of Mediterranean cultural circulation and mixture, deploying a wide range of informative anecdotes.

24. On Lithgow and his travel narratives, see Vitkus, "Trafficking with the Turk: English Travelers in the Ottoman Empire during the Early Seventeenth Century" in Kamps and Singh, *Travel Knowledge* 35–52.

25. In Hakluyt, *Principall Navigations* (1589), 231.

26. For a detailed picture of English and European merchants in the Ottoman Empire, see the studies by Goffman.

27. On the history of Ottoman tolerance toward Christians and Jews, see chapter 1, "The Limits of Tolerance: The Social Status of Non-Muslims in the Ottoman Arab Lands," of Masters.

28. *State Papers* 16/269/51. Cited in Matar's "Introduction" to Vitkus, *Piracy, Slavery, and Redemption* 36. Matar argues, "Captivity was destabilizing the emergent [English] national identity," which was being "undermined by the indignities that Muslim privateers, among others, were inflicting" (36).

29. See Maclean, "Ottomanism before Orientalism?" in Kamps and Singh, *Travel Knowledge* 85–96.

30. For an account of England's developing nautical technologies and how they used these technologies to compete, commercially and militarily, with other maritime powers, see Glete, *Navies and Nations* (esp. 1:25 and 2:107–17); for an account of the development of aggressive maritime forces in early modern England and Europe, see Thomson, *Mercenaries, Pirates, and Sovereigns* (esp. chapter 2, "Nonstate Violence Unleashed").

2   THE ENGLISH AND THE EARLY MODERN MEDITERRANEAN: THEATER, COMMERCE, AND IDENTITY

1. For Braudel's definition of "world-economies," see *The Perspective of the World* 21 ff. For further information on this expansion, see Rabb 1966 and 1967, Brenner 1993, Andrews, and MacCaffrey. The work of Immanuel Wallerstein is also indispensable to a proper understanding of the English economy's participation in the global "world-system" (see especially Wallerstein's *The Modern World-System*).

2. For a better understanding of England's participation in the rise and development of international capitalism, one might begin by consulting Sweezy, Wood 1991, and McNally.

3. See the section on "The Growth of London" (1:197–213) and the chapter on "England and the Outside World" (2:103–202) in Clay 1984. Clay argues "The sixteenth and seventeenth centuries, which

saw the culmination of the process whereby London drew to itself so much of the foreign trade of the kingdom, also the final stages of its evolution unto a capital city in a modern sense" (1:203).

4. *S.P.D. Eliz*, vol. 230, no. 80 (February 23, 1590), quoted in Epstein 1908, 33 fn.

5. The term "imagined community," as Howard acknowledges in her essay, comes from Benedict Anderson's book, *Imagined Communities*. See Anderson 25–28.

6. In *King James VI and I and the Reunion of Christendom*, W.B. Patterson discusses James's peacemaking policies. James worked to establish Christian amity throughout Europe, and one of the supposed benefits of such a peace would be to enable a common crusade against an Islamic, Turkish empire that was pushing back the borders of Christendom. As early as 1589, James had begun to promote religious reconciliation among Christian nations and express hostility toward the Ottoman sultanate. In 1601 James wrote to the Shah of Persia, Abbas I, praising him for his military success against the Ottomans and implying that soon James himself would offer assistance to Persia.

7. For an account of the negotiations between the Levant Company and their new monarch, leading to the establishment of the 1605 charter, see Wood 37–41.

8. English and Dutch merchantmen were increasingly successful in this environment (due in large part to superior nautical technology) at the expense of Venetian seapower and prosperity. See Tenenti's chapter on "The English" in *Piracy and the Decline of Venice* 56–86.

9. In support of this point, Greene cites an early seventeenth-century document from the English Admiralty Court that refers to a "time of libertie and deceipte, when soe manie banners and collours are promiscuouslie used at sea to disguise themselves and intrapp others [that it is not possible] to knowe which ships are pyrattical or not" (52).

10. See Vaughan 1954.

11. On Mediterranean piracy, see Tenenti, Wolf, and Fisher.

12. See Matar 1994, 37.

3 MARLOWE'S MAHOMET: ISLAM, TURKS, AND RELIGIOUS CONTROVERSY IN *TAMBURLAINE, PARTS I AND II*

1. See esp. 69 and 71. The letter was originally in Latin. Skilliter reprints the English translation that also appeared in Hakluyt.

2. Compare the unofficial "praier unto God for the peace of Christendome, to defend and preserve it from Turkish invasion, to the destruction & overthrow of all Infidels" printed in *The Estate of Christians* (1595).

3. Preface to *Perimedes the Blacke-Smith* sig. A3.

4. Marginal commentary to Revelation 16.19 in the Geneva Bible.
5. For a detailed analysis of these texts, consult Setton's *Western Hostility to Islam and Prophecies of Turkish Doom.*
6. See the articles by Battenhouse (1973), Burton (2000), Goldberg, and Mary Elizabeth Smith.
7. See Bevington's *Mankind to Marlowe.*
8. On the Turk as ally of the Reformation, see Vaughan 1954, 134–46.
9. On the Turks and the early Lutherans, see Fischer-Galati, Kortpeter, and Setton's "Lutheranism and the Turkish Peril."
10. Jonathan Burton (2000) foregrounds this aspect of the contemporary context to show how Marlowe's play comments on "early modern England's need to produce a rhetoric that could justify its controversial dealings with the Turk" (129).
11. Walsingham's letter to Harborne is transcribed and printed in Read 1925, 3:226–28 (see esp. 226).
12. For scholarship that treats Luther's attitude toward the Turks, see Vaughan 1954, 134–46; Simon; and Forell.
13. Luther's fifth thesis is cited and discussed in Forell 257.
14. See Shapiro 138 for a discussion of the continuing controversy generated by these two books in the seventeenth century.
15. In "England and the Common Corps of Christendom," Baumer argues for the persistence of this principle in "official," popular, and literary spheres of cultural production in England.
16. See also Battenhouse's essay, "Tamburlaine: The Scourge of God."
17. A convincing interpretation of the play's ending, arguing that Tamburlaine's demise is caused by an excess of fiery humors in his body, is Parr's essay, "Tamburlaine's Malady."
18. Burton (2000) argues, "... Tamburlaine's shifting religious identity is not merely 'ambiguous'—as numerous critics suggest—but instead strategically reflective of the period's continual suspension and activation of anti-Islamic prejudice" (126). While it is certainly true that this ambiguity refers to historically specific discourses about Islam, the play does not simply "reflect" the pattern of "suspension and activation"; in fact, it is this unstable fluctuation that creates an ambiguity which ultimately demystifies any and all possible notions of divine agency—Islamic, Christian, or otherwise. Other critics who discuss this issue of ambiguity include David Bevington (*"Mankind" to Marlowe* 211–17) and Emily Bartels (*Spectacles of Strangeness* 60).
19. Much has been written about Marlowe's "atheism" and the subversive, blasphemous tendency in his writing. A good place to begin looking at the scholarship on this aspect of Marlowe's work is David Riggs's fine essay, "Marlowe's Quarrel with God." For further discussion of Marlowe's subversive or blasphemous tendencies, see Dollimore 107–19 and Kocher.
20. This statement appears in one of the letters that Kyd wrote to the Lord Keeper, Sir John Puckering, in the spring of 1593 (Maclure 35).

The full texts of the "note" by Richard Baines and the letter sent by Kyd to Puckering are reprinted in Maclure 32–38.

21. See Bartels's chapter, "East of England: Imperialist Self-Construction in Tamburlaine, Parts I and II" in *Spectacles of Strangeness*.

22. It is interesting to imagine Marlowe at Cambridge poring over this map in light of Lesley Cormack's argument that, beginning in 1580, at the English universities "young scholars found in the study of geography a set of attitudes and assumptions that encouraged them to view the English as separate from and superior to the rest of the world" (1). Cormack discerns "the development of an imperial *mentalité* by the last two decades of the sixteenth century" (7).

23. See Walsingham's memorandum, "A consideration of the trade into Turkey, 1580," printed in Epstein 1908, 245–51 (esp. 245).

24. David Bevington, the editor of the Revels edition of Lyly's play, glosses this passage by citing an English proverb, "The great thieves hang the little ones" (Dent T119).

25. See Greenblatt's classic discussion of anamorphosis in *Renaissance Self-Fashioning* 18–23.

26. There are many other passages from the Bible that employ this kind of imagery and could also be cited here. See, e.g., Joel 2:30–31, Acts 2:19–20, and Revelation 6:12.

27. For more information on Frobisher's voyages, see Hogarth et al. and Kenyon as well as Stefanasson's edition of George Best's 1578 *true discourse of the late voyages of discouerie*.

28. I have argued in my first chapter that this is jumping the gun in two ways: first, in Marlowe's day England had no empire; and second, Said's *Orientalism* offers an anachronistic framework for understanding the early modern context.

29. Marx introduces the term "primitive accumulation" at the end of volume 1 of *Capital*.

4 OTHELLO TURNS TURK

1. Vaughan's chapter, "Global Discourse: Venetians and Turks," makes apparent the importance of Turkey in the imaginative geography of Stuart England (13–34).

2. For historical studies of the Barbary pirates and the slave trade in the North African regencies, consult Hebb, G.N. Clark, Earle, Fisher, Friedman, and Wolf.

3. For a discussion of English writings on the Barbary pirates, see Matar 1993; Matar's introduction to Vitkus, *Piracy, Slavery, and Redemption: Barbary Captivity Narratives from Early Modern England*; and Potter. For a descriptive summary of early modern texts that include English accounts of Turkish culture in the early modern period, consult Chew, *The Crescent and the Rose* 100–86. See also the article by Hoenselaars.

4. Of course, some of these authors' statements are designed to make their subject matter sound exciting and important, but the tone of alarm goes beyond mere catchpenny rhetoric.

5. From "A Form to be used in common prayer... to excite all godly people to pray unto God for the delivery of those Christians that are now invaded by the Turk," reprinted in Clay 1847, 519–23 (esp. 519).

6. From "A Form to be used in common prayer... To excite all godly people to pray unto God for the preservation of those Christians and their Countries, that are now invaded by the Turk in Hungary, or elsewhere," reprinted in Clay 1847, 527–35, esp. 527.

7. On the strategic effect of the Turkish defeat at Lepanto, see Hess.

8. From King James Stuart, *His Maiesties Lepanto, or Heroical Song*. James's *Lepanto* was written ca. 1585, first published in Scotland in 1591, and then reprinted in London at the time of his accession to the English throne in 1603.

9. See Jones 1968 on "*Othello, Lepanto*, and the Cyprus Wars." Compare *Othello* 5.2.349–52 with the passages from James's *Lepanto*.

10. See Norman Sanders's comments in his introduction to the New Cambridge edition of *Othello* (Cambridge University Press, 1984) 1–51, esp. 2.

11. Bernard Harris gives an account of this Moroccan embassy in his essay, "A Portrait of a Moor."

12. See chap. 3, " 'The Present Terror of the World,' " in Chew; and Matar 1994.

13. Languet to Sidney, March 26, 1574, in *The Correspondence of Philip Sidney and Hubert Languet*, 47–50, esp. 49–50.

14. See Braudel 1973, 1:626.

15. According to Hebb, "by the early 17th century the character of the operations of the Barbary pirates had changed dramatically" (15). Increasingly, they used "tall ships" instead of galleys, and they began to move out of the Western Mediterranean into the Atlantic, taking captives from places as far north as Iceland.

16. See Edward Kellett's and Henry Byam's sermons, published together in *A Returne from Argier. A Sermon Preached at Minhead in the County of Somerset the 16. of March, 1627, at the re-admission of a relapsed Christian into our Church* (London, 1628). Another sermon of this kind is William Gouge, *A Recovery from Apostacy* (London, 1639), also delivered on the occasion of a readmission into Christianity from Islam.

17. The "Form of Penance and Reconciliation of a Renegado, or Apostate from the Christian Church to Turcisme" is reprinted in *The Works of Joseph Hall* 12:346–50.

18. See the discussion of conversion and religious controversy in Shapiro 131 ff. "In their enthusiasm to undermine the positions of their adversaries," observes Shapiro, "Protestant and Catholic writers alike hunted down instances of how their opponents had betrayed their own

faith" (138). A useful study of Roman Catholic–Protestant conversion
is Questier, *Conversion, Politics, and Religion in England, 1580–1625*.

19. See Burton's essay, "English Anxiety and the Muslim Power of
Conversion," for an account of Islam's appeal for English subjects.

20. John Donne, "Satire 3" in the Oxford Authors *John Donne* 29–31
(esp. ll.43 ff). For a vivid description of the condition of English
Catholics who were faced with persecution and the temptation to
"turn Protestant," see the chapter entitled "Apostasy" in John
Carey's biographical study *John Donne: Life, Mind, and Art* 15–36.

21. From Hall's *Quo Vadis? A Just Censure of Travel* reprinted in *The
Works of Joseph Hall*, 12:97–132.

22. *Oxford English Dictionary* 18:701. Shakespeare uses the word "turn"
in a similar sense when the Pucelle comments upon Burgundy's
betrayal of his English allies in *1 Henry VI*: "Done like a Frenchman,
turn and turn again" (3.3.85). This line is thought to be an interpo-
lated reference to Henry of Navarre and his conversion to Roman
Catholicism. Another relevant usage is in *Twelfth Night*, when
Malvolio, convinced by the false gospel of the forged letter, falls in
love with Olivia and is described by Maria: "Yon gull Malvolio is
turned heathen, a very renegado, for there is no Christian that means
to be saved by believing rightly can ever believe such impossible passages of grossness" (3.2.59–62).

23. Even as late as the eighteenth century, Europeans continued to
believe that epilepsy or "the falling sickness" was brought on by
demonic possession. Other medical authorities argued, following
humoral theory, that an excess of black bile in the body causes the fits
(for the latter explanation, see Robert Burton, *The Anatomy of
Melancholy* 1.2.1.6). For a discussion of the early modern understanding of epilepsy and the long-standing association between
epilepsy, prophecy, and possession, consult Temkin.

24. According to Leo Africanus, "This falling sicknes likewise possesseth
the women of Barbarie, and the land of Negros; who, to excuse it, say
that they are taken with a spirite (39)." On Muhammed's "falling
sicknes," see also Curio sig. 4v. Shakespeare's use of Leo Africanus as
a source is discussed in Whitney and in Johnson 1985.

25. Kellett also refers to "Mahomet, that rake-shame of the world…the
ravisher of his mistress, the known adulterer with one Zeid…(20). In
Byam's sermon, given later the same day, the Prophet is described in
similar terms:

> He was the very puddle and sink of sin and wickedness. A thief, a mur-
> derer, an adulterer, and a Wittal. And from such a dissolute life pro-
> ceeded those licentious laws of his. That his followers may avenge
> themselves as much as they list. That he that kills most infidels shall
> have the best room in Paradise: and he that fighteth not lustily, shall be
> damned in hell. That they may take as many wives as they be able to

keep, and lest insatiable lust might want whereon to feed, to surfeit, he
alloweth divorce upon every light occasion. He himself had but eleven
wives, besides whores; but the Grand Signior in our days kept three
thousand concubines for his lust. (62–63)

26. See Daniel 1958, 152, where he discusses the prevalent European
    notion that "Islam was essentially built upon a foundation of sexual
    licence which was plainly contrary to the natural and the divine law."
27. Compare Mandeville's *Travels*, where the description of Islamic reli-
    gious practice and doctrine does point to beliefs that Christians and
    Muslims hold in common; but when it comes to the Muslims'
    description of paradise in the Koran, Mandeville condemns it as one
    of the greatest and most absurd errors of the "saracens": "if they are
    asked what paradise they are talking about, they say it is a place of
    delights, where a man shall find all kinds of fruit at all seasons of the
    year, and rivers running with wine, and milk, and honey, and clear
    water; they say they will have beautiful palaces and fine great man-
    sions, according to their deserts, and that these palaces and mansions
    are made of precious stones, gold and silver. Every man shall have
    four score wives, who will be beautiful damsels, and he shall lie with
    them whenever he wishes, and he will always find them virgins"
    (104). Mandeville's narrative was frequently reprinted in sixteenth-
    century England and was still received in Shakespeare's day as a fac-
    tual account; it was also included in the first edition of Hakluyt's
    Principall Navigations (1589).
28. See also Donne's "Elegy 2: To his Mistress Going to Bed," in which
    the speaker compares a sexual experience to "a heaven like Mahomet's
    Paradice" (12–13 [esp.l.21]). The Turks, and especilly the Ottoman
    sultan with his harem, were proverbial for lust. For example, Edgar in
    King Lear refers to sexual indulgence, claiming to have "in woman
    outparamour'd the Turk" (3.4.92).
29. See Daniel 1958, 135–40.
30. On early modern connotations of "to turn Turk," see Rice.
31. See also the use of this phrase in *Much Ado About Nothing*, where
    Margaret tells Beatrice that she suspects her of loving Benedick:
    "Well, an you be not turned Turk, there's no more sailing by the star"
    (3.4.47–48).
32. *OED*, 3:374. Donne uses the word "convertite" in two of the poems
    that he wrote while in France, *Of the Progress of the Soul. The Second
    Anniversary* and the verse epistle "A Letter to the Lady Carey, and
    Mistress Essex Rich, from Amiens" (218–31 [l.518] and 231–33 [l.7]).
    In both of these poems, Donne refers ironically to those who convert to
    Catholicism for material gain. A note in W. Milgate's edition tells us that
    "…In French *converti* was a name given to beggars who made a pro-
    fession of their change of religion in order to extract alms from passers-
    by" (Donne, *The Epithalamions, Anniversaries, and Epicedes* 176n).

33. For one example of this genre, see the section entitled "The Conversion of an English Courtizan, reformed this present year, 1592" in Robert Greene's *Disputation betweene a Hee Conny-catcher and a Shee Conny-catcher.*

34. For a brief description of this trend (without reference to *Othello*), see Hoy 2:10–14.

35. For discussion of the comic conventions in *Othello*, see de Mendonça, Snyder 70–90, and Teague.

36. See D'Amico 63 ff. and Jones 1965, 1–26.

37. For more information about the figure of the Moor on the London stage, consult Barthelemy, Cowhig, D'Amico, and Tokson.

38. According to Gillies's study of the Shakespearean "mythology of geographic difference" (10), Othello is both "other" and "voyager." He is also the figure of the barbarian, from outside the circuit of civilization. The periphery of civilization was defined by the Romans as the *orbis terrarum* or *orbis terrae* (literally, "the circle of lands"), and the civilized center defines itself against the periphery, with which it is fascinated. "Monstrous, savage, and barbarous" races inhabit the marginal spaces. This mythology establishes "the link between monstrosity, margins, and sexual 'promiscuity'" (13). Other useful studies of the construction of "blackness" as racial difference in *Othello* and its historical and theatrical contexts include Braude 1997, Callaghan 1996, Habib, Hall 1995, Oldenburg, Orkin, Smith 1998, Vaughan and Vaughan; Little 72–101; Neill 237–84; and Lim 104–41.

39. On the early modern etymology of "Moor," see Barthelemy (8 ff.), whose conclusions confirm those of G.K. Hunter: "'Moor' can mean... non-black Muslim, black Christian, or black Muslim. The only certainty a reader has when he sees the word is that the person referred to is not a European Christian" (7).

40. See Chew 518–21 on English Renaissance stereotyping of Moors in literary texts.

41. A modern English translation of Cinthio's 1566 Italian text is provided in *Narrative and Dramatic Sources of Shakespeare*, ed. Geoffrey Bullough, 7:239–52.

42. See Newman, "'And wash the Ethiope white.'"

43. See also the discussion in D'Amico, 63 ff. If he consulted the English translation of Leo Africanus, Shakespeare may have been influenced by Pory's account of Africanus, who was himself a Moorish convert to Christianity. For analysis of the similarities between Othello and Africanus, see Whitney, Johnson 1985, Bartels 1990, and Burton 1998.

44. One contemporary source defines "Turk" in the following way: "... the word Turke (being a Tartarian word) signifieth one that is accursed and a vagabond" (*The Policy* 1597, sig. 7r). Thomas Dallam, who visited the Ottoman sultan's court at the end of the sixteenth century, referred to his guide and translator (or "drugaman") as "a Turke, but a Cornish man borne" (Dallam, *The Account of an Organ Carried to the Grand Seigneur and Other Curious Matter* 1–98, esp. 79).

45. There was a Morisco uprising in Spain during 1568–70, supported, to a limited degree, by Muslims from North Africa. It was put down by a Spanish army under Don John of Austria. During this war thousands of Moorish captives were taken by the Spanish and sold into slavery in Italy. Many of them became galley slaves, and some would have served as rowers at the battle of Lepanto, in ships that fought against their fellow Muslims; See Braudel 1973, 2:1069–87.

46. The most famous renegade admiral was Aruj, known as Kheyr-ed-Din (or Barbarossa), a Greek who converted to Islam and rose to command the Ottoman fleet in the Mediterranean. He was the founder of the corsair center at Algiers, where construction of the Great Mole began under his sponsorship in 1529.

47. The English had been granted commercial capitulations by the Ottoman sultan, allowing trade in the Turkish Levant, in May of 1580. See Skilliter, Davis 1961, Davis 1973, Rawlinson, and Willan on Anglo-Ottoman trade.

48. See MacNeill 183 ff.

49. Protestant polemics against Roman Catholicism frequently equated Islam and Roman Catholicism (see Chew 101). The notion of Islam (the religion of "Turks," "Moors," "Mahometans," and "Saracens") as a variety of pagan idol worship begins in romance tradition (in the *Chanson de Roland*, the Islamic knights worship an unholy trinity of pagan idols—Mahound, Apollin, and Jupiter) and had a remarkable persistance among educated Europeans. See Daniel 1984, 263–64. Spenser, for example, draws upon this tradition when presenting Roman Catholic lawlessness, joylessness, and faithlessness in the form of three Saracen knights in Book I of *The Faerie Queene*.

50. On the English "myth of Venice," consult McPherson. For further information on the early modern Venetian context and the English perception of Venice, consult Queller, Mulier, Hale, Lane, Valensi, and MacNeill.

51. See Tenenti on Venice's struggle to maintain her economy in a commercial climate of maritime aggression and violence.

52. Quoted here from McPherson 32 (McPherson's translation).

53. See also D. Vaughan 16–21.

54. Cyprus was conquered by crusaders under Richard Coeur de Lion in 1190. It was controlled by the Lusignan dynasty until the island was annexed by the Venetian republic in 1489. During the fifteenth century the Mamluks raised armies and attacked Cyprus on several occasions, most notably in 1426 when an invading force sent by the Sultan Baybars conquered Nicosia and forced the Lusignan monarchs to pay an annual tribute. When it fell to the invading Turks under Sultan Selim II in 1571, it was the last remaining "*outre-mer*" territory conquered by the Frankish crusaders that was still in Christian hands. See Hill's *History of Cyprus*.

55. After a violent seige, Nicosia was taken in September of 1570, many of its inhabitants put to the sword (Knolles claimed that more than 14,000 Christians were slain), its wealth pillaged, and a large number of its citizens taken away to be slaves. Famagusta followed, after a courageous resistance. Knolles reports that Mustapha, the Ottoman general, betrayed the governor and officials who came into his camp to parley, killing and torturing all of them (848–68). Emrys Jones shows how some of Shakespeare's lines echo Knolles's account of the Turkish invasion of Cyprus, and Jones claims in his conclusion that "Shakespeare had the events of 1570–1 [on Cyprus] in mind" when composing *Othello* (50). For a contemporary account of the seige of Famagusta by an eyewitness, see Martinego.

56. The play also refers to Rhodes as a potential target for Turkish aggression (1.3.14–35). It was taken by the Ottomans in 1522 and was still in Turkish hands when Shakespeare wrote *Othello* eighty years later.

57. See the section titled "Of Arms and Beards: The Loss of Cyprus and the Myth of Venice" in McPherson 75–81.

58. The marginal menace of the Turks frames the action in several of Shakespeare's plays set in the Mediterranean, including *Othello*, *Twelfth Night*, *Much Ado About Nothing*, *The Taming of the Shrew*, and *All's Well That Ends Well*. In these plays this offstage power is associated with piracy, captivity, and war.

59. In fact, there were a number of plays written in early modern England that featured "the Great Turk." Those extant include [Thomas Kyd], *The Tragedie of Solyman and Perseda* (ca. 1589–92); Robert Greene, *The Tragical Reign of Selimus* (ca. 1586–93); Fulke Greville's closet plays, *Mustapha* (ca. 1594–96) and *Alaham* (ca. 1598–1600); John Mason's *The Turke* (1610); and two plays written by Thomas Goffe, *The Raging Turk, or Bajazet the Second* (1631) and *The Couragious Turk, or Amurath the First* (1632). See Simon Shepherd's chapter "Turks and Fathers" in his *Marlowe and the Politics of Elizabethan Theatre* (142–77).

60. On the connection between these armada-dispersing tempests and the one in *Othello*, see the comments of Bullough in *Narrative and Dramatic Sources of Shakespeare* 7:213–14.

61. Quoted here from Mattingly 390.

62. On the English Protestant seige mentality, see Fernandez-Armesto and Weiner.

63. Many of the scholarly debates on *Othello* conducted in the last century have raised literal-minded questions about the moral or religious "character" of Othello (questions that perhaps have been invalidated by our poststructuralist understanding of textual "character"). See, for example, the debate on damnation and the "Christianness" of *Othello* in Barnet, Bethell, Hubler, Siegel, and West.

64. Spivak explores this pattern in his study of *Shakespeare and the Allegory of Evil*.

65. The punishment of an adulteress was stopped by Christ in a biblical scene that resonates ironically with the religious language of the murder scene and with Othello's claim to be "merciful." The final verse of John 8:1–11 reads "And Jesus saide unto her, Neither doe I condemn thee: Goe, and sinne no more" (*The Holy Bible* 1611, sig. K2v). The Elizabethan homily "Against whordome and adulterie" refers to allegedly severe punishment for adultery among various Islamic peoples: "If anye amonge the Egyptians had been taken in adulterye, the Law was, that he should be openly in ye presence of all the people bee scourged naked with whipps, unto the number of a thousande stripes, the woman that was taken with him had her nose cut off whereby shee was knowen ever after, to bee a whore, and therfore to be abhorred of all men. Among the Arabians, they that were taken in adulterie, had their heads strike[n] from their bodies. ... Amonge the Turks, even at this day, they that be taken in adulterie, both man & woman, are stoued [stoned] straight waye to death without mercie" (*Certaine Sermons* sig. L3v–L4r).

66. Take, for example, the character of Mullisheg, King of Fez, in Heywood's *Fair Maid of the West, Part I*, who declares,

> If kings on earth be termed demigods,
> Why should we not make here terrestrial heaven?
> We can, we will: our God shall be our pleasure;
> For so our Meccan Prophet warrants us. (4.3.37–40)

67. See Chew's thorough reconstruction of the origin and reproduction of this narrative in early modern England (478–90). The tragic story of the sultan and the slave girl was staged in a lost play by George Peele ("the famous play of *The Turkish Mahomet and Hyrin the Fair Greek*"), in Thomas Goffe's *The Couragious Turke*, in Lodowick Carlell's *Osmond the Great Turk* (ca. 1637–42), and in Gilbert Swinhoe's *Unhappy Fair Irene* (ca. 1640).

68. For dating and commentary on sources, consult the introduction in *A Critical Old-Spelling Edition of Thomas Goffe's "The Courageous Turk,"* ed. Susan Gushee O'Malley. Quotations from the play follow this edition. A helpful gloss to the term "Hiren" is provided by Gordon Williams in his *Dictionary of Sexual Language and Imagery in Shakespearean and Stuart Literature*. A typical version of the story, one available to Shakespeare, appears in William Painter, *The Palace of Pleasure*, I.40 (190–97).

69. For further analysis of the "O" in Othello, see Vitkus, "The 'O' in *Othello*: Tropes of Damnation and Nothingness."

70. See Barthelemy 4.

71. For further commentary on this genealogy of blackness and its function in early modern culture, see Oldenburg and the articles by Alden T. and

Virginia Mason Vaughan and by Benjamin Braude in the special issue of *William and Mary Quarterly* on "Constructing Race" (January 1997). Ania Loomba also discusses this issue and its connection to representations of religious difference in the drama: see her chapter, "'Delicious traffick': racial and religious difference on early modern stages" in *Shakespeare and Race*.

72. See also Hall, *Things of Darkness.*
73. For further discussion of circumcision in *Othello*, see the article by Lupton.
74. See, for example, the circumcision scene in Daborne's *A Christian Turned Turk* (scene 9). According to De Nicolay, those who change "from baptisme to circumcision," converting to Islam from Christianity, bring upon themselves "the eternall perdition of their soules" (sig. 8r). Kellett takes verse 5.2. from Paul's epistle to the Galatians as his text: "If yee be circumcised, Christ shall profit you nothing"; he also refers to the renegades' "stayning and ingrayning of the Christal clere-saving water of Baptisme, with the bloud of Circumcision" (1 and 18).
75. In *Lenten Stuffe*, Thomas Nashe refers to the Ottomans as "curtaild skinclipping pagans" (*Works* 3:173). At the end of Heywood's play *The Fair Maid of the West*, the clownish tapster, Clem, foolishly asks to receive the "honor" of an appointment as Mullisheg's "chief eunuch" in the royal harem, and discovers his folly when he is about to be castrated (see 4.2.91–131). In that play and in other English representations of Christians converting to Islam, there is a confusion of castration and circumcision, of eunuchs and renegades who "turn Turk." See also Shapiro's comments on the theological and cultural significance of circumcision in his chapter entitled "The Pound of Flesh" (113–30).
76. See the entry for "dog" in Gordon Williams's *Dictionary of Sexual Language and Imagery.* In Aleppo for a Christian to strike a Muslim was a crime punishable by death, and the only way for a Christian to avoid the penalty would be to convert to Islam (see Matar 1994, 35).
77. See Battenhouse 1994 on "Othello as a Judas."
78. Samuel Rowlands's epigram on the renegade pirate Ward also underscores the connection between conversion to Islam and damnation: "Perpetuall flames is reprobates Re-warde" ("To a Reprobate Pirat that hath renounced Christ and is turn'd Turk" reprinted in vol. 2 *The Complete Works of Samuel Rowlands* sig. B2).

5   SCENES OF CONVERSION: PIRACY, APOSTASY, AND THE SULTAN'S SERAGLIO

1. Africanus goes on to describe the spread of Islam from the Mideast to parts of South Asia. His account of how the Muslims spread their religion through trade, intermarriage, and the use of force is remarkable

in its resemblance to English colonial strategies of the seventeenth century. See esp. 383–84.

2. See Matar's lengthy discussion on patterns of Christian (and English) conversion to Islam (1998, 14–19, 22–49).

3. For a complete list of the Barbary captivity narratives printed in England during the sixteenth and seventeenth centuries, consult the bibliography at the end of Vitkus, *Piracy, Slavery and Redemption*.

4. For a more detailed account of this international culture in North Africa, see Matar's chapter, "Soldiers, Pirates, Traders, and Captives: Britons among the Muslims," in *Turks, Moors & Englishmen*.

5. A version of this text was originally published in Purchas. It was reprinted in 1650 and 1653. See the editor's introduction to Bon.

6. Early modern accounts of the seclusion of women and the imperial seraglio at Topkapi palace that were produced by Christian, European authors often mix fantasy and exaggeration with more accurate reportage. For a more accurate picture of the lives of Turkish women, in and out of the seraglio, consult the following studies: Peirce, *The Imperial Harem*; Necipoglu, *Architecture, Ceremonial and Power: The Topkapi Palace in the 15th and 16th Centuries*; Tuglaci, *The Ottoman Palace Women*; Goodwin, *The Private World of Ottoman Women*; Freely, *Inside the Seraglio*; Barnet Miller, *Beyond the Sublime Porte*.

7. John J. Murray, whose edition of the play is used here, makes some untenable claims in his introduction to the text, but I am in agreement with him when he makes the case for *The Spanish Tragedy* being written before *Soliman and Perseda*. See Kyd, *The Tragedye of Solyman and Perseda*, ed. Murray, x–xi.

8. Another complex layering of textual interrelations occurs when Shakespeare draws upon Marlowe's *Tamburlaine* and Kyd's *Soliman and Perseda*, using parodic imitation in the character of Pistol, who resembles Kyd's Piston, and Falstaff, who owes something to Kyd's vainglorious knight, Basilisco. Compare *2 Tamburlaine*, 5.3.67–71; *Soliman and Perseda* 4.2.22 ff.; and *1 Henry IV*. All of these characters are modeled after the *miles gloriosus* of Latin comedy and the stock character, Basilisco, from *commedia dell'arte* (see John J. Murray's introduction xvii–xx).

9. See Murray's discussion of the dating for *Soliman and Perseda* x–xii, of his edition. Andrews (1984, 92–93) describes English relations with the Ottomans at this time, including the successful efforts of William Harborne, the English ambassador to the Sublime Porte, in preventing Spain from extending its truce with the Ottomans in 1587. For more information on possible Anglo-Ottoman or Anglo-Moroccan conspiracies or alliances against Spain during the 1580s, see Vella.

10. Kyd's word "porpuse" implies both "prepuce" and "purpose," and Burton argues that it signifies "pore-puss." See Burton's discussion of "porpuse" in "English Anxiety and the Muslim Power of Conversion" (2002, 50–51).

11. See Matar (1997) on the significance of the turban in early modern England.

12. For more information on the medieval anti-Islamic tradition in literature and religious polemic, see Daniel 1984, Metlitzki, the two articles by Comfort, the articles in Frassetto and Blanks, and Paull's dissertation.

13. Fuchs argues, "The confrontation with Islam, in its many incarnations, was crucial for Europe's cultural construction of itself as a geographic and imperial center" (2–3).

14. On John Harrison's activities as the agent of in Morocco, see Matar, *Turks, Moors & Englishmen*, 10 and passim.

15. See Chew 437 for more information on these prophecies.

16. "Queer virginity" is a concept developed by Theodora Jankowski in her study, *Pure Resistance: Queer Virginity in Early Modern English Drama*.

17. In *Empire and Mimesis*, Barbara Fuchs also discusses what she calls "the imprecise boundary between the categories of privateer and pirate" (123).

18. See Senior 90–91 for a full account of Carosman and Ward's relationship.

19. "The Ballad of Ward and Danseker" was listed in the Stationers' Register on July 3, 1609. It is reprinted in *The Roxburghe Ballads*, 6:784–85.

20. See *Calendar of State Papers, Venice 1607–10*, 49.

21. One of the English corsairs who served under Ward, Captain Bishop, surrendered and declared, "I will die a poor labourer in mine own country, if I may, rather than be the richest pirate in the world," *Calendar of State Papers, Ireland, 1611–14*, 91.

22. Lithgow goes on to say, "Yet old Ward their master was placable, and joined me safely with a passing land conduct to Algier; yea, and diverse times in my ten days staying there, I dined and supped with him..." (315).

23. The opening sentence of King James's 1605 "Proclamation for revocation of mariners from foreign services": "...within this short time since the Peace concluded between Us and the King of Spain and the Archduke our good brothers, it hath appeared unto Us that many mariners and seafaring men of this realm, having gotten a custom and a habit in the time of the war to make profit by spoil, do leave their ordinary and honest vocation and trading in merchantly voyages... and do betake themselves to the service of diverse foreign states... to have thereby occasion to continue their unlawful and ungodly course of living by spoil, using the services of those princes but for color and pretext, but in effect making themselves no better than pirates to rob both Our own subjects their countrymen and the subjects of other princes our neighbors..." *Stuart Royal Proclamations* 1:108 (#50).

24. Cited by Jack Beeching in his edition of Hakluyt, *Voyages and Discoveries* 23.

25. This incident is mentioned in L'Estrange-Ewan 9.

26. His career can be traced in the *Calendar of State Papers, Venetian*, vols. 11 and 12, 1607–10 and 1610–13. See esp. vol. 11:348.

27. See *CSPV* 11:348.

28. See *CSPV* 11:916, p. 492; 12:59, pp. 45–46.

29. A similar account of Danseker's demise is given by Lithgow, who claims that in February of 1616 Danseker was tricked and executed by the Bashaw of Tunis (*Totall Discourse* 334–35).

30. See *CSPV* 11:629, p. 346.

31. For the best recent attempts to estimate the number of captives held in North Africa during this period, see Nabil Matar's introduction to Vitkus, *Piracy, Slavery and Redemption*, and Robert C. Davis's article, "Counting Slaves on the Barbary Coast."

32. See *The Policy* 24 and the account of Arthur Edwards in Hakluyt, *Principall Navigations* 1:418.

33. See the article by MacDonald, "'The Fearefull Estate of Francis Spira': Narrative, Identity, and Emotion in Early Modern England."

34. Friedman (1983) discusses the role of Roman Catholic priests, including "redemptionist" friars in freeing Spanish captives from bondage in Muslim North Africa.

35. See Hutcheon, *A Theory of Parody*.

6   MACHIAVELLIAN MERCHANTS: ITALIANS, JEWS, AND TURKS

1. See the articles by Griffin and Everett on phobic representations of Spanish or Italo-Spanish figures in *Othello* and other English texts. Much more could be said about English culture's engagement with Spain and the Spanish Mediterranean, in the theater and in other media, but I have not been able to include such discussion in this study.

2. On the image of the Jew in English Renaissance drama and literature, see Rosenberg, Cardozo, Michelson, and especially Shapiro's *Shakespeare and the Jews*.

3. See also the chapter on "The Marranos and Crypto-Judaism" in Zagorin, *Ways of Lying*.

4. See Andrews 1984, 87 ff., for a good summary account of the English trade in the Levant at this time.

5. From the *Merchants Mappe of Commerce* (1638), cited in Brenner 1993, 4.

6. Based on customs records, W.G. Hoskins concludes, "for the period 1485 to 1547.... Foreign merchants had a large hold in [overseas] trade, taking between 40 and 50 per cent at different times" (178).

7. On the controversy involving Velutelli's monopoly, consult Read 3:375.

8. See Tawney 1925 where he observes that at mid-century, "The prominence of the Italian colony in connection with the money market is significant, since it suggests that the more highly-specialized and intricate type of financial business, involving international connections and an accurate knowledge of foreign conditions, was still something of an exotic" (64).

9. On religious objections to the new economic practices brought by capitalism, see the classic essay by Tawney, "Religious Thought on Social and Economic Questions in the Sixteenth and Seventeenth Centuries."

10. Other primary texts on usury include Nicholas Sanders's *A Briefe Treatise of Usurie* (1568), Philip Caesar's *A General Discourse Against the Damnable Sect of Usurers* (1578), Miles Mosse's *The Arraignment and Conviction of Usurie* (1595), Roger Fenton's *A Treatise of Usurie* (1611), Sir Thomas Culpeper's *Tract Against Usurie* (1621), and John Blaxton's *The English Usurer* (1634). Two useful surveys of the topic of usury are Jones 1989 and Nelson, and David Hawkes's *Idols of the Marketplace* should also be consulted by anyone interested in usury and commercial ideology in early modern England.

11. On "dry exchange" and "fictitious exchange," see De Roover's article, "What is Dry Exchange?" and De Roover 1949, 7–11, 161–65, 178–80; esp. pp. 179–80 on dry exchange, fictitious exchange, and public hostility toward dealers who used these and other practices.

12. This text was printed in Raymond de Roover, *Gresham on Foreign Exchange*. It was not Gresham, but Thomas Smith, who wrote this treatise. See the review of de Roover's edition by Mary Dewar, "The Memorandum 'For the Understanding of the Exchange': Its Authorship and Dating." See also D.R. Fusfeld, "On the Authorship and Dating of 'For the Understanding of the Exchange" and "Appendix A" "The Dating of the Memorandum 'For the Understanding of the Exchange'" in Gould, *The Great Debasement*. The text was probably prepared initially in 1576 for the commission appointed to investigate the foreign exchanges. A manuscript copy dated 1578 was owned by John Dee.

13. Kenneth R. Andrews provides a good overview of colonial and commercial aggression in *Trade, Plunder, and Settlement: Maritime Enterprise and the Genesis of the British Empire, 1480–1630.* For a more recent and more specific case study in English maritime plundering, consult Harry Kelsey's *Sir Francis Drake: The Queen's Pirate*, especially 11–89.

14. For an account of how piracy affected the Venetian republic and its empire, see Tenenti.

15. See Glete 1:116 ff. for a description of the dangers a typical merchantman from England had to face when trading in the Mediterranean.

16. See also Challis 183–98 on "Trade, Politics and Spanish Treasure." Also helpful for understanding early mercantilism and the import–export issue are J.D. Gould, *The Great Debasement*; and Thirsk, *Economic Policy and Projects*. Those who defended foreign trade and the importation of luxury goods were opposed by those whom Thirsk calls "Commonwealth men" and by some early mercantilists.

17. Building on Shapiro's work, Peter Berek maintains, "Marranism is the particular form of Jewishness which is most pertinent to our understanding" of "the way that Jewishness figured in the theater of the 1590s" (130). When Berek asserts that Elizabethan and Jacobean stage Jews are focal points for English anxieties about unstable or unknowable identity, this confirms many of my own arguments, but Berek looks more closely at the converted Jews living in England while downplaying the crucial features of geographic mobility and international commerce that were associated with stage Jewishness. In the section of his article titled "The Jew Abroad," Berek's claim that the "overt Judaism" of Jews outside England "doesn't seem to have been viewed as a serious threat" (140) fails to acknowledge the threatening commercial power of merchant Jews that English subjects frequently encountered in the Mediterranean, and it is that power (and the alliance of that power with Islamic forces) that underlies the portrayal of Jewishness in theatrical characters like Barabas, Shylock, and Benwash.

18. The English movement into the Eastern Mediterranean after 1570 has been well documented (see Brenner, Davis, Foster, Rabb, Willan, and Wood). For various discussions of Jewish merchants in the Mediterranean and their role in the sixteenth and seventeenth-century economy, consult Braude and Lewis, Arbel, Cooperman, M.A. Epstein, and Levy.

19. For an account of English involvement in both trade and piracy based in North Africa, as profiteers and victims, see Fisher's study.

20. See Inalcik's article on "Capital Formation in the Ottoman Empire," which provides a detailed picture of the relationship between the Ottoman state and the maritime economy that included foreign trade partners.

21. On the career of Nasi, see Roth, and for an informative discussion of connections between Nasi and Marlowe's Barabas, consult Bawcutt's introduction to *The Jew of Malta* 7–9.

22. This proverb is cited and discussed by the Cutlers (98). The massacre of both Muslims and Jews at the conquest of Jerusalem during the First Crusade in 1099 is perhaps the best-known example of this. An account of this massacre may be found in Runciman 188.

23. Brian Pullan's article, "Jewish Moneylending in Venice: From Private Enterprise to Public Service," provides a fascinating gloss on Shakespeare's play about moneylending in Venice.

24. Shapiro, Tanner, Moisan, and others have pointed to Portia's question as a crucial statement about the play of cultural difference and similarity in *The Merchant of Venice*.
25. See Hawkes for a fuller treatment of this issue in English Renaissance literature.

BIBLIOGRAPHY

Adams, Stephen. *The Best and Worst Country in the World: Perspectives on the Early Virginia Landscape.* Charlottesville: University Press of Virginia, 2001.

Africanus, Johannes Leo. *A Geographical Historie of Africa.* Trans. John Pory. London, 1600.

Ahmad, Aijaz. *In Theory: Classes, Nations, Literatures.* London: Verso, 1992.

Anderson, Benedict. *Imagined Communities: Reflections on the Origin and Spread of Nationalism.* London: Verso, 1983.

Andrews, Kenneth R. *Trade, Plunder and Settlement: Maritime Enterprise and the Genesis of the British Empire, 1480–1630.* Cambridge University Press, 1984.

Andrews, K.R., N.P. Canny, and P.E.H. Hair, eds. *The Westward Enterprise: English Activities in Ireland, the Atlantic, and America, 1480–1650.* Liverpool University Press, 1978.

Arbel, Benjamin. *Trading Nations: Jews and Venetians in the Early Modern Mediterranean.* Leiden: Brill, 1995.

Armitage, David. *The Ideological Origins of the British Empire.* Cambridge University Press, 2000.

—— ed. *Theories of Empire, 1450–1800.* Aldershot, 1998.

Aston, Edward. *The Manners, lawes and customes of all Nations.* London, 1611.

Barker, Andrew. *True and Certaine Report of the Beginning, Proceedings, Overthrowes, and now present Estate of Captaine Ward and Dansiker, the two late famous Pirates.* London, 1609.

Barnet, Sylvan. "Some Limitations of a Christian Approach to Shakespeare." *ELH* 22 (1955): 81–92.

Bartels, Emily C. "*Othello* and Africa: Postcolonialism Reconsidered." *William and Mary Quarterly* 54.1 (January 1997): 45–64.

——. *Spectacles of Strangeness: Imperialism, Alienation, and Marlowe.* Philadelphia: University of Pennsylvania Press, 1993.

——. "Making More of the Moor: Aaron, Othello, and Renaissance Refashionings of Race." *Shakespeare Quarterly* 41.4 (Winter 1990): 433–54.

Barthelemy, Anthony Gerard. *Black Face, Maligned Race: The Representation of Blacks in English Drama from Shakespeare to Southerne.* Baton Rouge and London: Louisiana State University Press, 1987.

222 BIBLIOGRAPHY

Battenhouse, Roy W. "Othello as a Judas" in *Shakespeare's Christian Dimension.* Ed. Battenhouse. Bloomington: Indiana University Press, 1994. 423–27.

——. "Protestant Apologetics and the Subplot of *2 Tamburlaine.*" *ELR* 3 (1973): 30–43.

——. "Tamburlaine: The Scourge of God." *PMLA* 56 (1941): 337–48.

Baumer, Frank L. "England, the Turk, and the Common Core of Christendom." *The American Historical Review* (1945): 26–48.

Beard, Thomas. *The Theatre of Gods Judgements or, a collection of histories out of sacred, ecclesiasticall, and prophane authours concerning the admirable judgements of God upon the transgressours of his commandements. Translated out of French and augmented by more than three hundred examples.* London, 1597.

Berek, Peter. "The Jew as Renaissance Man." *Renaissance Quarterly 51.1* (Spring 1998): 128–62.

Best, George. *A true discourse of the late voyages of discouerie, for the finding of a passage to Cathaya, by the Northweast, under the conduct of Martin Frobisher Generall: devided into three bookes.* London, 1578.

Bethell, S.L. "Shakespeare's Imagery: The Diabolical Images in *Othello.*" *Shakespeare Survey* 5 (1952): 62–80.

Beverley, John. "Marvelous Dispossession: On 1492, Stephen Greenblatt's *Marvelous Possessions*, and the Academic Sublime." *Romance Quarterly* 40 (1993): 131–40.

Bevington, David M. *From Mankind to Marlowe: growth of structure in the popular drama of Tudor England.* Cambridge, MA: Harvard University Press, 1962.

Bhabha, Homi, K. "The Other Question: The Stereotype and Colonial Discourse." *Screen* 24.6 (1983): 18–36. Repr. in *Contemporary Postcolonial Theory: A Reader.* Ed. Padmini Mongia. London: Arnold, 1996.

——. *The Location of Culture.* London and New York: Routledge, 1994.

——. "Remembering Fanon: Self, Psyche and the Colonial Condition" in *Colonial Discourse and Poscolonial Theory.* Ed. P. Williams and L. Chrisman. New York: Columbia University Press, 1994. 112–23.

——ed. *Nation and Narration.* London: Routledge, 1990.

Blanks, David R. and Michael Frassetto, ed. *Western Views of Islam in Medieval and Early Modern Europe.* New York: St. Martin's Press, 1999.

Blaxton, John. *The English Usurer.* London, 1634.

Blount, Sir Henry. *A Voyage into the Levant: A Breife Relation of a Journey, Lately Performed by Master H. B., Gentleman, from England by the way of Venice, into Dalmatia, Sclavonia, Bosnia, Hungary, Macedonia, Thessaly, Thrace, Rhodes and Egypt unto Gran Cairo: With Particular Observations Concerning the moderne condition of the Turkes and other people under that Empire.* London, 1636.

Bon, Ottaviano. *The Sultan's Seraglio.* Trans. Robert Withers as *A Description of the Grand Signor's Seraglio, or Turkish Emperours Court.* London, 1625. Ed. Godfrey Goodwin. London: Saqi Books, 1996.

Bradley, William Aspenwall, ed. *The Correspondence of Philip Sidney and Hubert Languet.* Boston: Merrymount Press, 1912.

Braude, Benjamin. "The Sons of Noah and the Construction of Ethnic and Geographical Identities in the Medieval and Early Modern Periods." *William and Mary Quarterly* 54.1 (January 1997): 103–42.

Braude, Benjamin and Bernard Lewis. *Christians and Jews in the Ottoman Empire*. 2 vols. New York: Holmes & Meier Publishers, 1982.

Braudel, Fernand. *Civilization and Capitalism, 15th–18th Century*. Vol. 3 of 3. *The Perspective of the World*. Trans. S. Reynolds. New York: Harper & Row, 1984.

——. *The Mediterranean and the Mediterranean World in the Age of Philip II*. 2 vols. 1966. Trans. S. Reynolds. Berkeley: University of California Press, 1973.

Brenner, Robert. *Merchants and Revolution: Commercial Change, Political Conflict, and London's Overseas Traders, 1550–1653*. Princeton University Press, 1993.

——. "The Social Basis of English Commercial Expansion, 1550–1650." *Journal of Economic History* 32 (1972): 361–84.

Bruster, Douglas. *Drama and the Market in the Age of Shakespeare*. Cambridge University Press, 1992.

Bullough, Geoffrey, ed. *Narrative and Dramatic Sources of Shakespeare*. 8 vols. New York: Columbia University Press, 1957–75.

Burton, Jonathan. "English Anxiety and the Muslim Power of Conversion: Five Perspectives on 'Turning Turk' in Early Modern Texts." *Journal for Early Modern Cultural Studies* 2.1 (2002).

——. "Anglo-Ottoman Relations and the Image of the Turk in *Tamburlaine*." *Journal of Medieval and Early Modern Studies* 30.1 (2000): 125–57.

——. "'A Most Wily Bird': Leo Africanus, Othello and the Trafficking in Difference" in *Postcolonial Shakespeares*. Ed. Ania Loomba and Martin Orkin. New York and London: Routledge, 1998. 43–63.

Burton, Robert. *The Anatomy of Melancholy*. Oxford, 1621.

Caesar, Philip. *A General Discourse Against the Damnable Sect of Usurers*. Trans. Thomas Rogers. London, 1578.

Calderwood, James L. *The Properties of "Othello."* Amherst: University of Massachusetts Press, 1989.

Calendar of State Papers, Domestic series, of the reigns of Edward VI, Mary, Elizabeth, James I, 1547–[1625]. 12 vols. London: Her Majesty's Stationary Office, 1856–72.

Calendar of State Papers and Manuscripts, Existing in the Archives and Collections of Venice (CSPV). 37 vols. Ed. Rawdon Brown. London: Longman, 1864–1909.

Calendar of the State Papers, relating to Ireland, of the reign of James I . . . Preserved in Her Majesty's Public Record Office and elsewhere. 5 vols. Ed. C.W. Russell and John P. Prendergast. London: Longman, 1872–80.

Callaghan, Dympna. *Shakespeare Without Women: representing gender and race on the Renaissance stage*. London and New York: Routledge, 2000.

Callaghan, Dympna. "'Othello Was a White Man': Properties of Race on Shakespeare's Stage" in *Alternative Shakespeares, II*. Ed. Terence Hawkes. London: Routledge, 1996.

Canny, Nicholas, ed. *The Oxford History of the British Empire*, Vol. 1. *The Origins of Empire: British Overseas Enterprise to the Close of the Seventeenth Century*. Oxford University Press, 1998.

——. *Kingdom and Colony: Ireland in the Atlantic World 1560–1800*. Baltimore: Johns Hopkins University Press, 1988.

Cardozo, Jacob Lopes. *The Contemporary Jew in Elizabethan Drama*. Amsterdam: H.J. Paris, 1925.

Carey, Daniel. "Questioning Incommensurability in Early Modern Cultural Exchange." *Common Knowledge* 6.2 (Fall 1997): 32–50.

Carey, John. *John Donne: Life, Mind, and Art*. New York: Oxford University Press, 1980.

Carruthers, Bruce G. *City of Capital: Politics and Markets in the English Financial Revolution*. Princeton University Press, 1996.

Cavendish, Harrie. *Mr. Harrie Cavendish, his journey to and from Constantinople, 1589, by Fox, his servant. Camden Miscellany*. Vol. 17.2. Ed. A.C. Wood. London: Royal Historical Society, 1940 [from a manuscript].

Certaine Sermons appointed by the Queens Majestie, to be declared and read .... London, 1595.

Challis, C.E. *The Tudor Coinage*. Manchester University Press, 1978.

Chew, Samuel. *The Crescent and the Rose: Islam and England during the Renaissance*. 1937. Repr. New York: Octagon Books, 1965.

Clark, G.N. "Barbary Corsairs in the Seventeenth Century." *Cambridge Historical Journal* 8 (1945–46): 22–35.

Clay, C.G.A. *Economic Expansion and Social Change: England 1500–1700*. 2 vols. Cambridge University Press, 1984.

Clay, William Keatinge, ed. *Liturgical Services of the Reign of Queen Elizabeth: Liturgies and Occasional Forms of Prayer Set Forth in the Reign of Queen Elizabeth*. Cambridge University Press, 1847.

Clifford, James. *The Predicament of Culture: twentieth-century ethnography, literature, and art*. Cambridge, MA: Harvard University Press, 1988.

Cohen, Walter. "The undiscovered country: Shakespeare and mercantile geography" in *Marxist Shakespeares*. Ed. Jean E. Howard and Scott Cutler Shershow. London and New York: Routledge, 2001.

Comfort, William Wistar. "The Saracens in Italian Epic Poetry." *Proceedings of the Modern Language Association* 59 (1944): 882–910.

——. "The Literary Role of the Saracens in the French Epic." *Proceedings of the Modern Language Association* 55 (1940): 628–59.

Cooperman, Bernard Dov. "Venetian Policy Towards Levantine Jews in Its Broader Italian Context." *Gli Ebrei e Venezia*. Milano: Edizioni di Comunita, 1987.

Cormack, Lesley B. *Charting an Empire: Geography at the English Universities, 1580–1620*. University of Chicago Press, 1997.

Cowhig, Ruth. "Blacks in English Renaissance Drama and the Role of Shakespeare's Othello" in *The Black Presence in English Literature*. Ed. D. Dabydeen. Manchester University Press, 1985.

Crashaw, William. *A Sermon Preached in London before the Right Honorable Lord Lawarre*. London, 1610.

Crowley, Robert. *Way To Wealth Wherein Is Plainly Taught A Most Present Remedy For Sedicion*. London, 1550.

The [Croxton] Play of the Sacrament in *Non-Cycle Plays and Fragments*. Ed. Norman Davis. London: Oxford University Press, 1970.

Culpeper, Sir Thomas. *A Tract Against Usurie*. London, 1621.

Curio [Curione], Augustine. *A Notable History of the Saracens*. Trans. Thomas Newton. London, 1575.

Cutler, Alan and Helen. *The Jew as Ally of the Muslim: Medieval Roots of Anti-Semitism*. South Bend, IN: Notre Dame University Press, 1986.

Dallam, Thomas. *The Account of an Organ Carried to the Grand Seigneur and Other Curious Matter*. [1599–1600] MS publ. in *Early Voyages and Travels in the Levant*. Ed. J.T. Bent. Hakluyt Society, 1893.

D'Amico, Jack. *The Moor in English Renaissance Drama*. Tampa: University of South Florida Press, 1991.

Daniel, Norman. *Heroes and Saracens: An Interpretation of the Chansons de Geste*. Edinburgh University Press, 1984.

——. *Islam and the West: The Making of an Image*. Edinburgh University Press, 1958.

Davis, Robert C. *English Overseas Trade, 1500–1700*. London: Macmillan, 1973.

——. "England and the Mediterranean, 1570–1670" in *Essays in the Social and Economic History of Tudor and Stuart England*. Ed. F.J. Fisher. Cambridge University Press, 1961.

Davis, Robert C. "Counting European Slaves on the Barbary Coast." *Past & Present* 172:1 (2001): 87–124.

Day, John, William Rowley, and George Wilkins, *The Travailes of the Three English Brothers*. London, 1607. Repr. in *Three Renaissance Travel Plays*. Ed. Anthony Parr. Manchester University Press, 1995.

de Baudier, Seigneur Michael [de Languedoc]. *Histoire Generalle du Serrail, et de la Cour du Grand Seigneur Empereur des Turcs*. Paris, 1624. Trans. Edward Grimestone. *The History of the Imperiall Estate of the Grand Seigneurs*. London, 1635.

de Busbecq, Ogier Ghiselin. *The Turkish Letters of Ogier Ghiselin de Busbecq, Imperial Ambassador at Constantinople, 1554–1562*. Trans. Edward Seymour Foster. Oxford: Clarendon Press, 1968.

de Mendonça, Barbara Heliodora C. "*Othello*: A Tragedy Built on Comic Structure." *Shakespeare Survey* 21 (1968): 31–38.

de Nicolay, Nicholas. *Navigations et Peregrinations Orientales* (Lyons, 1568). Trans. T. Washington the Younger. *Navigations and Voyages made into Turkie*. London, 1585.

de Roover, Raymond. *Gresham on Foreign Exchange: An Essay on Early English Mercantilism with the Text of Sir Thomas Gresham's Memorandum for the Understanding of the Exchange.* Cambridge, MA: Harvard University Press, 1949.

———. "What is Dry Exchange? A Contribution to the Study of English Mercantilism." *Journal of Political Economy* 52 (1944): 250–66.

de Sousa, Geraldo U. *Shakespeare's Cross-Cultural Encounters.* New York: St. Martin's Press, 1999.

Dekker, Thomas. *The Dramatic Works of Thomas Dekker.* Ed. Fredson Bowers. 4 vols. Cambridge University Press, 1953–80.

———. *The Second Part of the Honest Whore.* London, 1630.

Dekker, Thomas, John Day, and William Haughton. *Lust's Dominion, or The Lascivious Queen.* Ed. J. Le Gay Brereton. Louvain: Librarie Universitaire, Uystpruyst, 1931.

Derrida, Jacques. *The Gift of Death.* Trans. D. Wills. University of Chicago Press, 1994.

Dessen, Alan C. "The Elizabethan Stage Jew and Christian Example: Gerontus, Barabas, and Shylock." *Modern Language Quarterly* 35 (1974): 231–45.

Dewar, Mary. "The Memorandum 'For the Understanding of the Exchange': Its Authorship and Dating." *Economic History Review* 17.3 (April 1965): 476–87.

Dollimore, Jonathan. *Radical Tragedy: Religion, Ideology, and Power in the Drama of Shakespeare and His Contemporaries.* Brighton: Harvester, 1984.

Donne, John. *John Donne.* ("Oxford Authors" series) Ed. John Carey. Oxford University Press, 1990.

———. *The Epithalamions, Anniversaries, and Epicedes.* Ed. W. Milgate. Oxford: Clarendon Press, 1978.

Earle, Peter. *Corsairs of Malta and Barbary.* London: Sidgwick & Jackson, 1970.

Ellis, Steven. *Ireland in the Age of the Tudors, 1447–1603: English expansion and the end of Gaelic rule.* London: Longman, 1998.

———. *Tudor Ireland: Crown, Community and the Conflict of Cultures, 1470–1603.* London: Longman, 1985.

Epstein, Mark Alan. *The Ottoman Jewish Communities and Their Role in the Fifteenth and Sixteenth Centuries.* Freiburg: K. Schwarz, 1980.

Epstein, Mortimer. *The Early History of the Levant Company.* London, 1908.

Everett, Barbara. " 'Spanish Othello': The Making of Shakespeare's Moor." *Shakespeare Survey* 35 (1982). Repr. in *Shakespeare and Race.* Ed. Catherine M.S. Alexander and Stanley Wells. Cambridge University Press, 2000. 64–81.

The Estate of Christians, living under the subjection of the Turke. London, 1595.

Fanon, Frantz. *The Wretched of the Earth.* 1961. Trans. C. Farrington. New York: Grove Press, 1968.

Fenton, Roger. *A Treatise of Usurie*. London, 1611.

Fernandez-Armesto, F. "Armada Myths: The Formative Phase" in *God's Obvious Design: Papers for the Spanish Armada Symposium, Sligo, 1988*. Ed. P. Gallagher and D.W. Cruikshank. London: Tamesis Books, 1990. 19–39.

Fischer-Galati, Stephen A. *Ottoman Imperialism and German Protestantism, 1521–1555*. Cambridge, MA: Harvard University Press, 1959.

Fisher, Godfrey. *Barbary Legend: War, Trade, and Piracy in North Africa 1415–1830*. Oxford: Clarendon, 1957.

Fitz-Geffry, Charles. *Compassion Towards Captives chiefly towards our brethren and country-men who are in miserable bondage in Barbarie*. Oxford, 1637.

Forell, George. "Luther and the War against the Turks." *Church History* 14 (1945): 256–71.

Foster, Sir William. *England's Quest of Eastern Trade*. London, 1933.

Foucault, Michel. *Power/Knowledge: Selected Interviews and Other Writings, 1972–1977*. Ed. Colin Gordon. New York: Pantheon, 1980.

Foxe, John. *Actes and Monuments of matters most speciall and memorable, happening in the Church, with an universall history of the same*. 2 vols. London, 1596.

Freely, John. *Inside the Seraglio: private lives of the sultans in Istanbul*. London: Viking, 1999.

Friedman, Ellen G. *Spanish Captives in North Africa in the Early Modern Age*. Madison: University of Wisconsin Press, 1983.

——. "Christian Captives at 'Hard Labour' in Algiers: Sixteenth-Eighteenth Centuries." *The International Journal of African Historical Studies* 13.4 (1980): 616–32.

Fuchs, Barbara. *Mimesis and Empire: The New World, Islam, and European Identities*. Cambridge University Press, 2001.

——. "Conquering Islands: Contextualizing *The Tempest*." *Shakespeare Quarterly* 48:1 (Spring 1997): 45–62.

Fuller, Mary. *Voyages in Print: English Travel to America, 1576–1624*. Cambridge University Press, 1995.

Fusfeld, D.R. "On the Authorship and Dating of 'For the Understanding of the Exchange.'" *Economic History Review* 20.1 (April 1967): 145–50.

Gandhi, Leela. *Postcolonial Theory: A Critical Introduction*. New York: Columbia University Press, 1998.

Geuffroy, Antoine. *The order of the greate Turckes courte, of hys menne of warre, and of all hys conquestes, with the summe of Mahumetes doctryne*. Trans. Richard Grafton. London, 1542.

Gillies, John. *Shakespeare and the Geography of Difference*. Cambridge: Cambridge University Press, 1994.

Glete, Jan. *Navies and Nations: Warships, Navies and State-Building in Europe and America, 1500–1860*. 2 vols. Stockholm: Almquist & Wiksell International, 1993.

Goffe, Thomas. *A Critical Old-Spelling Edition of Thomas Goffe's "The Courageous Turk."* Ed. Susan Gushee O'Malley. New York and London: Garland, 1979.

Goffe, Thomas. *The Raging Turke, or Bajazet the Second*. London, 1631. Ed. Meighen. Malone Society reprints. Oxford University Press, 1974.

Goffman, Daniel. *Britons in the Ottoman Empire, 1642–1660*. Seattle: University of Washington Press, 1998.

———. *Izmir and the Levantine World, 1550–1650*. Seattle: University of Washington Press, 1990.

Goldberg, Dena. "Whose God's on First? Special Providence in the Plays of Christopher Marlowe." *ELH* 60.3 (Fall 1993): 569–87.

Goodall, Baptist. *The Tryall of Travell*. London, 1630.

Goodwin, Godfrey. *The Private World of Ottoman Women*. London: Saqi Books, 1997.

Gouge, William. *A Recovery from Apostacy*. London, 1639.

Goughe, Hugh. *Ofspring of the house of Ottomano*. London, n.d. [1569?].

Gould, J.D. *The Great Debasement: currency and the economy in mid-Tudor England*. Oxford: Clarendon Press, 1970.

Graff, Gerald and James Phelan, eds. *Case Studies in Critical Controversy: William Shakespeare, The Tempest*. Boston and New York: Bedford/ St. Martin's, 2000.

Greenblatt, Stephen. "Invisible Bullets: Renaissance authority and its subversion, Henry IV and Henry V" in *Political Shakespeare: New Essays in Cultural Materialism*. Ed. Jonathan Dollimore and Alan Sinfield. Ithaca: Cornell University Press, 1985.

———. *Renaissance Self-Fashioning from More to Shakespeare*. University of Chicago Press, 1980.

Greene, Molly. "Beyond the Mediterranean Invasion: The Mediterranean in the Seventeenth Century." *Past & Present* 174:1 (2002): 42–71.

Greene, Robert. *Disputation betweene a Hee Conny-catcher and a Shee Conny-catcher*. London, 1592.

———. *Perimedes the Blacke-Smith*. London, 1588.

Griffin, Eric. "Un-Sainting James; or, Othello and the 'Spanish Spirits' of Shakespeare's Globe." *Representations* 62 (1998 Spring): 58–99.

Grosrichard, Alain. *The Sultan's Court; European Fantasies of the East*. 1979. Trans. Liz Heron. New York: Verso, 1998.

Guicciardini, Francesco. *The historie of Guicciardin containing the warres of Italie and other parts, continued for manie yeares vnder sundrie kings and princes, together with the variations and accidents of the same*. 3rd edn. Trans. Geffray Fenton. London, 1618.

Habib, Imtiaz. "*Othello*, Sir Peter Negro, and the Blacks of Early Modern England: Colonial Inscription and Postcolonial Excavation." *Literature Interpretation Text* 9 (1998): 15–30.

Hadfield, Andrew. *Literature, Travel, and Colonial Writing in the English Renaissance, 1545–1625*. Oxford: Clarendon Press, 1998.

Hakluyt, Richard. *Voyages and Discoveries*. Ed. Jack Beeching. New York: Penguin, 1972.

———. *The Principal Navigations, Voyages, and Discoveries of the English Nation*. London, 1589; second edition 1598–1600 in 3 vols. Repr. Glasgow: J. MacLehose and Sons, 1903–05. 12 vols.

Hale, John R. ed. *Renaissance Venice*. London: Faber and Faber, 1973.

Hall, Jonathan. *Anxious Pleasures: Shakespearean Comedy and the Nation-State.* Madison and Teaneck, NJ: Fairleigh Dickinson University Press, 1995.

Hall, Joseph. *The Works of Joseph Hall.* 12 vols. Oxford: D.A. Talboys, 1837–39.

Hall, Kim. *Things of Darkness: Economies of Race and Gender in Early Modern England*. Ithaca, NY: Cornell University Press, 1995.

Haller, William. *The Rise of Puritanism*. New York: Harper, 1957. Orig. publ. 1938.

Harris, Bernard. "A Portrait of a Moor." *Shakespeare Survey* 11 (1958): 89–97. Repr. in *Shakespeare and Race*. Ed. Catherine M.S. Alexander and Stanley Wells. Cambridge University Press, 2000. 37–63.

Harrison, G.B. *The Life and Death of Robert Devereux Earl of Essex*. London: Cassell, 1937.

Hawkes, David. *Idols of the Marketplace: Idolatry and Commodity Fetishism in English Literature, 1580–1680*. New York: Palgrave, 2001.

Hebb, David Delison. *Piracy and the English Government, 1616–1642.* Brookfield, VT: Ashgate, 1994.

Helgerson, Richard. *Forms of Nationhood: The Elizabethan Writing of England*. Chicago: University of Chicago Press, 1992.

Hess, Andrew. "The Battle of Lepanto and Its Place in Mediterranean History." *Past and Present* 57 (1972): 53–73.

Heywood, Thomas. *The Fair Maid of the West, Parts I and II*. Ed. Robert K. Turner. Lincoln: University of Nebraska Press, 1967.

——. *Londini Emporia, or London's Mercatura*. London, 1633.

Hill, George F. *A History of Cyprus*. 4 vols. Cambridge University Press, 1940–52.

Hoenselaars, A.J. "The Elizabethans and the Turk at Constantinople." *Cahiers Elizabethains* 47 (1995): 29–42.

Hogarth, D.D., P.W. Boreham, and J.G. Mitchell. *Martin Frobisher's Northwest Venture, 1576–1581: Mines, Minerals & Metallurgy*. Hull, Quebec: Canadian Museum of Civilization, 1993.

Holland, Philemon. *The historie of the world Commonly called, the naturall historie of C. Plinius Secundus*. London, 1601.

The Holy Bible, Conteyning the Old Testament and the New. London, 1611.

Hoskins, W.G. *The Age of Plunder: The England of Henry VIII, 1500–1547*. London and New York: Longman, 1976.

Howard, Jean E. "An English Lass Amid the Moors: gender, race, sexuality, and national identity in Heywood's *The Fair Maid of the West*" in *Women, "Race," and Writing in the Early Modern Period*. Ed. Margo Hendricks and Patricia Parker. London and New York: Routledge, 1994. 101–17.

Hoy, Cyrus. *Introductions, Notes, and Commentaries to Texts in "The Dramatic Works of Thomas Dekker."* 4 vols. Cambridge University Press, 1980.

Hubler, Edward. "The Damnation of Othello: Some Limitations on the Christian View of the Play." *Shakespeare Quarterly* 9 (1958): 295–300.

Hulme, Peter and William Sherman, ed. *"The Tempest" and Its Travels*. Philadelphia: University of Pennsylvania Press, 2000.

Hunter, G.K. "Elizabethans and Foreigners." *Shakespeare Survey* 17 (1964): 37–52.

Hutcheon, Linda. *A Theory of Parody: the teachings of twentieth-century art forms.* New York: Methuen, 1985.

Inalcik, Halil. "Capital Formation in the Ottoman Empire." *Journal of Economic History* 29 (March 1969): 97–140.

Jankowski, Theodora A. *Pure Resistance: Queer Virginity in Early Modern English Drama.* Philadelphia: University of Pennsylvania Press, 2000.

Jardine, Lisa and Jerry Brotton. *Global Interests: Renaissance Art between East & West.* Ithaca: Cornell University Press, 2000.

Johnson, Robert. *The New Life of Virginea.* London, 1612.

Johnson, Rosalind. "African Presence in Shakespearean Drama: Parallels between Othello and the Historical Leo Africanus." *Journal of African Civilizations* 7.2 (1985): 276–87.

Jones, Eldred. *Othello's Countrymen: The African in English Renaissance Drama.* London: Oxford University Press, 1965.

Jones, Emrys. "*Othello, Lepanto,* and the Cyprus Wars." *Shakespeare Survey* 21 (1968): 47–52.

Jones, Norman. *God and the Money-lenders: Usury and Law in Early Modern England.* Cambridge: Blackwell, 1989.

Journals of the House of Lords. 123 vols. London: H.M.S.O., 1800–1891.

Kamps, Ivo and Jyotsna Singh, eds. *Travel Knowledge: European "Discoveries" in the Early Modern Period.* New York: Palgrave, 2000.

Kastan, David Scott. *Shakespeare After Theory.* New York: Routledge, 1999.

Kellett, Edward [and Henry Byam]. *A Returne from Argier. A Sermon Preached at Minhead in the County of Somerset the 16. of March, 1627, at the re-admission of a relapsed Christian into our Church.* London, 1628.

Kelsey, Harry. *Sir Francis Drake: The Queen's Pirate.* New Haven: Yale University Press, 1998.

Kenyon, Walter A. *Tokens of Possession: The Northern Voyages of Martin Frobisher.* Toronto: Royal Ontario Museum, 1975.

Kermode, Lloyd Edward. "The Playwright's Prophecy: Robert Wilson's *The Three Ladies of London* and the 'Alienation' of the English." *Medieval and Renaissance Drama in England* 11 (1999): 60–87.

Knapp, Jeffrey. *An Empire Nowhere: England, America, and Literature from "Utopia" to "The Tempest."* Berkeley: University of California Press, 1992.

Knolles, Richard. *The Generall Historie of the Turkes.* London, 1603.

Knorr, Klaus E. *British Colonial Theories, 1570–1850.* Toronto: University of Toronto Press, 1944.

Kocher, Paul. *Christopher Marlowe: A Study of his Thought.* Chapel Hill: University of North Carolina Press, 1946.

Kortpeter, Carl Max. *Ottoman Imperialism during the Reformation.* University of London Press, 1973.

Kupperman, Karen Ordahl. *Indians and English: facing off in early America.* Ithaca, NY: Cornell, 2000.

——. *Roanoke: The Abandoned Colony.* Totowa, NJ: Rowman & Allenheld, 1984.

——. *Settling with the Indians: The Meeting of English and Indian Cultures in America, 1580–1640.* Totowa, NJ: Rowman and Littlefield, 1980.

[Kyd, Thomas]. *The Tragedye of Solyman and Perseda.* Ed. John J. Murray. New York: Garland, 1991.

L'Estrange-Ewan, C. *Captain John Ward, Arch-Pirate.* Privately printed, 1939.

Lane, Frederick C. *Venice: A Maritime Republic.* Baltimore: Johns Hopkins University Press, 1973.

Larkin, James F. and Paul L. Hughes, eds. *Stuart Royal Proclamations.* 2 vols. Oxford: Clarendon Press, 1973–83.

Leinwand, Theodore. *Theatre, Finance, and Society in Early Modern England.* Cambridge University Press, 1999.

Lenman, Bruce. *England's Colonial Wars, 1550–1688: Conflicts, Empire and National Identity.* New York: Longman, 2001.

Levy, Avigdor. *The Jews of the Ottoman Empire.* Princeton, NJ: Darwin Press, 1994.

Lim, Walter S.H. *The Arts of Empire: The Poetics of Colonialism from Ralegh to Milton.* Newark: University of Delaware Press, 1998.

Lithgow, William. *The Totall Discourse of the Rare Adventures and Painefull Peregrinations of long Nineteene Years Travayle From Scotland to the most famous Kingdoms in Europe, Asia, and Affrica.* London, 1632.

Little, Arthur, Jr. *Shakespeare Jungle Fever: National-Imperial Re-Visions of Race, Rape, and Sacrifice.* Stanford University Press, 2000.

Loomba, Ania. "'Delicious traffick': racial and religious difference on early modern stages" in *Shakespeare and Race.* Ed. Catherine M.S. Alexander and Stanley Wells. Cambridge University Press, 2000.

——. *Gender, Race, Renaissance Drama.* Manchester University Press, 1989.

Lupton, Julia Reinhard. "*Othello* Circumcised: Shakespeare and the Pauline Discourse of Nations." *Representations* 57 (Winter 1997): 73–89.

Luther, Martin. *On War Against the Turk* in *The Works of Martin Luther.* 5 of 6 vols. Trans. Charles M. Jacobs. Philadelphia: A.J. Holman & Castle Press, 1931. 5.77–123.

Lyly, John. *Galatea; Midas.* Ed. David Bevington. New York: Manchester University Press, 2000.

MacCaffrey, Wallace T. *Queen Elizabeth and the Making of Policy, 1572–1588.* Princeton University Press, 1981.

MacDonald, Michael. "'The Fearefull Estate of Francis Spira': Narrative, Identity, and Emotion in Early Modern England." *Journal of British Studies* 31 (January 1992): 32–61.

Maclure, Millar, ed. *Marlowe: The Critical Heritage, 1588–1896.* London: Routledge & Kegan Paul, 1979.

MacNeill, William H. *Venice: The Hinge of Europe, 1081–1797.* University of Chicago Press, 1974.

The Mahumetane or Turkish Historie. Trans. Robert Carr. London, 1600.

Mandeville, Sir John. *The Travels of Sir John Mandeville.* Ed. C.W.R.D. Moseley. London: Penguin, 1983.

Marlowe, Christopher. *Tamburlaine the Great.* Ed. J.S. Cunningham. Manchester University Press, 1981.

——. *The Jew of Malta.* Ed. N.W. Bawcutt. Manchester University Press, 1978.

Marshall, Tristan. *Theatre and Empire: Great Britain on the London Stages under James VI and I.* Manchester University Press, 2000.

Marston, John. *The Dutch Courtesan* in *The Selected Plays of John Marston.* Ed. Macdonald P. Jackson and Michael Neill. Cambridge University Press, 1986.

Martinego, Nestore. *The True Report of all the Successe of Famagosta.* Trans. William Malim. London, 1572.

Marx, Karl. *Capital: A Critique of Political Economy.* 3 vols. New York: International Publishers, 1967.

Masters, Bruce. *Christians and Jews in the Ottoman Arab World: The Roots of Sectarianism.* Cambridge University Press, 2001.

Matar, Nabil I. *Turks, Moors & Englishmen in the Age of Discovery.* New York: Columbia University Press, 1999.

——. *Islam In Britain, 1558–1685.* Cambridge University Press, 1998.

——. "Renaissance England and the Turban" in *Images of the Other: Europe and the Muslim World Before 1700. Cairo Papers in Social Science* 19:2. Ed. David Blanks. Cairo: American University in Cairo Press, 1997. 39–54.

——. " 'Turning Turk': Conversion to Islam in English Renaissance Thought." *Durham University Journal* 86 (1994): 33–42.

——. "The Renegade in English Seventeenth-Century Imagination." *SEL* 33 (1993): 489–505.

Mattingly, Garrett. *The Armada.* Boston: Houghton Mifflin, 1959.

McEachern, Claire. *The Poetics of English Nationhood, 1590–1612.* Cambridge University Press, 1996.

McNally, David. *Political Economy and the Rise of Capitalism.* Berkeley: University of California Press, 1988.

McPherson, David C. *Shakespeare, Jonson, and the Myth of Venice.* London and Toronto: Associated University Presses, 1990.

Metlitzki, Dorothee. *The Matter of Araby in Medieval England.* New Haven, CT: Yale University Press, 1977.

Michelson, Hijman. *The Jew in Early English Literature.* Amsterdam: H.J. Paris, 1926.

Middleton, Thomas. *The Triumphs of Truth.* London, 1613. In *Jacobean Civic Pageants.* Ed. Richard Dutton. Ryburn: Keele University Press, 1995.

——. *The Revenger's Tragedy.* Ed. Brian Gibbons. 2nd edn. New York: W.W. Norton, 1991.

Miller, Barnet. *Beyond the Sublime Porte: The Grand Seraglio of Istanbul* 1931. With an intro. by Halidé Edib. New Haven: Yale University Press; London: H. Milford, Oxford University Press, 1931. Repr. New York: AMS Press, 1970.

Minadoi, Giovanni Tommaso. *Historia della Guerra fra Turchi e Persiani.* Venice, 1588. Trans. Abraham Hartwell, *History of the Warres between the Turkes and the Persians.* London, 1595.

Moisan, Thomas. "'Which is the merchant here? And which the Jew?': Subversion and Recuperation in *The Merchant of Venice*" in *Shakespeare Reproduced: The Text in History and Ideology.* Ed. Jean Howard and Marion F. O'Connor. New York: Methuen, 1987.

Moore-Gilbert, Bart. *Postcolonial Theory: Contexts, Practices, Politics.* London: Verso, 1997.

Morison, Fynes. *Shakespeare's Europe: A Survey of the Condition of Europe at the End of the 16th century. Being Unpublished Chapters of Fynes Moryson's "Itinerary" (1617).* Ed. Charles Hughes. 2nd edn. New York: Benjamin Blom, 1967.

Mosse, Miles. *The Arraignment and Conviction of Usurie.* London, 1595.

Muldrew, Craig. *The Economy of Obligation: The Culture of Credit and Social Relations in Early Modern England.* Macmillan, 1998.

Mulier, Eco O.G. Haitsma. *The Myth of Venice and Dutch Republican Thought in the Seventeenth Century.* Trans. Gerald T. Moran. Assen, the Netherlands: Van Gorcum, 1980.

Mullaney, Steven. *The Place of the Stage: license, play, and power in Renaissance England.* University of Chicago Press, 1988.

Nashe, Thomas. *Works.* Ed. Ronald B. McKerrow. Repr. from the original edn. with corrections and supplementary notes. Edited by F.P. Wilson. 5 vols. Oxford: Blackwell, 1958.

Necipoglu, Gulru. *Architecture, Ceremonial and Power: The Topkapi Palace in the 15th and 16th Centuries.* New York: Architectural History Foundation; Cambridge, MA: MIT Press, 1991.

Neill, Michael. *Putting History to the Question: Power, Politics, and Society in English Renaissance Drama.* New York: Columbia University Press, 2000.

Nelson, Benjamin. *The Idea of Usury: From Tribal Brotherhood to Universal Otherhood.* 2nd edn. University of Chicago Press, 1969.

Newes from Sea, of Two Notorious Pirates, Ward . . . and Dansiker. London, 1609.

Newman, Karen. "'And wash the Ethiope white': Femininity and the Monstrous in *Othello*" in *Shakespeare Reproduced: The text in history and ideology.* Ed. Jean E. Howard and Marion F. O'Connor. New York and London: Methuen, 1987. 143–62.

Oldenburg, Scott. "The Riddle of Blackness in England's National Family Romance." *Journal for Early Modern Cultural Studies* 1.1 (2001): 46–62.

Olster, David M. *Roman Defeat, Christian Response, and the Literary Construction of the Jew.* Philadelphia: University of Penn Press, 1994.

Orkin, Martin. "*Othello* and the Plain Face of Racism." *Shakespeare Quarterly* 38.2 (1987): 166–88.

Oxford English Dictionary. Prep. J.A. Simpson and E.S.C. Weiner. 2nd ed. 20 vols. Oxford: Clarendon Press, 1989.

Pagden, Anthony. *Lords of All the World: Ideologies of Empire in Spain, Britain, and France c. 1500–c. 1800.* New Haven: Yale University Press, 1995.

Painter, William. *The Palace of Pleasure*. Ed. Joseph Jacobs. London: D. Nutt, 1890.

Palmer, Daryl. "Merchants and Miscegenation: *The Three Ladies of London, The Jew of Malta*, and *The Merchant of Venice*" in *Race, Ethnicity and Power in the Renaissance*. Ed. Joyce Green MacDonald Fairleigh Dickinson University Press, 1997.

Palmer, Sir Thomas. *An essay of the meanes how to make our travailes more profitable*. London, 1606.

Parker, Patricia. *Shakespeare from the Margins: Language, Culture, Context*. University of Chicago Press, 1996.

Parr, Johnstone. "Tamburlaine's Malady" reprinted in *Marlowe... A Casebook*. Ed. John Russell Brown. Macmillan, 1982.

Patterson, W.B. *King James VI and I and the Reunion of Christendom*. Cambridge University Press, 1997.

Paull, Michael R. *The Figure of Mahomet in Middle English Literature*. Diss., University of North Carolina at Chapel Hill, 1968.

Peckham, Sir George. *A True Report... of the Newfound Landes*. London, 1583.

Peirce, Leslie P. *The Imperial Harem: women and sovereignty in the Ottoman empire*. New York: Oxford University Press, 1993.

The Policy of the Turkish Empire. London, 1597.

Porter, Dennis. "*Orientalism* and its Problems" in *The Politics of Theory*. Ed. Francis Barker et al. Colchester: University of Essex Press, 1983.

Potter, Lois. "Pirates and 'turning Turk' in Renaissance drama," in *Travel and Drama in Shakespeare's Time*. Ed. Jean-Pierre Maquerlot and Michèle Willems. Cambridge University Press, 1996.

Powell, Timothy, ed. *Beyond the Binary: reconstructing cultural identity in a multicultural context*. New Brunswick, NJ: Rutgers University Press, 1999.

Pratt, Mary Louise. *Imperial Eyes: Travel Writing and Transculturation*. London and New York: Routledge, 1992.

Procter, Thomas. *Of the knowledge and conducte of warres*. London, 1578.

Pullan, Brian. "Jewish Moneylending in Venice: From Private Enterprise to Public Service." *Gli Ebrei e Venezia*. Milano: Edizioni di Comunita, 1987.

———. *The Jews of Europe and the Inquisition of Venice, 1550–1670*. Oxford: Blackwell, 1983.

Queller, Donald. *The Venetian Patriciate: Reality Versus Myth*. Urbana and Chicago: University of Illinois Press, 1986.

Questier, Michael C. *Conversion, Politics, and Religion in England, 1580–1625*. Cambridge University Press, 1996.

Quinn, D.B. *The Elizabethans and the Irish*. Ithaca: Cornell University Press, 1966.

Rabb, Theodore K. *Enterprise and Empire: Merchant and Gentry Investment in the Expansion of England, 1575–1630*. Cambridge, MA: Harvard University Press, 1967.

——. "Investment in English Overseas Enterprise, 1575–1630." *Economic History Review*. 2nd series, 19 (1966): 70–81.

Rainolds, William. Completed by William Gifford. *Calvino-Turcismus, Id Est, Calvinisticae Perfidiae cum Mahumetana Collatio*. Antwerp, 1597; Cologne, 1603.

Rawlinson, H.G. "Early Trade between England and the Levant." *Journal of Indian History* 2.1 (1922): 107–16.

Read, Conyers. *Mr. Secretary Walsingham and the Policy of Queen Elizabeth*. 3 vols. Cambridge, MA: Harvard University Press, 1925.

Rice, Warner G. "'To Turn Turk.'" *Modern Language Notes* 46 (1931): 153–54.

Riggs, David. "Marlowe's Quarrel with God" in *Marlowe, History and Sexuality*. Ed. Paul W. White. New York: AMS Press, 1998.

Rosen, Alan. "The Rhetoric of Exclusion: Jew, Moor, and the Boundaries of Discourse in *The Merchant of Venice*" in *Race, Ethnicity and Power in the Renaissance*. Ed. Joyce Green MacDonald. Fairleigh Dickinson University Press, 1997.

Rosenberg, Edgar. "The Jew in Western Drama: An Essay and a Checklist." *Bulletin of the New York Public Library* 72 (1968): 442–91.

Roth, Cecil. *The House of Nasi, The Duke of Naxos*. Philadelphia: The Jewish Publication Society of America, 1948.

Rowlands, Samuel. *The Complete Works of Samuel Rowlands, 1598–1628*. 3 vols. Glasgow: R. Anderson, 1880. Repr. New York, 1930.

Roxburghe Ballads. Ed. Charles Hindley. London: Reeves and Turner, 1873–74.

Rushdie, Salman. *The Satanic Verses*. New York: Viking, 1988.

Runciman, Steven. *The First Crusade*. Cambridge University Press, 1980.

Said, Edward. *Orientalism*. 1978. 2nd edn. rev. New York: Pantheon, 1994.

Sanders, Nicholas. *A Briefe Treatise of Usurie*. London, 1568.

Sandys, Sir George. *A Relation of a Journey... Containing a descripion of the Turkish Empire*. London, 1615.

Scanlon, Thomas. *Colonial Writing and the New World, 1583–1671*. Cambridge University Press, 1999.

Schick, Irvin C. *The Erotic Margin: Sexuality and Spatiality in Alteritist Discourse*. London: Verso, 1999.

Seaton, Ethel. "Marlowe's Map" in *Essays and Studies by Members of the English Association* 10 (1924): 13–35. Reprinted in *Marlowe: A Collection of Critical Essays*. Ed. Clifford Leech. Englewood Cliffs, NJ: Prentice-Hall, 1964.

The Seconde Tome of Homilies: Of such matters as were promised, and entituled in the former part of homilies. Set out by the authoritie of the Queenes Maiestie: and to be read in euerie parish church agreeably. London, 1595.

Senior, C.M. *A Nation of Pirates: English Piracy in Its Heyday*. New York: Crane, Russak & Co., 1976.

Setton, Kenneth M. *Western Hostility to Islam and Prophecies of Turkish Doom*. Philadelphia: American Philosophical Society, 1992.

Setton, Kenneth M. "Lutheranism and the Turkish Peril." *Balkan Studies* 3.1 (1962): 136–65.

Shakespeare, William. *The Norton Shakespeare*. Ed. Stephen Greenblatt et al. New York: W.W. Norton, 1997.

Shapiro, James. *Shakespeare and the Jews*. New York: Columbia University Press, 1996.

Shepherd, Simon. *Marlowe and the Politics of Elizabethan Theatre*. Brighton: Harvester, 1986.

Siegel, Paul N. "The Damnation of Othello." *PMLA* 68 (1953): 1068–78.

Simon, G. "Luther's Attitude toward Islam." *Moslem World* 21 (1931): 257–62.

Sisson, C.J. "A Colony of Jews in Shakespeare's London." *Essays and Studies* 23 (1938): 38–51.

Skilliter, S.A. *William Harborne and the Trade with Turkey, 1578–82: A documentary study of the first Anglo-Ottoman relations*. Oxford University Press, 1977.

Sleidanus, Johann Philippson. *De quatuor summis imperiis… Lebri tres*. Strasbourg, 1556; trans. Stephen Wythers, *A Briefe Chronicle of the Foure Principall Empyres*. London, 1563.

Smith, Ian. "Barbarian Errors: Performing Race in Early Modern England." *Shakespeare Quarterly* 49.2 (1998): 168–86.

Smith, Captain John. *The True Travels, Adventures, and Observations of Captaine John Smith, …from… 1593 to 1629*. London, 1630.

Smith, Mary Elizabeth. " 'Hell Strives With Grace': Reflections on the Theme of Providence in Marlowe" in *Elizabethan Theatre XI*. Ed. A.L. Magnusson and C.E. McGee. Port Credit: P.D. Meany, 1990.

Snyder, Susan. *The Comic Matrix of Shakespearean Tragedy*. Princeton University Press, 1979.

Soranzo, Lazaro. *L' Ottomano*. Ferrara, 1594. Trans. Abraham Hartwell. *The Ottomano of L.S. Wherein is delivered as well a full and perfect report of the might and power of Mahomet the Third, Great Emperour of the Turkes now raigning*. London, 1603.

Spivak, Bernard. *Shakespeare and the Allegory of Evil*. New York: Columbia University Press, 1958.

Steensgard, Niels. *The Asian Trade Revolution of the Seventeenth Century*. University of Chicago Press, 1974.

Stefansson, Vilhjalmur, ed. *The Three Voyages of Martin Frobisher in Search of a Passage to Cathay and India by the North-west*, A.D. *1576–8. From the original 1578 text of George Best, together with numerous other versions, additions, etc*. London: Argonaut Press, 1938.

Stuart, King James. *His Maiesties Lepanto, or Heroical Song*. London, 1603. Repr. in *The Poems of James VI of Scotland*. Ed. James Craigie 1 of 2 vols. Edinburgh and London: William Blackwood & Sons, 1955.

Stuart Royal Proclamations. Ed. Paul L. Hughes and James F. Larkin. Vol. 1. New Haven: Yale University Press, 1988.

Sutcliffe, Matthew. *De Turco-Papismo: Hoc Est De Turcarum et Papistrarum Adversus Christi Ecclesiam & Fidem Conjuriatione*. London, 1599 and 1604.

Sweezy, Paul et al. *The Transition from Feudalism to Capitalism*. London: Verso, 1976.

Tanner, Tony. "'Which is the Merchant Here? And Which the Jew?': The Venice of Shakespeare's *Merchant of Venice*" in *Venetian Views, Venetian Blinds: English Fantasies of Venice*. Ed. Manfred Pfister and Barbara Shaff. Amsterdam: Rodopi, 1999.

Taussig, Michael. *Mimesis and Alterity: A Particular History of the Senses*. New York and London: Routledge, 1993.

Tawney, R.H., ed. and intro. *Thomas Wilson. A Discourse Upon Usury*. 1925. Repr. New York: Augustus M. Kelley, 1963.

——. "Religious Thought on Social and Economic Questions in the Sixteenth and Seventeenth Centuries." *Journal of Political Economy* 31.5 (1923): 637–74.

Tawney, R.H. and Eileen Power, eds. *Tudor Economic Documents*. 3 vols. London and New York, 1924.

Teague, Francis. "*Othello* and New Comedy." *Comparative Drama* 20 (1986): 54–64.

Temkin, Owsei. *The Falling Sickness: A History of Epilepsy from the Greeks to the Beginnings of Modern Neurology*. 2nd edn. Baltimore and London: Johns Hopkins University Press, 1971.

Tenenti, Alberto. *Piracy and the Decline of Venice, 1580–1615*. Berkeley: University of California Press, 1967.

Thirsk, Joan. *Economic Policy and Projects: The Development of a Consumer Society in Early Modern England*. Oxford: Clarendon Press, 1978.

Thomson, Janice E. *Mercenaries, Pirates, and Sovereigns: State-Building and Extraterritorial Violence in Early Modern Europe*. Princeton University Press, 1994.

Tokson, Elliot. *The Popular Image of the Black Man in English Drama, 1550–1688*. Boston: G.K. Hall, 1982.

Tuglaci, Pars. *The Ottoman Palace Women*. Istanbul: Cem Yayinevi, 1985.

Valensi, Lucette. *The Birth of the Despot: Venice and the Sublime Port*. Trans. Arthur Denner. Ithaca: Cornell University Press, 1993.

Vaughan, Alden T. and Virginia Mason Vaughan. "Before Othello: Elizabethan Representations of Subsaharan Africans." *William and Mary Quarterly* 54:1 (January 1997): 19–44.

Vaughan, Dorothy M. *Europe and the Turk: A Pattern of Alliances, 1350–1700*. Liverpool, 1954.

Vaughan, Virginia Mason. "*Othello*": *A Contextual History*. Cambridge: Cambridge University Press, 1994.

Vella, Andrew P. *An Elizabethan-Ottoman Conspiracy. Royal University of Malta Historical Studies* 3. Malta: Royal University of Malta, 1972.

Vitkus, Daniel J. "The 'O' in *Othello*: Tropes of Damnation and Nothingness" in "*Othello*": *New Critical Essays*. Ed. Philip Kolin. New York and London: Routledge, 2001.

Vitkus, Daniel J., ed. *Piracy, Slavery, and Redemption: Barbary Captivity Narratives from Early Modern England*. Introduction by Nabil Matar. New York: Columbia University Press, 2001.

——, ed. *Three Turk Plays from Early Modern England*. New York: Columbia University Press, 2000.

Wallerstein, Immanuel. *The Modern World-System*. New York: Academic Press, 1974.

Weiner, Carol Z. "The Beleaguered Isle. A Study of Elizabethan and Early Jacobean Anti-Catholicism." *Past and Present* 51 (1971): 27–62.

West, Robert H. "The Christianness of Othello." *Shakespeare Quarterly* 15 (1964): 333–43.

Wheeler, John. *A Treatise of Commerce: Wherein are shewed the commodities arising by a well ordered and ruled trade, such as that of the Societie of Merchants Aduenturers is proued to be: written principally for the better information of those who doubt of the necessarinesse of the said societie in the state of the realme of England*. London, 1601.

Whitney, Lois. "Did Shakespeare know Leo Africanus?" *PMLA* 37 (1922): 470–83.

Willan, Thomas S. "Some Aspects of English Trade with the Levant in the Sixteenth Century." *English Historical Review* 70 (1955): 399–410.

Williams, Gordon. *A Dictionary of Sexual Language and Imagery in Shakespearean and Stuart Literature*. London and Atlantic Highlands, NJ: Athlone Press, 1994.

Wilson, Robert. *An Edition of Robert Wilson's "Three Ladies of London" and "Three Lords and Three Ladies of London."* Ed. H.S.D. Mithal. New York: Garland, 1988.

Wolf, John B. *The Barbary Coast: Algiers under the Turks, 1500 to 1830*. New York: W.W. Norton, 1969.

Wood, Alfred C. *A History of the Levant Company*. Oxford University Press, 1935.

Wood, Ellen Meiksins. *The Pristine Culture of Capitalism*. New York: Verso, 1991.

Yver, Jacques. Trans. Henry Wotton. *A Courtlie Controversie of Cupids Cautels Conteyning Five Tragicall Histories*. London, 1578.

Zagorin, Perez. *Ways of Lying: Dissimulation, Persecution and Conformity in Early Modern Europe*. Cambridge, MA: Harvard University Press, 1990.

INDEX

Achelley, John, 70–71
Adams, Stephen, 4
Africanus, Leo, 85, 87, 90, 91,
    108–09, 159–60, 179, 207n,
    209n, 213n
Ahmet I, 118–19
Aijaz, Ahmad, 201n
Amurath III, 51, 59, 72
Anderson, Benedict, 203n
Andrews, Kenneth, 214n, 216n,
    217n
Arbel, Benjamin, 218n
Armitage, David, 200n
Aston, Edward, 87

Baines, Richard, 205n
Barbarossa, 210n
Barker, Andrew,
    A True and Certaine Report of. . .
    Captaine Ward and
    Dansiker, 145–49
Bartels, Emily, 5, 71, 200n, 204n,
    205n, 209n
Barthelemy, Anthony, 209n, 210n,
    212n
Battenhouse, Roy, 204n, 213n
Baumer, Frank, 204n
Beard, Thomas,
    The Theatre of Gods Judgements,
    169
Beaumont, Francis and John Fletcher,
    The Woman Hater, 89
Berek, Peter, 218n
Best, George,
    A true discourse of the late voyages
    of discoverie, 102–03, 205n
Beverly, John, 200n
Bevington, David, 56, 204n, 205n
Bhabha, Homi, 2, 12–13, 30
Bible, The, 205n, 212n
    Acts and Epistles, 34

Geneva Bible, 55, 204n
    maps in, 34
    Matthew, 54, 69
    Revelation, 55–56
Blanks, David, 215n
Blaxton, John, 217n
Blount, Sir Henry, 20–21,
    117–18
Bon, Ottaviano, 116, 181, 214n
Bottingham, Karl S., 199n
Bragdin, Piero, 19
Braude, Benjamin, 209n, 213n, 219n
Braude, Benjamin and Bernard
    Lewis, 218n
Braudel, Fernand, 14–15, 25, 35,
    202n, 206n, 210n
Brenner, Robert, 26, 218n
Brotton, Jerry, 201n
Bruster, Robert, 27
Bullough, Geoffrey, 209n, 211n
Burton, Jonathan, 8, 51, 124–25,
    204n, 207n, 209n, 214n
Burton, Robert, 207n
Byam, Henry, 83, 87, 105, 206n,
    208n

Caesar, Philip, 217n
Calderwood, James, 96
Callaghan, Dympna, 103, 209n
Calvino-Turcismus, 62
Canny, Nicholas, 4
Cardozo, Jacob Lopez, 216n
Carey, Daniel, 3
Carllel, Lodowick,
    The Famous Tragedy of Osmond
    the Great Turk, 212n
Carr, Ralph,
    The Mahumetane or Turkish
    Historie, 66, 82, 105
Cavendish, Harry, 159
Challis, C.E., 218n

Chanson de Roland, 210n
Charles I, 5, 20, 110
Chew, Samuel, 81, 205n, 209n, 212n, 213n, 215n
Cinthio, Geraldo,
  Gli Hecatommithi, 91, 94, 209n
Clark, G.N., 205n
Clay, William, 202n, 206n
Cohen, Walter, 29
Coke, John, 20
Comfort, William, 215n
Cooperman, Bernard Dov, 179–80, 218n
Cormack, Lesley B., 199n, 205n
Cotgrave, Randle, 88
Cowhig, Ruth, 209n
Crashaw, William,
  A Sermon Preached in London before the Right Honorable Lord Lawarre, 10
Crowley, Robert,
  Way To Wealth, 167
[Croxton] Play of the Sacrament, The, 165–68, 173, 181
Culpeper, Sir Thomas,
  A Tract Against Usurie, 217n
Curio [Curione], Augustine,
  A Notable History of the Saracens, 81, 207n
Cutler, Alan and Helen, 182, 218n

Daborne, Robert,
  A Christian Turned Turk, 23, 108, 114, 122, 124, 127, 141–45, 148–49, 152–58, 161, 163, 165, 177, 178, 180, 183, 185, 192–94, 213n
Dallam, Thomas, 116–17, 209n
D'Amico, Jack, 5, 103, 209n, 210n
Daniel, Norman, 208n, 211n, 215n
Dansiker, Simon, 144, 151–53, 155, 157, 160, 161, 216n
Davis, Robert C., 216n, 218n
Day, John, William Rowley, and George Wilkins,
  The Travels of the Three English Brothers, 183

De Baudier, Michel,
  The History of the Imperiall Estate of the Grand Seigneurs, 115
De Breves, Le Sieur, 153
De Busbecq, Ogier Ghiselin, 19
Dee, John, 217n
Dekker, Thomas,
  The Honest Whore, 88–9
  Lust's Dominion (with Day and Haughton), 102–03
  The Shoemaker's Holiday, 28, 133–34
De La Warre, Lord, 10
De Mendonça, 209n
Denball, Sampson, 148
De Nicolay, Nicholas,
  Navigations. . .into Turkie, 36, 164, 179, 184, 213n
De Roover, Raymond, 172, 217n
Derrida, Jacques, 12
De Sousa, Geraldo, 191
De Turco-Papismo, 62
Dewar, Mary, 217n
Dollimore, Jonathan, 204n
Donne, John, 83–84, 207n, 208n
Drake, Sir Francis, 30, 70, 150
Du Bellay, Guillaume, 93

Earle, Peter, 205n
Edward I, 164
Eldred, John, 16
Elizabeth I, 4, 32, 51, 59, 110, 124, 133, 141, 150, 168, 189
Ellis, Steven, 4
Epstein, Mark Alan, 203n, 219n
Essex, Earl of, 189
Estate of Christians, living under the subjection of the Turke, The, 16, 203n
Everett, Barbara, 216n

Fajardo, Don Luis, 153
Famous and Wonderful Recovery of a Ship of Bristol, The, 111, 113
Fanon, Frantz, 7, 201n
Fenton, Roger, 185, 217n
Fernandez-Armesto, F., 211n
Fischer-Galati, Stephen, 204n, 205n

Fisher, Godfrey, 218n
Fitz-Geffry, Charles,
    Compassion Towards Captives, 197
Forell, George, 204n
Foscarini, Antonio, 152
Foster, Sir William, 218n
Foucault, Michel, 6, 11, 200n, 201n
Fox, John, 53–54, 63
Foxe, John,
    Acts and Monuments, 61, 69
Friedman, Ellen, 205n, 216n
Frobisher, Martin, 70, 71
Fuchs, Barbara, 5, 6, 7, 129–30,
    139, 144, 200n, 201n, 215n
Fuller, Mary, 199n
Fusfield, D.R., 217n

Gandhi, Leela, 11
Georgievitz, Bartolomeo, 20
Geuffroy, Antoine,
    *The order of the greate Turckes
    courte*, 49
Gifford, Captain, 153
Gillies, John, 35, 90, 188, 209n
Glete, Jan, 172–73, 202n, 217n
Goffe, Thomas,
    The Courageous Turke, 99–101,
        102, 120, 123, 211n, 212n
    The Raging Turke, 183, 211n
Goffman, Daniel, 3, 199n, 202n
Goldberg, Dena, 47, 48, 204n
Goodall, Baptist, 145
Gouge, William, 206n
Goughe, Hugh,
    *The Ofspring of the House of
    Ottomanno*, 19
Gould, J.D., 218n
Grafton, Richard, 49
Gramsci, Antonio, 11, 201n
Graves, William, 146
Greenblatt, Stephen, 5, 28, 43, 63,
    71, 194, 199n, 200n, 205n
Greene, Molly, 36, 203n
Greene, Robert, 54, 209n
    Selimus, 57, 183, 211n
Gresham, Sir Thomas, 172, 217n
Greville, Fulke, 211n
Griffin, Eric, 216n

Grosrichard, Alain, 115, 128
Guicciardini, Francesco, 185
Gustinian, Zorzi, 148

Habib, Imtiaz, 209n
Hadfield, Andrew, 199n
Hakluyt, Richard, 21, 26, 33, 53,
    102, 109, 202n, 203n, 208n,
    216n
Hale, John, 210n
Hall, Bishop Joseph, 83–84, 207n,
    210n, 213n
Hall, Kim, 5, 200n, 209n, 213n
Haller, William, 110
Harborne, William, 59, 134, 204n,
    214n
Harris, Bernard, 206n
Harrison, John, 134, 215n
Hartwell, Abraham, 72, 97
Hawkes, David, 217n, 219n
Hawkins, Sir John, 69–70, 71
Hebb, David, 82, 205n, 206n
Helgerson, Richard, 27
Henry IV [of France], 151–52
Hess, Andrew, 206
Heywood, Thomas, 32, 121, 122,
    125, 127–28, 133, 136, 161,
    162, 195, 213n, 214n
    The Fair Maid of the West, Part I,
        107, 114, 124, 128–36,
        141–43, 195, 196, 212n,
        214n
    *The Fair Maid of the West,
    Part II*, 136–41, 162
Hoenselaars, A.J., 206n
Hogarth, D.D., 205n
Holland, Philemon, 33
Hoskins, W.G., 216n
Howard, Jean E., 27, 129, 135
Hoy, Cyrus, 209n
Hunter, G.K., 90, 209n
Hutcheon, Linda, 161, 216n

Inalcik, Halil, 218n

James I, 4, 32, 110, 143, 148, 149,
    215n
    Lepanto, 80

Jankowski, Theodora, 215n
Jardine, Lisa, 201n
Jewel, Bishop John, 88
Johnson, Robert,
    The New Life of Virginea, 9–10
Jones, Emrys, 80, 206n
Jones, Inigo, 81
Jones, Norman, 217n
Jonson, Ben, 28, 81
    The Alchemist, 28
    Sejanus, 39

Kamps, Ivo and Jyotsna Singh, 202n
Kastan, David Scott, 6
Kellett, Edward, 83, 86, 106, 206n,
    207n, 213n
Kelsey, Harry, 217n
Keynes, J.M., 150
King, John, 151
Knapp, Jeffrey, 199n
Knolles, Richard,
    *The Generall Historie of the
    Turkes*, 49, 50, 81, 94, 105,
    180, 211n
Kocher, Paul, 204n
Koran, the, 17–18, 50, 55
Kortpeter, Carl, 204n
Kupperman, Karen, 201n
Kyd, Thomas, 162, 204n, 212n, 214n
    The Spanish Tragedy, 124, 126,
    133, 214n
    *The Tragedy of Soliman and
    Perseda*, 107, 114, 120–29,
    134–35, 136, 141, 156, 161,
    162, 211n, 214n

Lane, Frederick, 210n
Languet, Hubert, 81, 206n
Laud, Archbishop William, 83
Leinwand, Theodore, 189
Lenman, Bruce, 4, 199n
L'Estrange-Ewan, 216n
Levy, Avigdor, 182, 218n
Lewis, Bernard, 219n
Lim, Walter S.H., 209n
Lithgow, William, 15–16, 18, 54,
    148, 154, 202n, 215n
Little, Arthur L., Jr., 6, 200n, 209n

Loomba, Ania, 8–9, 213n
Lupton, Julia, 213n
Luther, Martin, 60
    On War Against the Turk,
    47, 60
    Table Talk, 60
Lyly, John,
    Midas, 37–38, 67, 205n

MacDonald, Michael, 216n
Maclean, Gerald, 21, 202n
MacNeill, William, 210n
Mahomet I, 181
Mandeville, Sir John, 208n
Marlowe, Christopher, 8, 22, 30,
    96, 192, 196, 204n, 205n,
    215n, 218n
    Doctor Faustus, 97
    The Jew of Malta, 23, 43, 46, 56,
    163, 164, 166, 167, 170,
    177, 178, 180, 183, 185–87,
    193–95
    Tamburlaine, Part I, 49, 56, 67,
    69, 72–74
    Tamburlaine, Part II, 46, 50, 57,
    63, 71, 73, 74, 214n
    Tamburlaine plays, 8, 23, 45–68,
    70–75, 107–08, 122, 155,
    156, 161, 191, 205n,
    215n
Marshall, Tristan, 200n
Marston, John,
    The Dutch Courtesan, 28, 88, 89
Marx, Karl, 75, 196, 205n
Mason, John, *The Turke*, 211n
Massinger, Philip, 108, 125
    The Renegado, 23, 88, 114, 122,
    124, 127, 139, 141, 149,
    152, 156, 158–61, 197
    The Roman Actor, 39
Masters, Bruce, 202n
Matar, Nabil, 3, 81, 109–10, 187,
    202n, 203n, 205n, 206n,
    213n, 214n, 215n, 216n
McEachern, Claire, 27
McPherson, David, 94, 210n, 211n
Metlitzki, Dorothee, 215n
Michelson, Hijman, 216n, 217n

Middleton, Thomas,
  Blurt, Master Constable, 89
  Michaelmas Term, 89
  The Revenger's Tragedy, 88
  The Triumphs of Truth, 140
  Your Five Gallants, 89
Minadoi, Giovanni, 72
Mitton, Thomas, 146
Moisan, Thomas, 219n
Moore-Gilbert, Bart, 10
Moryson, Fynes, 94
Mosse, Miles, 169, 217n
Muhammad, 17, 50–52, 56, 85–86,
  118, 207n
Mulier, Eco O. G. Haitsma, 210n
Mullaney, Steven, 28
Murray, John J., 124, 214n

Nashe, Thomas, 213n
Nasi, Joseph, 180, 218n
Neill, Michael, 188, 191, 209n
Nelson, Benjamin, 217n
*Newes from Sea, of Two Notorious
  Pirates, Ward… and Dansiker*,
  146–47, 155
Newman, Karen, 209n
Newton, Thomas,
  Sarracenicae Historiae, 81

Ohlmeyer, Jane H., 199n
Oldenburg, Scott, 209n, 212n
Olster, David M., 182
O'Malley, Susan Gushee, 212n
Orkin, Martin, 209n
Ortelius, Abraham,
  Theatrum Orbis Terrarum,
  64
Osbourne, Edward, 26
Osman, Cara, 146, 148
*Oxford History of the British Empire,
  The*, 199n

Painter, William, 212n
Palmer, Sir Thomas,
  *An essay of the meanes how to
    make our travailes more
    profitable*, 21
Patterson, W.B., 203n

Paull, Michael, 215n
Peckham, George, 69, 71
Peele, George, 212n
Philip II [of Spain], 38
Policy of the Turkish Empire, The,
  17, 66, 82, 114, 216n
Porter, Dennis, 201n
Pory, John, 85, 91, 109
Potter, Lois, 205n
Powell, Timothy, 2–3
Pratt, Mary Louise, 7, 201n
Procter, Thomas,
  *Of the knowledge and conducte of
    warres*, 82
Puckering, Sir John, 204n, 205n
Pullan, Brian, 218n
Purchas, Samuel, 21, 214n

Queller, Donald, 210n
Questier, Michael, 207n
Quinn, D.B., 199n, 201n

Rabb, Theodore, 25, 218n
Read, Conyers, 216n
Richard I, Coeur de Lion, 210n
Rawlins, John, 111–13
Roberts, Lewes, 168, 197
Rosen, Alan, 191
Rosenburg, Edgar, 216n
Roth, Cecil, 218n
Rowlands, Samuel, 213n

Said, Edward, 8, 13, 31, 201n,
  205n
  Orientalism, 10–11, 19
Sanders, Nicholas, 217n
Sanders, Norman, 206n
Sandys, George,
  *A Relation of a Journey…
    Containing a descripion of the
    Turkish Empire*, 118–19
Scanlon, Thomas, 199n
Seaton, Ethel, 64–65
Seconde Tome of Homilies, The,
  105
Selim II, 210n
Senior, C.M., 150, 215n
Setton, Kenneth, 204n

Shakespeare, William, 22, 29, 30, 34, 170, 207n, 209n, 212n
All's Well That Ends Well, 212n
Comedy of Errors, 39, 121
Measure for Measure, 89
Merchant Of Venice, 39, 43–44, 121, 143, 177–78, 188–96, 219n
Much Ado About Nothing, 39, 208n, 212n
Othello, 2, 14, 23, 35, 39, 77–79, 80–82, 84–87, 89–99, 101–08, 120, 123, 124, 127, 156, 157, 161, 165, 191, 206n, 211n, 213n, 217n
Pericles, 34, 40–43
Richard II, 39
Romeo and Juliet, 39
Taming of the Shrew, 39, 212n
The Tempest, 6, 17, 201n
Titus Adronicus, 102
Troilus and Cressida, 114
Twelfth Night, 207n, 212n
Shapiro, James, 177, 181, 204n, 206n, 213n, 216n, 218n
Sharpham, Edward, *The Fleer*, 89
Shepherd, Simon, 211n
Sidney, Philip, 81, 206n
Simon, G., 204n
Sisson, C.J., 181
Skilliter, S.A., 203n
Sleidanus, Johann, 66
Smith, John, 4–5, 154
Smith, Mary Elizabeth, 204n, 209n
Smith, Thomas, 170, 217n
Snyder, Susan, 209n
Soranzo, Lazaro, *L' Ottomano*, 97
Spenser, Edmund, 84, 210n
Spira, Francis, 160
Spivak, Bernard, 212n
Staper, Richard, 26
Stefansson, Vilhjalmur, 205n
Stukely, Thomas, 67
Suleiman I, 121, 184
Swinhoe, Gilbert, *Unhappy Fair Irene*, 213n

Tanner, Tony, 219n
Tasso, Torquato, *Jerusalem Delivered*, 62–63
Taussig, Michael, 14, 130
Tawney, R.H., 168, 170–71, 175, 217n
Teague, Francis, 209n
Tenenti, Alberto, 203n, 210n, 217n
Thirsk, Joan, 218n
Thomson, Janice, 202n
Tokson, Elliot, 209n

Valensi, Lucette, 210n
Vaughan, Alden T. and Virginia Mason, 209n, 213n
Vaughan, Dorothy M., 203n, 204n, 210n
Vaughan, Virginia Mason, 77, 205n
Velutelli, Acerbo, 168
Vendramin, Giacomo, 151
Vitkus, Daniel, 205n, 212n, 213n

Walsingham, Sir Francis, 59, 67, 204n, 205n
Ward, John, 67, 144–48, 151, 153, 155–58, 161, 192, 215n
Wheeler, John, *The Treatise of Commerce*, 195–96
Whitney, Lois, 209n
Willan, Thomas, 218n
Willet, Andrew, 165
Williams, Gordon, 212n, 213n, 214n
Wilson, Robert, *The Three Ladies of London*, 173–76, 183
Wilson, Thomas, 32, 171
Withers, Robert, 116
Wolf, John, 205n
Wood, Alfred, 203n, 218n
Wotton, Henry, 120

Yver, Jacques, 120

Zagorin, Perez, 216n